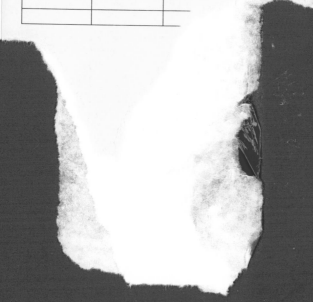

DATE			

The Lazarus Heist

From Hollywood to High Finance:
Inside North Korea's Global Cyber War

GEOFF WHITE

BUSINESS

PENGUIN BUSINESS

UK | USA | Canada | Ireland | Australia
India | New Zealand | South Africa

Penguin Business is part of the Penguin Random House group of companies
whose addresses can be found at global.penguinrandomhouse.com.

First published 2022

002

Copyright © Geoff White, 2022

By arrangement with the BBC
The BBC logo is a trademark of the British Broadcasting Corporation
and is used under licence
BBC logo © BBC, 2011; BBC News World Service logo © BBC, 2018

This book is based on the BBC News World Service podcast, *The Lazarus Heist*

The moral right of the copyright holders has been asserted

Set in 12/14.75 pt Dante MT Std
Typeset by Jouve (UK), Milton Keynes
Printed and bound in Great Britain by Clays Ltd, Elcograf S.p.A.

The authorized representative in the EEA is Penguin Random House Ireland,
Morrison Chambers, 32 Nassau Street, Dublin D02 YH68

A CIP catalogue record for this book is available from the British Library

HARDBACK ISBN: 978-0-241-55425-8
TRADE PAPERBACK ISBN: 978-0-241-55426-5

Follow us on LinkedIn: https://www.linkedin.com/company/penguin-connect

www.greenpenguin.co.uk

For my mum and my wife – my two guiding stars

Contents

Introduction

'North Korea? Really?'

It's the response I often get when I tell people I'm researching North Korean computer hackers.

Many people's image of this small Asian country – if they even have one – is of an idiosyncratic, isolated land whose limited technological skill is mainly spent on launching missiles and testing nukes. The idea that it has a force of computer hackers, let alone one of the world's most dangerous, seems outlandish.

As an investigative journalist covering cybercrime, I have a very different perspective. Over the last decade or so I've watched as the crimes being attributed to North Korea's cyber-warriors – nicknamed the Lazarus Group by security researchers – have increased in scale, ferocity and ingenuity. Computer hacks have become a key weapon in North Korea's arsenal, and they now pose a significant threat to global security and stability.

The Lazarus Group's hackers started out with low-level attacks defacing websites, but within a worryingly short amount of time they graduated to far bigger targets: taking out movie studios and TV stations, stealing millions from national banks and even shutting down hospital departments. The idea of a computer hacker disabling an emergency room was once the stuff of Hollywood film plots. Now it's reality.

But this story isn't just about computer hacking. As I've dug deeper into the group's alleged activities, I've unearthed the global criminal network that facilitates its operations: a dark realm encompassing dodgy bankers in the Philippines, hapless philanthropists in Sri Lanka, gambling sharks in Macau, used-car salesmen in Japan and Instagram millionaires in Dubai. It's a sprawling underworld of crooks and fixers wielding extraordinary power and handling vast quantities of money, most of whom operate way beyond the reach of any police or law-enforcement agency.

At the centre of it all is a small team of highly ambitious hackers seemingly capable of penetrating their targets with unsettling stealth. Most of the victims in this book had no idea they were under attack until it was too late – their money gone, their data leaked and their computers trashed.

To understand North Korea's alleged hacking campaigns is to understand the modern world of crime. It's bewilderingly swift, knows no borders and relies on a shadowy network of accomplices. These digital offensives are perhaps the biggest threat to our ever-growing online existence. In the UK cyber is now the most common type of crime, having long ago overtaken the thefts and murders that dominate the headlines.[1]

North Korea's cyber-activity graphically illustrates why the threat from hackers is becoming increasingly pernicious. The more our world shifts online, the more vulnerable we all become to the Lazarus Group's machinations. And the more we rely on technology, the more likely we are to be held to ransom (literally, in some cases) by these digital assailants and others like them.

We now face the monumental challenge of defending ourselves against this new threat. Currently, standing against the likes of the Lazarus Group is an army of technologists who spend their lives developing all sorts of tools and tactics to fend off the attacks and keep us safe. You'll find them in government, in law enforcement and probably in your organization's own IT department. But, as you'll learn in this book, no matter how good their defences are, none of them can stop the hackers every time. That's up to us: the people who use this technology day in, day out. Usefully, protecting yourself against most of these online assaults doesn't necessarily require costly kit or advanced cyber-skills. While some of the hackers' tactics are frighteningly smart, a lot of the time they simply reuse tried-and-tested methods that are easily defeated once you know what you're looking for. Defending yourself against them can be as simple as hitting the 'delete' button on a dodgy-looking email. Your main weapon is knowledge, and you'll find plenty of that in the pages that follow.

I

Jackpot

They came from all over central India: a taxi driver from Mumbai, a pharmacist from Pune, a caterer from Nanded, an auditor from Virar. Along with dozens of others, they journeyed for hour after hour through the humid downpours of the rainy season, some by car, some on India's redoubtable train network, eventually converging on one location: Kolhapur, a city of just over half a million people in Maharashtra state.

What drew them on that August weekend in 2018 was not a religious event, nor a festival or a concert. They came to carry out a secret task for which they had been specially recruited.[1] They were almost certainly unaware of the full scale of the crime into which they had been co-opted. For at that exact moment, all around the world, hundreds of others were setting out on similar journeys with the same mission. They were all doing the bidding of a group of elite cybercriminals who were pulling the strings from thousands of miles away using an international network of collaborators.

This group of hackers was about to stage one of its most audacious and complex crimes to date. It would pull in millions of dollars and was the culmination of years of hacking activity, according to the US Federal Bureau of Investigation (FBI), which has tracked the gang's work. Over time the group has honed its skills and developed its contacts to make it one of the most unpredictable and formidable cybercrime forces in the world.

The timing of the men's arrival in the Indian city of Kolhapur was critical. Once in place, they would have only a few hours to carry out their allotted task and then disappear safely back into the crowd – or, at least, that's what they were promised.

The men looked innocuous enough. Casually dressed, they were mostly in their late twenties and early thirties. The only hint of their covert endeavour was the stacks of bank cards they each carried. Their task was simple: use the cards in as many ATMs as possible, pocket the cash and keep moving. They would later pass on the proceeds of their activities to their handlers and receive their cut.

At 3 p.m., on Saturday, 11 August, the men sprang into action.[2] Some worked alone, others in small groups. On the streets of Kolhapur they hit dozens of ATMs. It didn't matter which bank the machines belonged to: all they had to do was to insert the card, enter a PIN and withdraw as much cash as they could.

Two of the men were later quoted as saying they walked for miles through the city, attempting withdrawals from every cash machine they could find.[3]

By 10 p.m. the operation was over. The men handed the cash to their bosses and pocketed their share. They were reportedly paid up to $500 – a big payday in a country in which the average income for an entire year is less than $2,000.[4] But, for those controlling this network of so-called 'money mules', the pay-offs were well worth it. By running so many mules in so many places, in just a few hours they had netted more than $350,000 from the group's cashpoint spree.[5] In some Indian ATMs, the highest denomination note is 500 rupees, meaning the gang was now potentially looking at a pile more than 50,000 banknotes high.

But that was just the tip of the iceberg. The seven-hour operation in India was only one of dozens being carried out simultaneously across the globe. Bank cards were being used to withdraw money in the US, Canada, UK, Turkey, Poland, the Russian Federation and more. In all, twenty-nine different countries were involved.[6] The total amount stolen in one day in August made the Indian operation pale by comparison: worldwide, more than $11m had been withdrawn in 12,000 transactions in two hours and thirteen minutes.[7]

It was a tightly co-ordinated raid on the international banking system, carried out with breath-taking efficiency.

Those who co-ordinated the crime had not only the technical

skill to make ATMs around the world spew out banknotes on demand but also the global reach to mobilize a worldwide network of mules, who would now pass the stolen funds back up the chain to those who had masterminded the job.

For many of those who investigated the heist, the signs pointed to one culprit. It's a hacking unit that's been christened with a variety of enigmatic names: Stardust Chollima, Zinc, Hidden Cobra, Nickel Academy. But most often it's referred to as the Lazarus Group. According to the law-enforcement officials who've followed its online crime spree, this isn't just another bunch of crooks on the make. The unit is working for the government of North Korea. Well funded and highly motivated, this force of computer hackers operates within the country's rigidly controlled military structure. And it has one main goal: to make cash for the regime. Many perceive North Korea, formally known as the Democratic People's Republic of Korea, or DPRK, as a backward state, disconnected from the modern world and trapped in the clutches of its capricious leaders, the Kim Dynasty. But, while this state of affairs may be true for the bulk of its society, Western law-enforcement and security researchers see an entirely different side to the so-called 'Hermit Kingdom'.

Over the last few years investigators claim that North Korea's government hackers have become some of the most effective and dangerous on the planet. That the regime has an online army shouldn't come as a surprise: many nations now have such cyber-divisions, including the UK and the US, and in North Korea's highly militarized society such a unit is an inevitable addition to its forces. But researchers who've tracked North Korea's operations see something very different about the country's hacking behaviour: whereas many countries' cyber-teams are focused on stealing information for strategic advantage, North Korea's online war is part of a battle for economic survival.

The country is trapped in a financial death spiral triggered by a damaging series of events that has unfolded over the course of its relatively short history and accelerated rapidly in the last three decades. At one point North Korea ran so short of money that it failed in its most basic duty to its people, millions of whom are believed to have starved to death thanks to economic mismanagement and dogmatic adherence to ideological goals. Simultaneously, its pursuit of nuclear weapons saw it hit with international sanctions – all of which will be explored in the following chapters. The net result is that one of the poorest countries in the world has little chance of making money legitimately.[8] According to many experts, North Korea has instead turned to crime, in the past experimenting with forgery, smuggling and even crystal-meth production, before finally discovering a far more reliable and lucrative form of income: computer hacking.

Researchers have watched with growing concern as the country's cyber-warriors have been blamed for increasingly sophisticated attacks, moving from basic tactics aimed at defacing and disrupting websites to highly complex raids on major organizations and financial institutions worldwide.

Since at least 2015 North Korea's cyber-teams have been targeting banks, mastering the arcane world of international money transfers to steal hundreds of millions of dollars. Researchers at the United Nations Security Council (UNSC) – which tracks potential infringements of the sanctions placed on North Korea – have attributed twenty-one different bank attacks to the country. In a 2019 report the UNSC lists the institutions that have been hit and gives details of the methods used to transfer and launder the money. It paints a dizzying picture of computer hackers whose online activities seem to circumnavigate the globe with ease: they hack into a bank in South Africa, steal account information and use it to forge cash cards for use in Japan. They raid a bank in Chile, moving the money to accounts in Hong Kong while distracting employees by crashing thousands of computers. They transfer money from a bank in Malta and within hours the funds are being withdrawn to buy Rolexes and fast cars in the UK.[9]

It is the cutting edge of crime: stateless, instant and seemingly with little chance of the perpetrators ever being caught. And in 2018 the group behind this global crime wave turned its attention to a little-known but very wealthy bank in India.

Cosmos Co-Operative Bank is the second-largest and second-oldest bank in India, established in 1906.[10] Such co-op institutions were set up at the turn of the century to serve India's rural economy, often running on a not-for-profit basis. In the West they might have been described as credit unions. But over time some of these co-ops morphed into modern, complex finance houses. Sadly, according to several Indian tech sources, their IT security hasn't kept pace, leaving some fatally vulnerable to digital attack.

Cosmos Co-Operative Bank now runs operations in seven Indian states, with $2bn of deposits.[11] Its headquarters is Cosmos Tower, a twelve-storey block of gleaming silver and glass in Pune around a hundred miles inland from Mumbai. The building is surrounded by high, heavy fences, and guards police the entrance. None of these security measures presented a problem for the hackers, however. Their route inside would bypass them all easily.

According to a financial-industry source in India, from September 2017 carefully crafted phishing emails began to arrive in the inboxes of staff at the bank's branches. The exact content of the messages has never been made public, but it's likely the hackers used well-worn tricks to tempt the recipients into opening them, perhaps disguising them as urgent financial information or an attractive job offer. Getting someone to fall for such an email is often a numbers game: send enough of them, and sooner or later someone will take the bait, click on a link in an email or open an attachment, and unwittingly install a virus allowing the hackers access. Over the next few months the hackers' game paid off.

Once inside the bank's systems, the cyber-attackers began stealthily to explore their target's network. Much of it may have been familiar territory for them: according to the United Nations Security Council, by this time North Korea's hackers had hit at least fourteen banks in the preceding two years, so they would have been well experienced in the kinds of systems and software used.

This time, however, they tried something different, zeroing in on the programs that control the bank's ATM withdrawals. Cashpoints are an amenity that almost all of us use without a second thought, but behind the machines in every bank and high street worldwide is an intricate system of computerized checks and controls. Between the moment you insert your card and the moment you walk off with the cash, dozens of staccato messages whizz back and forth across the globe to make sure that the right person is getting the right amount of money. For the hackers targeting Cosmos Co-Operative Bank, this flow of data would be the key to a multimillion-dollar payday.

Take a look at one of the bank cards in your pocket. In addition to the bank name, it's very likely there'll be a logo somewhere for Visa, Mastercard or another big financial firm. It's not just branding: these companies' details are coded into the card, and, when you insert it into a cashpoint in a high street, petrol station or super-market, one of the first things the ATM checks is which payment company the card is registered to. After you type in your PIN, it's scrambled and sent off to Visa, Mastercard, etc., along with a unique number that identifies which bank you're with.

The payment company checks the bank ID, then sends the encrypted PIN to that bank, which unscrambles it and checks whether it's correct. The bank's software then looks at the amount you're trying to withdraw and checks whether you have enough in your account. If so, it sends a message via the payment company to the ATM, giving the machine the okay to provide the cash.

This system is the reason why you can visit pretty much any ATM in the world, insert your card and receive cash, even if the ATM isn't run by the bank where you have your account. Payment companies like Visa and Mastercard hold a prime position in the middle of billions of transactions, passing information back and forth between ATMs and banks to make sure transactions get approved. At regular intervals there's a settling-up process to make sure that the ATM that just gave you $100 is reimbursed by the bank where you have your account.

Thanks to Internet technology, all of this takes place in the blink of an eye. Most of us are blissfully unaware that it's happening, and for the vast majority of transactions the system is safe and secure. That's because, in most cases, criminals don't have access to the software that runs it. Inside Cosmos Co-Operative Bank, however, by July 2018 the hackers had worked their way to exactly this ATM approval software. They now had control over how Cosmos Bank's systems dealt with every cashpoint withdrawal, and were preparing to make subtle changes that would allow them to hijack the system and steal millions of dollars.

One option for the hackers was simply to tweak the software to approve every transaction that came along, without even checking whether the PIN was correct or the cardholder was good for the money. However, that might have aroused suspicion: if all of Cosmos's customers around the world were suddenly able to withdraw as much as they wanted without even having entered the right PIN, pretty soon someone in the bank would have cottoned on.

Instead, the hackers wanted to narrow the field so that the only people who would benefit from the hack would be the money mules working on their behalf. First, they picked 450 accounts (it's unclear quite how the hackers chose them: some reports state they were grabbed at random from legitimate bank customers; other reports suggest they were specially created in advance by the hackers' accomplices).[12] Next, they needed to make sure that the bank's computers would authorize withdrawals of large sums of money from those accounts. But that presented a problem. Despite their access to the bank's computer systems, the hackers couldn't control how much money was actually in those 450 accounts. If they didn't contain much money, they'd be of little value in the ensuing raid. The hackers found a neat workaround. According to the chairman of the bank, Milind Kale, they used their access to its computer systems to fool the ATM software into thinking that the balance on each of the accounts was around $10,000, regardless of the true amount of money held there. That's way in excess of the maximum amount most cashpoints will allow in a single withdrawal. As a result of the hackers' changes, no matter how much was requested to be withdrawn, the bank's systems would now say yes.

With the 450 accounts prepared and ready for big withdrawals, the hackers next needed to create bank cards attached to each of the accounts, which is not necessarily as hard as it sounds. Many people believe that the raised numbers on the front of the card are important, and are what the ATM looks at when they insert their card. So they probably think that creating a fraudulent bank card means being able to print something with raised digits. But that's no longer true (which is why some card companies are now issuing flat, smooth versions without raised numbers). In fact, the most sensitive information on the card is held on the black stripe on the back.

This magnetic stripe is scanned as it's pushed into the cashpoint slot, and it contains the unique number for the bank that issued the card, along with the full card number, expiry date and customer name.

To create a bank card that's readable by an ATM, all you need is a blank card with a magnetic stripe on the back and a machine that can electronically imprint the required information on to the stripe. Blank cards are no problem to acquire: even everyday gift cards now come with a magnetic stripe, and the information on them can easily be overwritten with other data. A machine to encode the card can be bought online for less than $200. So . . . does that mean that if someone has your bank card number, expiry date, name and so on they can just create a duplicate of your bank card and withdraw your money? Surely it can't be that easy? No, it isn't. Because there's a key element that they're missing: your PIN number. Yes, a fraudster can create a card with your details on it, but if he or she inserts it into a cashpoint and tries to make a withdrawal, your bank will ask for the PIN, and if the fraudster doesn't have it, they won't get any money. The PIN unlocks the account.

But, usefully for the hackers who raided Cosmos Co-Operative Bank, they had full control over the part of the bank's system that checked the PIN. They changed the software so that it would look out for incoming withdrawal requests from any of the 450 accounts they'd prepared and approve the withdrawals without verifying the PIN. It would then check the account balance, and thanks to the hackers' tricks it would see that there was, apparently, $10,000 available, and therefore send a message to the ATM giving it the okay to issue as much money as the person had requested.

In the hacking underworld, it's a process known as 'jackpotting'.

The criminal scheme was set and ready to go, but now the hackers needed accomplices to withdraw the money. They wanted to use people in as many different locations as they could. This would make it much harder for law enforcement to trace the whole operation and work out who was behind it. A source close to the investigation in India told me that the accomplices were recruited through the dark web – a hidden, encrypted part of the Internet that's rife with criminal sites. In this digital underground, 'carding' (as credit-card fraud is known) is a thriving and lucrative trade. Finding people with the skills, experience and willingness to take part in an ATM jackpotting campaign wouldn't be hard.

Using contacts made in this criminal underworld of credit-card fraudsters, the hackers would be able to send the information on the 450 rigged accounts to their accomplices around the globe, who could then encode it on to blank cards, which were then passed to the money mules for use.

'International gangs and distributing agencies were involved in this process,' said the source. 'All the buyers [of the stolen data] were allotted a time slot on 11 August when the card would be active and cash could be drawn from the ATMs.'

But, as the date of the heist neared, it seems the FBI got wind of what might be about to happen. A US security journalist reported that the day before the money mules set off for their cashpoint targets, the FBI issued a confidential alert to banks. It warned that the agency had 'obtained unspecified reporting indicating cybercriminals are planning to conduct a global Automated Teller Machine (ATM) cash-out scheme in the coming days . . . commonly referred to as an "unlimited operation" '.[13]

The FBI also had a handle on the tactics that would be used: 'The cybercriminals typically create fraudulent copies of legitimate cards by sending stolen card data to co-conspirators who imprint the data on reusable magnetic stripe cards, such as gift cards purchased at retail stores.'

The Feds were bang on target. But, sadly, it seems their urgent alert didn't spread widely enough to include Cosmos Co-Operative Bank. As Saturday approached and its staff went home for the weekend, it had no idea that the cash-out gangs were preparing to hit the jackpot.

In India at least twenty-three people were issued with the cloned bank cards. Local media reports claimed a gang in Dubai had sent the account information to colleagues in Mumbai, where 109 of the cloned cards were produced.[14]

Many of the suspected money mules arrived in Kolhapur ready for the 11 August raid, and went from ATM to ATM with their stacks of fake bank cards. One pair allegedly pulled out $121,000 during the few hours they were at work, targeting 52 cashpoints belonging to 31 banks.

Around the world, similar withdrawals were taking place. In total, $11m in cash was pulled out in less than four hours, according to the bank's reports.[15]

After each withdrawal, the money mules faded back into the crowd, between them quietly accumulating the wads of cash to pass on to their handlers.

Simultaneously, Cosmos Bank's IT system was starting to run into problems. Despite all their careful preparation, the hackers' control of the ATM system had gone awry. Customers reportedly started to complain that their cashpoint transactions were being declined. Others experienced the opposite problem: withdrawals were being approved even if they didn't have the money. Some of them took advantage and pulled out wads of cash, only to be overcome by their consciences and hand it back.[16] The bank's staff began to suspect something serious was up and took drastic action. They shut down all online banking for two days and disabled ATM withdrawals. Genuine customers were thrown into disarray as their transactions failed, and they were unable to get hold of banknotes – this would have been an especially big problem in a country like India, where access to banking was limited and low-level workers traditionally operated on a cash-only basis.[17] Cosmos's Chairman, Milind Kale, later took to YouTube to record a statement in an attempt to reassure customers and investors. 'The bank's position is very sound,' he said. 'Our banking system is very strong and we are capable of facing this situation.'[18]

Relentlessly, even as Kale's bank raced to deal with the ATM issue, the hackers were preparing yet another raid on its finances.

As part of their exploration of Cosmos's internal systems, the hackers had also gained access to a system called SWIFT. The Society for Worldwide Interbank Financial Telecommunication is, as the name suggests, a way for the world's banks to send messages to each other. Billions of dollars are dispatched between financial institutions on the basis of SWIFT communication.

Why are banks willing to send such massive amounts of money solely on the basis of a SWIFT message? Because they assume (rightly, in most cases) that the communication is legitimate since it could come only from someone working inside another bank. It's not as though you or I can simply install SWIFT software on our home computers and start demanding money from banks worldwide.

Of course this logic doesn't hold up quite so well if hackers are able to break into the bank and manoeuvre their way towards the SWIFT system, which is exactly what happened in the case of Cosmos Co-Operative.

Two days after the ATM attack, as the bank scrambled to comprehend the scale of the heist and how it was carried out, the hackers struck again, using SWIFT messages to transfer $2m to an account belonging to a Hong Kong company.[19] This time the bank was quicker on the uptake – it claims it was able to trace the payment in just fifteen minutes. Because some of the money was still within the financial system, Cosmos Co-Operative was able to recover a portion of it, clawing back half of the stolen funds.

But, as for the ATM withdrawals, the money was long gone. Not only had the bank been robbed of around $11m, but, to add insult to injury, it had also lost $500,000 in the commission payments it would normally have received for such withdrawals.[20] It's not clear how the losses were covered. The bank has insurance policies, but they were never mentioned when its officials talked of the hack. It's possible that customers will eventually end up paying indirectly, in the form of higher fees and so forth.[21]

Meanwhile, the money mules who'd done the legwork in India didn't have long to enjoy their winnings. Within weeks the police began to make arrests. They had been analysing CCTV footage from the ATMs and managed to identify several of the suspects. They were helped in this process by the fact that, for some of those arrested, this wasn't the first time they'd been involved in such cash-out activity. Police claimed four of the suspects had been caught on CCTV the year before illicitly withdrawing money from another Indian bank, City Union in Chennai.[22]

Gradually, the police dragnet expanded, pulling in suspected money mules from Mumbai and its surrounding suburbs. At the time of writing, none have been charged. Perhaps more importantly, the arrests in India stalled at the level of the mules. The country's police believed they had identified a key figure higher up the chain of command living in the Middle East, but they struggled to make more progress.

In a way, the bank got lucky: the police cyber-unit in Maharashtra is considered to be one of the best in the country (partly because of the prevalence of financial institutions based in the state). But, even with its investigative experience, its officers were stymied by the staggeringly global nature of the theft. With more than two dozen different countries affected, it faced a mountain of paperwork to get the information that would reveal who was behind the cash-out campaign. The hackers who originally attacked Cosmos Bank almost certainly knew this, and deliberately seeded the ATM cash-out gangs in many different countries across the globe to frustrate attempts to track them down.

As for identifying who originally hacked into the bank and started the whole heist (and who was presumably set to receive a big chunk of the stolen money), local police faced another uphill struggle. 'What's worrisome is they have wiped out all tracks, leaving no evidence; it's well planned,' said Brijesh Singh, Inspector General of Maharashtra Police, who headed up its special investigation team.[23] This is a common tactic among hackers: once they've completed their work, they carefully delete the malicious software they used, along with the victims' digital records of what happened when.

Indian law enforcement may have been struggling to work out who was behind the raid on Cosmos Co-Operative Bank in August 2018, but, once again, the US agencies' considerable resources seem to have put them one step ahead. In October the Cybersecurity and Infrastructure Security Agency (CISA) released an alert about a criminal campaign they nicknamed FASTCash, which, in the dry language of US cybercops, 'targeted the retail payment system infrastructure within banks to enable fraudulent ATM cash withdrawals across national borders'. In other words, FASTCash was targeting cashpoints all over the world.[24]

CISA said the FASTCash gang had hit banks in Asia and Africa, stealing tens of millions of dollars, including an 'incident in 2018' in which cash was simultaneously withdrawn from ATMs in dozens of different countries. To many security researchers it left little doubt that the US was now laying the blame for the Cosmos hack at the door of whoever was behind FASTCash.

CISA believed this was the work of Hidden Cobra, the code-name US law enforcement gives to North Korean government hackers. Security researchers have christened them with an even more enigmatic name thanks to their ability to survive inside their victims' computer networks: the Lazarus Group. It was these cyber-troops, they claim, who stealthily wormed their way into Cosmos, tweaked the ATM software to authorize thousands of fraudulent withdrawals and then attempted to send millions of dollars more to Hong Kong using SWIFT.

But if, as the US government apparently suspects, North Korea really is behind the Cosmos Co-Operative Bank heist, it leaves some big questions. How did this isolated regime co-ordinate the dozens of money mules across the globe, sending them to their cashpoint targets inside such a tight time window? And, once the job was done, how did North Korea get its hands on the millions of dollars that spewed forth from the ATMs?

Those who've tracked the regime's recent history believe they have the answers: they say North Korea has spent decades developing its links with the criminal underworld, partly because of the catastrophic series of events that have befallen the country from the 1990s – which have left North Korea desperate for cash and set it on an escalating path of cyber-conflict.

As a result of these underground connections, both online and in the real world, North Korea's operatives would have known exactly whom to approach in each country to set up the kind of money-muling networks used in the Cosmos hack. A deal would have been struck: some of the cash would go to the ATM gang bosses, while the rest would make its way back to the regime.

But it didn't stop at financial attacks. As North Korea's hacking prowess developed in the wake of raids on institutions like Cosmos Bank, its cyber-teams have become increasingly brazen, according to investigators, targeting critical services in its enemies' territory. Ultimately, even hospital departments and COVID-vaccine-makers would be swept up in the country's online attacks. Urgent operations would be affected, and Accident and Emergency departments shut down. North Korea's hacking would become literally a matter of life and death.

How did we end up here? How did this one tiny state end up accused of pursuing such a relentless and damaging cybercrime campaign? For the answers, you have to go right back to the earliest days of North Korea's birth as a nation, and piece together the tragic series of miscalculations that led North Korea right to the very brink of collapse.

2

Going Broke

At first, Jihyun Park's memories of her childhood summers sound like the sun-tinged recollections many of us cherish. Raised in Chŏngjin, a major North Korean city near the Chinese border, she grew up with the mountains on one side and the beach on the other.

With her friends she would head out after school and catch dragonflies among the rivers that meandered through the nearby farmland. 'There were always so many dragonflies in summer in North Korea. We used to see how many we could catch. Hundreds sometimes. We'd hold them by the wings in our fingers and count how many we'd got.'

It sounds idyllic. But for Park these trips were not the innocent nature rambles of a young girl exploring the world. What motivated her and her friends to catch bugs was something heartbreaking: a need that no child should ever experience.

'We took the heads off the dragonflies and ate them. It was food,' she tells me. 'We were so hungry.'

Stunned to hear this, I find myself asking her what dragonflies taste like. 'I don't remember,' she says; 'we were just hungry.'[1]

What Park couldn't have known – what almost no one in North Korea was allowed to know – was the real reason behind the gnawing hunger that drove her and her friends to hunt whatever they could find in the fields and rivers of Chŏngjin. North Korea's infrastructure was collapsing around them. The government was failing in its most basic role: to provide enough food to keep its people alive. And young Park had no idea just how bad things were going to get. It was a harrowing era that would be seared on to the memories of all who endured it, including Park. And it helped to steer

North Korea on a path towards criminality, one which would have global consequences for decades to follow.

North Korea is the world's oldest surviving socialist state. The Soviet Union took form in 1917 but collapsed by the century's end, along with most of its adherents. China's Communist Party only came to power in 1949. North Korea was established in 1948 and has outlasted dozens of other hard-left countries.

From 1910 the whole Korean peninsula was occupied by Japan, but, with its defeat at the end of the Second World War, the Japanese were gone and Korea was carved up between the capitalist US, which controlled the South, and the communist Soviet Union, which controlled the North. It was destined to become one of the first battlegrounds of the proxy war fought by the two superpowers.

The boundary was set at the 38th parallel, a line which circumnavigates the globe and also cuts through Athens in Greece and Charlottesville in the US. It was an arbitrary border picked by the Americans, because it divided the country roughly in two.[2] Almost overnight Koreans who just a few years previously had been one people now found themselves divided under competing administrations, with the border between them becoming increasingly fortified. Perhaps inevitably, this hastily agreed division of territory didn't hold up long.

War broke out in June 1950, and the opposing political systems fought to take control of the entire peninsula, the frontline shifting back and forth as their forces' fortunes waxed and waned.

After three gruelling years of conflict in which an estimated 2 million Koreans died, along with a million Chinese and many thousands among the international forces, the division line ended up, depressingly, back in almost exactly the same position that it had been at the beginning. This time, however, it would remain in place for decades, seemingly set in stone and divided by the Demilitarized Zone (the DMZ), a no-man's-land two miles across which is widely acknowledged as the most heavily fortified border in the world.

The two Koreas may have settled into their respective territories, but the conflict between them never ended. Instead, a truce was declared. Officially speaking, North Korea is still at war with the South and its allies. This enduring conflict has come to define the country in the most complete way imaginable, underpinning almost everything about daily life in this tiny nation of about 25 million people.

The war and North Korea's reaction to it form the first of a series of ratchet effects which have locked North Korea in its current, grinding, seemingly inescapable position. The country's leaders do not feel they can back down: realistically, they cannot win the war, but they cannot admit defeat either, for fear of being overrun by enemies they have hated and isolated the country from for so many decades.

This unenviable scenario became the lot of Kim Il Sung, the man who founded North Korea.

Piecing together Kim's life has been made immeasurably harder by the layers of myth and disinformation built up by him and his propagandists during his near-half-decade as a dictator in the Stalinist mould, increasingly controlling every aspect of his citizens' lives. His early biography is fairly uncontentious: born in 1912, he became part of the resistance against the Japanese occupation and later fought guerrilla battles against it in China. He endured considerable hardship and discovered a zeal for socialism along the way, according to his militia colleagues.

Things get murkier when the story moves on to his rise to power in North Korea. His own historians will tell you that Kim almost single-handedly led the ejection of Japan's forces from the North, bravely charging in to take over the territory. Other accounts (probably more accurately) say that he was brought in on a Soviet ship and placed in power by Moscow, where the communists were keen to see a friendly leader at their southern border.[3] North Korea shares most of its northern boundary with China, but there's also a tiny strip on the eastern side bordering Russia, meaning the capital, Pyongyang, is as close to Vladivostok as it is to Beijing. Kim was perceived by the Soviets as a pliable, safe pair of hands with a solid backstory of fighting for socialist goals.

What's beyond contention is that by 1946 Kim was effectively in charge of the North, aged just thirty-four.

Kim's role in the subsequent Korean War also varies according to who's telling the tale. In reality Kim wanted conflict and had pushed the Soviet Union to support his military plan, hoping he could reunite Korea on the North's terms (an aim still shared by North Korea's leaders today). But, again, his own historians will tell you that the war was started by the South, led by the US, in a bid to take over the entire peninsula. This origin story about the war is pivotal, because it is an important driver in keeping North Korea's population keyed up in a perpetual state of conflict – the unending war is, their leaders tell them, an enduring injustice inflicted on North Korea by the South and its US allies, which were the aggressors in the 1950s and continue to be so today. Against the backdrop of the earlier Japanese occupation, this creates a powerful underdog narrative: North Koreans are cast as the victims who must fight back, tolerating any hardships thrown at them along the way (a narrative that's proved highly convenient for their totalitarian rulers imposing those hardships).

With the truce declared in 1953, Kim set about rebuilding the damage that years of war had inflicted on his country. He took an incredibly hands-on approach, reportedly making more than 1,300 on-the-spot inspections of collective farms, factories, mines, highways, housing complexes, childcare facilities, museums and other public buildings over the following few years.[4] He dished out advice on everything from signage to crop-growing. This, in turn, created a bounty of stories for Kim's propagandists, who recounted tales of grateful citizens gazing in awe as their benevolent leader deigned to advise them on some mundane task, before pledging to put an end to their drudgery in his new socialist utopia.

Tragically for the North Koreans, some of Kim Il Sung's homespun advice would turn out to have the most devastating consequences, almost destroying his country for good, but it would be decades before those consequences became manifest.

However, during the late 1950s and into the 1960s, Kim Il Sung's reform and rebuilding worked out well (albeit he was starting from a very low base), and some began to see North Korea as a role model of reformist socialism in developing countries.

There are reasons to take some of the glowing recollections about Kim's early years in power with a pinch of salt. Much is made, for example, of his equality reforms and empowerment of women. But this may have been driven by the fact that his push to expand his military left a dearth of labourers for the farms and factories, and these positions had to be filled by women. Also, the reality of 'equality' often meant women taking on traditionally male functions in addition to the considerable burdens of housework and child-rearing they already had.[5]

There is reason to be sceptical about the statistics pointing to North Korea's success too. Often cited is the fact that per capita Gross Domestic Product in the North and South were neck and neck in 1953, but that GDP quadrupled in the North by 1960. However, this seems to come from a US Central Intelligence Agency (CIA) assessment, and at least one report admits it's not clear where they got the numbers from.[6] If the statistics about GDP were generated by North Korea itself, then, given the regime's deep-seated propaganda habit, they should be treated with great care.

But the final reason for a sideways look at North Korea's post-war boom is that, rather than the homegrown success story Kim's supporters want to paint, it seems to have been largely bankrolled by the Soviet Union, something that became obvious during the 1960s. Up until that point, Kim had been able to play off his two big backers – the USSR and China – against each other and gain support from both. But then Moscow and Beijing fell out over a dispute about their visions of communism. North Korea was forced to choose sides. China had come to Kim's aid during the Korean War, so he chose Beijing. The Soviets clearly weren't happy, and they withdrew aid to North Korea. As a result, North Korea's Seven-year Plan for breakneck growth was stretched to become a Ten-year Plan.[7] The Soviets eventually swung back to support North Korea, but the episode left little doubt that Kim's economic advances were tied by a leash to Moscow's benevolence.

An American politician once described the Russia–North Korea relationship as being 'Walt Disney and Donald Duck'.[8] It's hard to imagine a comparison more offensive to a proud and paranoid leader like Kim Il Sung. The idea that North Korea's success might be built on Russian patronage was deeply problematic, because it undermined a key plank of Kim Il Sung's ideology: the concept of *Juche*, usually translated as 'self-reliance'. In Kim's particular brand of socialism, North Korea had to be an all-providing, self-reliant state. Not only would this restore the pride of the North Korean people, he believed, but it would avoid the fate of becoming a puppet state of either Russia or China. Kim outlined his *Juche* twist on socialism in 1955, and it became a guiding star in his decisions, governing everything from overarching policy to the minutiae of daily life.[9]

It led to some bizarre moments. At one point in the late 1950s the North Koreans decided to build their own tractors. Moscow was less keen on the idea, preferring to sell them its farm machinery rather than give them the designs and let them make their own. So North Korean engineers set about disassembling a model and trying to replicate it. They succeeded, with just one problem: the tractor would only work in reverse gear. For anyone looking for a pithy analogy about North Korea's patchy progress towards a left-wing utopia, it was a godsend. Its engineers, however, eventually found the forward gears, and the country successfully set up its own factory to churn out the machines.[10]

Self-reliance proved even trickier in other areas, thanks to a quirk of topography unintentionally created by the Americans' arbitrary border decision. Whereas the South has some land for grazing and farming, North Korea is 80 per cent mountainous.[11] This throws up a critical issue for a state aiming for total independence: with a marked lack of sheep for wool and fields for cotton, what will the people wear?

North Korea found a remarkable answer in the dankness of the coalmines that it inherited from the post-war carve-up.

If you take anthracite and limestone and subject them to an industrial process, you create fibres that can be spun into cloth. It was a technique developed jointly by Korean and Japanese scientists before the Second World War, and the resulting material was christened vinylon, or vinalon.[12] If you want to find out what this wonder fabric feels like, find one of the Kånken backpacks made by Swedish luggage-maker Fjällräven – they're made of Vinylon F. As you'd expect from a material used for rucksacks, vinylon is rough and hardwearing. Yet North Korea hit upon this as a solution to its clothing-supply problems. Coal was one of its major resources, and now its citizens could wear it. Of course, it was starchy, scratchy and hard to dye into different colours, but this would almost certainly have been sold to the people as another noble hardship to bear, and better than the unthinkable option of buying more comfortable, colourful clothes from a capitalist supplier.

North Korea's efforts to carve out indigenous industry may sound quaint, but the underlying dynamics are very serious indeed. Because, as the century wore on, the concept of *Juche* would ultimately become yet another ratchet effect, helping to lock North Korea into a trajectory that would finish in near-disaster.

Meanwhile, as the 1960s came to an end, *Juche* could go only so far in meeting North Korea's needs. With Russian patronage proving shaky and the early post-war wins petering out, the country was beginning to struggle. But it couldn't let its people know – Kim Il Sung's pride and his reputation as a successful provider could not be tarnished. So around this time reports started to show a gradual sealing-off of the country. Western visitors were all but forbidden except in extremely rare cases. Even arrivals from friendly communist countries found themselves allowed to see only the highlights (including, of course, a museum dedicated to Kim Il Sung).[13] It was a process that continued and escalated over the following decades, eventually earning the country its modern sobriquet: the Hermit Kingdom.

This extreme isolationist approach created yet another ratchet effect: the more the outside world raced ahead of North Korea, the harder it became for the country's authoritarian regime to allow its citizens even a glimpse of how far they were falling behind. The drive to shut out the wider world has become an industry in itself: radio sets imported into North Korea are carefully soldered so that the reception dial can't be shifted away from the government-approved station.[14] One person who escaped the regime's clutches claimed that the country's broadcasters transmitted the football results only if the North Korean team won.[15] North Korea's citizens are kept in an information bubble unlike anything else on earth.[16]

Inside the country, meanwhile, Kim Il Sung's role as founding father was being turned into something much more powerful and far more sinister. The country was being shaped into a rigidly controlled and policed system of classes. And, at the top of the tree, Kim was becoming almost akin to a god. Inevitably, absolute power would end in abuse.

One of the most surprising things about Kim's dominance of North Koreans' personal lives is the relative ease with which he achieved it. He faced opposition of course, but, compared with upheavals such as the Cultural Revolution in China, his wholesale re-engineering of North Korean society seemingly faced little resistance. What emerged was called *songbun* – a class system which, far from being an organic reflection of existing social norms, was an artificial construct based strongly on Kim's own personal history and his citizens' proximity to it.

North Koreans are grouped into three classes: elite, middle and 'hostile'. These were the words used to explain it to me by Jihyun Park, the woman quoted at the beginning of this chapter, who as a child had foraged for food near her hometown of Chŏngjin. Others, however, have described it in more blackly humorous terms: 'tomatoes' versus 'apples' versus (green) 'grapes'. 'Tomatoes', which are red to the core, are worthy communists; 'apples', which are red only on the surface, need ideological improvement; and 'grapes' are hopeless.[17]

The family of Jihyun Park were of course no exception and were categorized according to this system. Her father drove a mechanical digger for an industrial company. In the West that might sound like a ticket to a lowly socioeconomic status, but in North Korea Park's father was actually in the elite class.

It may seem surprising that someone doing a job considered blue collar in most of the world would be in the top 10–15 per cent of North Korean society. But the class system, as with so much in the country, is unlike almost anything else on the planet. A citizen's place in this system is often directly related to their forebears' relationship to Kim Il Sung during his guerrilla years and the early formation of North Korea.

For example, Jihyun Park's grandfather had worked with Kim Il Sung's uncle during the 1930s, and she says this tenuous historical family connection was all it took to secure his descendants a permanent place among the elite, which generally means better housing, better job prospects, perhaps even foreign assignments, and an easier ride with the authorities in case of trouble.

Park's family situation was complicated by her mother's background, however Park's maternal grandfather had left Korea during the war of the 1950s. This perceived act of betrayal condemned her mother's side of the family to a place in the 'hostile' class.

The *songbun* regime is monitored and enforced with all the bureaucratic zeal that totalitarian regimes often apply to their various bigotries. The Workers' Party of Korea (the ruling political organization and, in reality, the only party that wields any power) researches citizens' backgrounds and histories, and keeps detailed records of their place in the system.[18]

Park says that, up until the age of sixteen, this didn't greatly affect her and her siblings, as they were judged on their father's elite background. But, as they moved into employment, there was further scrutiny from the authorities, and their maternal history came back to haunt them. Her sister, a talented computer programmer, failed in her applications for plum jobs. Her brother was shunned by the prestigious army institutions he applied to. Their mother's 'hostile' status was dragging down the family.

These weren't just the kind of early career setbacks most of us go through: in North Korean society a failure of this kind can condemn you to a miserable life of continuing low food rations, bad housing and harassment by suspicious officials. The kids' career prospects were pretty much the one chance the family had to win a better life, and they'd failed.

'At this time we really hated our mother, because our future was gone,' recalls Park.

Some explain the relative ease with which Kim Il Sung enforced this institutional nepotism by pointing to Korea's history of Confucianism, a philosophy which places the individual in a series of escalating relationships (thereby mentally preparing North Koreans to accept their fate under *songbun*). Others point to Korea's long history of feudalism (for centuries it had an elite class called the *yangban* and a serf class called the *nobi*). Still others believe it's at least partly the legacy of Japanese occupation, which forced Koreans to accept authoritarian bureaucracy.[19]

Whatever the truth, Kim Il Sung became the sun around which North Korean society revolved. The closer you are to the sun, the more light shines on you. Even today, the families who gained elite status thanks to their connection with him have passed it on to their offspring. But, as some would find out, getting too close can be very dangerous indeed.

As this system of extreme patriarchy bedded in, and as North Korea became more disconnected from the world and more beholden to Kim's *Juche*-driven leadership, he ascended to semi-divine status. Seats on which he sat on the subway in the capital, Pyongyang, were roped off as memorials upon which no others may sit; objects Kim Il Sung touched while on his many visits to schools and factories were covered and kept out of reach, like sacred objects.[20]

But, while those inside the country were increasingly taught to idolize him, by the late 1970s it was clear to many outside that Kim was not the genius of socialism some had believed he was in the post-war years. The wheels were starting to fall off his creation, and it was increasingly hard to disguise this. North Korea began to trade with capitalist Western countries and Japan, and by the mid-1970s 40 per cent of its business was with non-communist states.[21] This didn't come about because North Korea was wielding a powerful trading position; it was because it was desperate. Its debts to foreign countries at this point were estimated to be around $2bn, and there were reports that its cheques were starting to bounce. China and the Soviet Union stopped the supply of subsidized aid and materials in the 1980s.[22] People's food rations started to decrease from an already dangerously low level.

Already tottering, Kim then made two disastrous miscalculations.

In 1984 South Korea was hit by a famine. North Korea thought it could win a quick PR victory, making itself look superior to the South by offering to provide aid, including 7,200 tons of rice, from a stockpile it almost certainly didn't have.[23] Kim's advisers firmly believed the South would refuse out of principle. Instead, it said yes, and North Korea found itself on the hook. Those who escaped North Korea and were interviewed later reported watching with dismay as a small but sorely needed percentage of their rice ration was siphoned off to help a country they'd been taught was a mortal enemy.

The second error was North Korea's decision to host the 13th World Festival of Youth and Students in Pyongyang in 1989. Perhaps Kim was trying to make up for the ire of seeing a glitzy and successful Olympic Games held in the South Korean capital, Seoul, the previous year.[24]

Pyongyang offered to play host and reportedly splurged $4.5bn to do so – almost certainly borrowed dollars.[25] Not only did this risk incurring the wrath of North Korea's existing creditors, which still hadn't been paid back, but the festival brought to a partial end the decades of careful isolation from the outside world that Kim and his cadre had built up in his citizens. Suddenly, many North Koreans involved with the event saw foreigners arriving with nice clothes, gadgets, and tales of an outside world that looked very different from the dangerous and impoverished capitalist hellscape that North Koreans like Park had been told of.

Far from being a global PR victory for Kim Il Sung, some claim the Youth Festival, along with declining living standards, kicked off an industry of bribery and black marketeering. North Koreans increasingly realized the worth of foreign goods and currency, and some began to smuggle them into the country to supplement their dwindling resources.[26]

The world was changing. Kim Il Sung had adopted the King Canute approach, and now the water was up to his knees and rising. By the beginning of the 1990s China was doing more trade with South Korea than with the North.[27] But the big blow was yet to come. In 1991 the USSR broke up and quickly descended into chaos. Kim's biggest backer was on the ropes. Inside North Korea, of course, the vast majority of people knew nothing of this. All Park and her compatriots saw was the decreasing rice ration. 'They always said it was "weather problems" or "American problems",' she says. 'They always blamed something else; it was never socialism's problem.'

Meanwhile Kim Il Sung had morphed from a fatherly leader into a sexual predator. He had begun to recruit young women and schoolgirls to join what can only be described as an army of hostesses and sex slaves.[28] He had mansions dotted around the country, and set about populating them with women and girls. Sadly, he's by no means the first dictator to indulge his whims in such a way, but what makes Kim Il Sung different is the scale of his project. Some estimate as many as 2,000 women and girls were pulled into this system each year.[29] So extensive was the female pool that they came to be divided into three contingents: some were hostesses kept on to entertain dignitaries at parties; some were kept solely for sex; while others were kept for housework but were inevitably pulled into sexual favours too. Kim Il Sung's officials scoured schools to find new candidates. Some of those who fled the country recalled seeing girls being measured by inspectors to check if they fitted Kim's exacting standards before being taken away. The families of these 'successful' candidates were told their daughters were going to a prestigious career in service of the regime. Some were as young as twelve.[30]

It's possible that part of the motivation for this grim trade in prepubescent girls was a concern over Kim's life expectancy. While his citizens were taught he was near-invincible, Kim and his coterie knew his days were numbered, and great efforts were made to shore up his health. Some former aides have said that Kim's interest in girls went beyond sexually assaulting them, and that he believed mixing with young people might somehow stave off death.[31] It didn't. In 1994 Kim Il Sung, the leader who'd outlived nine US presidents, died, aged eighty-two.

By this time Park, always a talented mathematician, had found work as a high-school maths teacher (remarkably, Kim's ideology crept into even this abstract world – she tells me a typical arithmetic problem: 'If you kill five American soldiers and three South Korean ones, how many have you killed?').

'We were told there would be an emergency meeting at noon. There weren't usually emergency meetings during the daytime,' Park recalls. She started to ponder what such a big announcement might be. 'I thought, "Oh my God, they're going to announce unification [of North and South Korea]!"'

Instead, in front of the assembled school and similar gatherings right across the country, two newsreaders appeared on TV and solemnly told them of the sudden, unexpected death of the man many regarded as akin to a god.

Park remembers the silence lasting for a full five minutes. 'No one breathed.' Once the crying started, she recalls, it went on for days. While there were genuine outpourings of grief, the population was also monitored by regime officials looking for signs of insufficient mourning behaviour. 'The government told us: don't smile, don't drink alcohol, don't shout. If you did something wrong, your whole family would be punished.'

Rationally, North Koreans might have known this day would come. But decades of inculcation had suppressed the idea. As Park says: 'We never thought Kim Il Sung would die, because we learned that he's a god, we never talked about his death. We learned in history that in the 1930s Japanese soldiers would fire guns [at him], but he always survived.'

Waiting in the wings was his son Kim Jong Il. For decades he'd been groomed as the heir, and now his turn had come. But in addition to the ratchet effects set in motion by his father, the younger Kim would add his own, finally tipping North Korea over the edge.

The effort made by North Korea's propagandists to establish Kim Jong Il's reputation in the decades before he took power was arguably even more impressive than that made for his father. To their advantage, they had more of a clean slate to work from, so they started at the beginning, by faking his place of birth.

Kim Jong Il was born in Russia, where his father was working with the Soviets to retake Korea. This fact obviously doesn't chime well with the narrative of a strong, native-born hero, so North Korea's regime historians changed it.

One of the most sacred sites in North Korea is Mount Paektu, a breath-taking extinct volcano almost 10,000 feet high, its gleaming, water-filled caldera now christened the Lake of Heaven. It was here, according to a high-profile defector who recounted his story to the journalist Bradley Martin, that Kim Il Sung decided to reinvent his son's life story with a little help from his old guerrilla mates:

> He summoned the people who had participated in the partisan struggle and ordered them to find the site of the secret camp in Mount Paektu where Kim Jong Il was born. Obviously they could not find something that did not exist. So Kim Il Sung said that he would have to do it himself. He looked around and picked a scenic spot and claimed this was where the secret encampment had been . . . And this was where Kim Jong Il was born. He supposedly grew up in this hut listening to the sounds of gunshots of the partisans.[32]

There were good reasons to make an early start on the task of grooming Kim Jong Il to inherit his father's land. North Korea's political elite had no doubt watched the aftermath of the deaths of

Stalin in the Soviet Union and Mao in China, and perhaps concluded that a dynastic succession looked a hell of a lot less messy than a political process. So, in 1972, criticism of the hereditary system was taken out of the North Korean *Dictionary of Political Terminologies*.[33] Some believe that Korea's long feudal history and its Confucian emphasis on father–son relationships also helped to grease the wheels.

But the moment of Kim Jong Il's succession must still have felt like a time of maximum jeopardy for the new leader. No matter how much groundwork had been laid, there was still a chance that someone might stir up opposition to the inevitability of his succession; some powerful figure might see the chance to derail the Kim Dynasty and seize the throne.

On top of all this, the country that Kim Jong Il inherited was in crisis. Russia had gone from being a munificent communist ally to a failing state, and was now asking North Korea to pay for oil in hard currency. China too had other global trading priorities and was demanding market prices from North Korea (perhaps as a result, imports of coal from China dropped from 1.5m tons in 1988 to just 100,000 by 1996).[34] North Korea badly needed an overhaul. But Kim Jong Il couldn't provide it, thanks to another ratchet effect – one which he himself had been inadvertently cranking up for decades.

Kim Jong Il's inheritance was not a shoo-in. He'd worked extremely hard to secure it, mainly by bolstering the personality cult surrounding his father. At school he urged his classmates to read his father's works ten or twenty times to extract their deeper meaning. He arranged for busts of the old man to be manufactured and distributed to schools for prominent display.[35] He's even credited with coining the term 'Kimilsungism' to firmly nail North Korea's ideological roots to the man who created them.

But Kim Jong Il's boosterism created a downside (one which, to be fair, is always a risk in any dynastic succession). Having bought so totally into his father's reputation and urged so many others to do so, when Kim Jong Il came to power himself he could not immediately implement the desperately needed package of radical reform that would save his country from disaster, because it might be seen as unravelling the work of his now-hallowed father. Like his citizens, Kim Jong Il was trapped. North Korea stood on the brink of disaster, and one final push was all it took.

When you're constantly hungry, everything about food becomes an obsession. Seventeen years after she finally left North Korea, Jihyun Park still immediately recalls which two days of the month her mother was allowed to collect their food ration from the government store. 'The 4th and the 19th,' she says. Officially, workers were supposed to get between 700 and 900 grams of grain per day, students 400 grams and housewives 300 grams; around 30 per cent was in rice and the rest in corn, which is less nutritious. In practice, as the years wore on, the amounts bore little resemblance to the ration cards. It was even worse at the vegetable store: 'As soon as they brought the vegetables, everyone goes there. It's a war, shouting and fighting each other. There was never enough,' says Park.

To make crops grow on North Korea's challenging land often requires massive amounts of fertilizer, as well as electrical irrigation systems. Effectively its farmers have to replicate nature's usual bounty with man-made chemicals and machinery, and there's only a certain amount of punishment the land can take. Given this challenge, the idea of North Korea becoming self-sufficient for food was always a pipe dream, but it didn't stop Kim Il Sung from trying. Wedded unblinkingly to his *Juche* principles, the elder Kim advised his citizens to farm the hillsides. It was a classic piece of Kim's homespun, on-the-spot wisdom, but the consequences were a disaster. The hillsides were deforested to make way for farming but were not terraced, meaning they were perilously exposed. In 1995 summer downpours descended on the country. Crops and soil were sloughed down from the hillsides. Worse, this detritus ended up silting the rivers, which were then unable to cope with the ongoing deluge. So the rivers flooded, destroying yet more crops and then flowing into North Korea's coalmines, taking out a key energy source. People reacted by cutting down more trees for firewood, accelerating the vicious cycle of deforestation, erosion, silting, flooding and crop destruction. Supplies of subsidized oil and fertilizer from Russia dried up, further exacerbating the problems.[36]

With grim inevitability, the various ratchet mechanisms into which North Korea's leaders had tied the country began to wrench it almost to breaking point. Food supplies – always tenuous – now started to run out completely.

Even Park's elite family background couldn't insulate her from the consequences. More fights broke out over food. Children started to steal to feed themselves.

Then the dead, emaciated bodies appeared.

Park cannot forget the first one she saw: 'It was one of my students. He was really kind and passionate. He dreamed of becoming a doctor.' He was thirteen years old. 'When I saw his body I was really scared and just ran away.'

It would not be her last encounter with death in North Korea. She received news that her beloved uncle was gravely ill. 'We didn't say "famine", no one used the word, people just said, "They have an illness,"' she says. Her family managed to bring him to their home, but feeding him from their limited supply was a challenge. After seven days she watched him die, his body now just skin and bone, infested with lice. Unable to source a coffin, they buried his body in a sheet in the mountains overlooking Chŏngjin.

Park fled the following year. Her brother had been thrown out of the military, she says, and the regime was hunting for him; her father advised her to get out. Like many who escaped North Korea, she headed north to China. But the broker who engineered her escape tricked her, selling her as a slave to a Chinese man, with whom she had a son. She ended up in prison in China, from where she was repatriated back to a labour camp in North Korea. These camps are dotted around the country, and have been described as an 'essential component' of the regime's system of control. The stories told about them by former inmates who've subsequently escaped are horrific. Torture and starvation are commonplace. Prisoners are treated as slaves whose lives are barely worth preserving. Those who've tried to escape North Korea are treated particularly harshly.[37] Park recalls digging the land with her bare hands. Like most prisoners she was given very little food, and remembers eating seeds she'd picked out from animal dung. Her surviving uncle (still well connected as one of the elite class) managed to get her out, and she once again escaped through China, being reunited with her son along the way. She made her way to the UK, where in an unusual twist she ended up standing, albeit unsuccessfully, as a Conservative Party candidate for the local council in Bury in the north of England (asked why she stood for this particular party, she explains: 'Countries like North Korea don't care about the individuals and families, but Conservatives value these issues, so that's why I joined').

She's keen to share her story as someone who escaped North Korea, and she's not alone. As the famine kicked in, many more fled the growing hardship, despite North Korea's best efforts to stop them. Not only did these witnesses bolster the testimony of those who'd previously escaped (and whose accounts of life in North Korea had sometimes been looked on with scepticism), but they also alerted the world to the severity of the crisis in the isolated country.

By 1998 staff from the World Food Programme had arrived, discovering what North Koreans were already aware of: undernourished children and a food system on the brink of collapse.[38]

Estimates of the number of dead vary to an extent that seems astonishing at first: some as low as 240,000, some as high as 3 million. The truth is that putting a total number to the victims of the famine is hard, first, because of North Korea's predictable reluctance to give out any figures, but, second, because of the difficulty of categorizing which deaths are famine-related, against the 'background noise' of malnourishment and diminished life expectancy that had been going on for decades. Is it even possible to say when exactly the famine started? Park and others who escaped will tell you that it began long before the torrential summer of 1995.

Kim Jong Il's reaction to the famine and the exodus of citizens was telling. He established detention centres for captured escapees (effectively prison labour camps of the kind Park ended up in). And in 1995, right in the middle of the famine killing hundreds of thousands, he formalized the concept of *songun* – the policy of 'military first'.[39] From now on, priority across North Korean society would be given to the country's armed forces, already one of the world's largest per head of population. While his people starved, Kim Jong Il gorged the military with resources.

Those watching from the outside were not only horrified by North Korea's predicament and Kim Jong Il's reaction to it, but also confused. How was the country managing to stave off what looked like unavoidable economic collapse?

Thousands of miles from Pyongyang, in his office in Washington DC, one of those mulling this question was David Asher. At the time he was a senior adviser to the US State Department's North Korea Working Group and had been running the numbers, becoming increasingly perplexed about the regime's financial resilience.

'The North Korean economy was basically on its heels – I mean, near total bankruptcy,' he tells me. 'And then there comes a question as to how the heck is North Korea avoiding inflation? They had a huge trade deficit, which had gone on for over a decade. And there was no real sign of serious inflation, or basically much inflation at all. I mean, where did they get the money?'

An excellent question. And, as the millennium turned and Asher and his colleagues dug deeper, they believe they discovered an incredible answer. Caught in a trap of its own making and desperately short of income, North Korea had invented a unique solution to its financial woes. In a bizarre twist on the *Juche* self-reliance principle, it had created a potentially limitless source of illicit funds – something which led the country into ever-deeper links with the criminal community. North Korea had effectively given itself a licence to print money. All states have that ability, of course. The difference with North Korea was that it wasn't just churning out its own currency – it was printing someone else's.

3
Superdollars

The wedding was going to be a blow-out affair. Many of the guests had arrived in New Jersey from overseas, and they'd spent the lead-up to the big day partying hard in the gambling Mecca of Atlantic City.

The happy couple, Melissa Anderson and John Cavaricci, were splashing the cash. At a pre-wedding rehearsal they'd spent the night plying the guests with Dom Pérignon champagne. Melissa showed off an enormous engagement ring. The guests were also out to impress their hosts – some of them had bought Rolex watches as wedding presents.[1]

The attendees, mostly Chinese nationals who'd flown in specially for the occasion, assembled at the Trump Taj Mahal Hotel, nursing their hangovers as the limos arrived to take them to the wedding. The celebration was to be held on a yacht named *Royal Charm*, moored at Cape May, a picturesque beach resort at the very southern-most tip of New Jersey.

Under the summer sun the temperature was well into the 80s as the cars pulled up, driven by chauffeurs in tuxedos. The guests got in, and the cars whisked them away for the hour-long journey to the Cape. But none of them made it to the wedding. There was to be no ceremony, no exchange of vows, no lavish party. Because the men in tuxedos weren't chauffeurs; they were FBI agents. And, instead of driving them to the event, they delivered the wedding party into the waiting arms of a team of FBI officers who immediately arrested them all.

They had been snared in an incredibly elaborate sting operation – the culmination of a sprawling, fifteen-year campaign to crack down on what US law enforcement regarded as an existential threat to the very basis of American society. Someone had been trying to undermine America's financial system by flooding the world with fake dollar bills. And that someone, according to US investigators, was North Korea.

It all started in 1989. A cash handler at the Central Bank in the Philippines sensed something wasn't right with one of the $100 bills.[2] Maybe it was the feel of the paper, or perhaps there was something off about the printing. Some experts say that when you've run thousands of banknotes through your hands, you develop a sixth sense for detecting suspicious specimens.

The note was sent to the US, where it was examined by government experts. What they discovered deeply unnerved them.

Fake dollars are a fact of life: as long as there's value in a buck, there'll be criminals who try to counterfeit them. Every year US officials seize tens of millions of dollars' worth of fakes around the world. And so, for the US government, the Philippines $100 bill under their microscope back in 1989 was just a drop in the ocean.

However, what rang alarm bells was the quality of the counterfeit. Experts have repeatedly stated that it was by far the finest they'd ever seen – created using exactly the right paper, the right ink, the right printing press. Fear started to seep through the investigators' minds. If the fakes were up to this standard, they could have been slipping through the net for years. They could be everywhere. As one of them told a researcher: 'We have no idea how much they're counterfeiting, because it's so good.'[3]

Fear of counterfeiting is deeply embedded in American society, and its history goes right back to the origins of the modern US. During the Civil War it's estimated between a third and a half of all currency in circulation was fake.[4] This led to the creation of the US Secret Service, whose mission is to tackle currency crime (later it also took charge of protecting the President). As the US dollar has achieved apex status in global finance, America's job of keeping it secure has become commensurately more onerous.

So obsessive is the Secret Service about its task that every type of counterfeit banknote is assigned an ID number so it can be tracked and compared to other fakes as they emerge. The Philippines note was logged as C-14342. But then other notes started to turn up which seemed to be linked: the same printing process, the same paper. Not just $100 bills but $50 too – all, the Secret Service believed, the work of the same person or group. The original note had fathered a family of fakes, and now earned the designation PN-14342 (Parent Note).[5] It would eventually become known by a far more evocative title: the 'superdollar'.

Within years the high-quality counterfeit $100 bills started to arrive in more and more places. In 1993 they were sprouting in Japan, where police were seizing hundreds per year.[6] They were also turning up in the Middle East, notably Iran. Perhaps because of America's fractious relationship with the country, some US politicians concluded the notes were being produced in the region.[7]

But, in 1994, an incident occurred which led investigators to train their sights on North Korea instead. In June of that year a New York bank called Republic National reportedly bought $280,000 worth of $100 bills from a bank called Banco Delta Asia.[8] The latter was based in Macau, a former Portuguese colony that is now an enclave overseen by China.

On closer inspection, the notes turned out to include fakes, and further investigation revealed them to be superdollars. When Banco Delta Asia was asked where the dollars had come from, the trail led to a firm called Zokwang Trading. It was a tiny company on the fifth floor of a nondescript building in a residential district of Macau. Journalists who later visited and rang the bell (which played the French nursery rhyme 'Frère Jacques') found a normal-looking office. The only thing out of the ordinary was the artwork on the walls: portraits of Kim Il Sung and Kim Jong Il, the leaders of North Korea.[9]

As journalists circled Zokwang Trading, they sometimes described it as a 'front company' for the North Korean government. That might be a little unfair: in a closely managed socialist economy like North Korea's, it seems inevitable that its foreign trading operations will be overseen by the government. But, in this case, Zokwang's effective status as an arm of the state created a big headache for investigators trying to get to the bottom of the superdollars case: four Zokwang employees were arrested but later released because they had North Korean diplomatic passports.[10] It would become an enduring pattern, and one that would repeatedly frustrate attempts to track the superdollars' origin back to Pyongyang.

Meanwhile, spooked by the emergence of so many high-quality counterfeits, in 1996 the US redesigned the $100 bill, incorporating eight new security features. Among them was a watermark, micro-printed text apparently too small to be forged, and the number '100' in the corner, which was printed in special colour-shifting ink that appeared to change from green to black as it was moved in the light. They became known as the 'big-head' bills, because of the enlarged image of Benjamin Franklin in the centre.[11]

But the counterfeiters were undeterred. Within a few years new fakes had emerged that incorporated many of the security features built into the upgraded big-head notes. US experts were stunned to discover that not only were the new superdollars keeping pace with attempts to defeat them but were arguably even better than the real thing. One Treasury Department official told the *New York Times* that, under a magnifying glass, he noticed the hands on the clock tower of the Independence Hall were sharper than those on the genuine $100 note.[12] He, like other US officials, was convinced of North Korean involvement. During that year a remarkable story emerged that seemed to back up that theory.

In January 1995 a group of men walked into a photo shop in Pattaya, a beach resort in Thailand. The man who owned the shop reportedly ran an underground money-changing business, and the men wanted to sell $9,000 in $100 bills. Afterwards, the money-changer became suspicious. Sure enough, the notes were later found to be superdollars. The US Secret Service got involved and, along with Thai police, began to trace back the path of the money. It led them to Phnom Penh, the capital of Cambodia, around 400 miles east of Pattaya, and a man calling himself Kazunori Hayashi.[13] He was a frequent visitor to the North Korean Embassy.

The investigators looked more closely at their suspect. He wasn't Hayashi at all, they discovered. He was, in fact, Yoshimi Tanaka, one of the world's most-wanted terrorists.

Back in March 1970 Tanaka had been part of a far-left group in Japan called the Red Army. Like its more famous German equivalent, it was one of a slew of hard-left collectives around the world ready to use violent means to bring about an end to capitalism. Tanaka and his colleagues had risen to the cause with gusto. He and eight others hijacked a Japan Airlines plane carrying 129 passengers.[14] They released the hostages and forced the jet to fly to Pyongyang, where Tanaka was reportedly given a hero's welcome and enjoyed a comfortable life in North Korea. He later told journalists he and his fellow hijackers were given a team of helpers who would run their errands and 'repair our Mercedes-Benz cars'.[15]

After the hijack, Tanaka had gone to ground and not been heard of since. Then, in March 1996, thanks to the superdollars, investigators had tracked him down in Cambodia, where he was holed up in the North Korean Embassy. What happens next seems straight out of a film. According to media reports,[16] a Mercedes saloon with blacked-out windows and North Korean diplomatic number plates emerged from the embassy and raced for the border with Vietnam. Cambodian police pursued, but were slightly delayed after getting a flat tyre. By the time they caught up with the car, it was at the border, where its occupants were trying, unsuccessfully, to bribe a guard with $10,000 to let them through. The car turned tail and headed back to Phnom Penh, where it was finally stopped by police. Inside were three North Korean diplomats and Yoshimi Tanaka.

He was deported back to Thailand and stood trial for counterfeiting, but was acquitted in 1999 due to lack of evidence.[17] Nonetheless, his past had caught up with him. Within a year he was extradited back to Japan, where he pleaded guilty to the hijacking. He died in 2007 while still serving out his twelve-year sentence.[18]

Tanaka may have been acquitted of the counterfeiting offences, but, as the 1990s wore on, US officials were increasingly convinced that North Korea was not simply distributing the superdollars but actually printing them.

The argument goes like this: according to defectors, Kim Jong Il had been exhorting his overseas bureaucrats to pull in foreign currency since the 1970s to prop up the country's ailing economy. Each government department oversaw its own trading company, and foreign exchange was set for them as a key goal.[19] As North Korea's attempts to garner overseas cash became more desperate and the country battled famine and isolation, the theory goes, it took to creating its own supply and began to print $100 bills, gradually honing their quality to create the superdollar.

But how do you go about creating near-perfect replicas? Well, first, you need a printing press. And not just any press: to replicate greenbacks you'll need something like the mighty Koebau-Giori-De La Rue Intaglio Color 8, which is what churns out America's banknotes.[20] Usefully for North Korea, it has exactly such a machine. This is sometimes reported by the media as a shocking revelation, as in one BBC report which stated: 'In the late 1980s US intelligence discovered that the North Korean government had acquired a highly sophisticated printing press known as the Intaglio.'[21] In fact, it's no surprise that North Korea might have one of these printing presses. They're mainly made by an Italian firm called Giori (now part of German printing giant Koenig & Bauer)[22] and, as the firm's own website states: 'there is hardly a banknote in the world that has not been printed on a Giori machine.'[23] Like almost every government, North Korea issues paper currency, and so there's no reason why it wouldn't be able to buy – perfectly legitimately – an Intaglio press. (Koenig & Bauer refused to confirm whether a Giori press has been sold to North Korea, citing client confidentiality.)

To create the superdollars, North Korea would also need to use the right paper. Dollars are printed on a very specific type: it's a mix of 75 per cent cotton and 25 per cent linen sourced only from authorized manufacturers.[24] Any attempt to create an improvised version risks being spotted by US officials, who of course know exactly what the real thing is like. So how could North Korea get the right paper? Defectors have an explanation: they claim that they were told to acquire $1 bills and bleach them, then reprint them as $100 notes using the presses.[25]

What about the security features, like the special colour-changing ink? The major supplier of this ink (called OVI, Optically Variable Ink) is a firm called SICPA in Switzerland. It's been reported that it gave exclusive rights to the US for the green–black colour mix used in the $100 big-head note. Then North Korea approached SICPA and ordered colour-change ink to use on its own notes. Why on earth would North Korea want to use expensive counterfeit-prevention ink on its banknotes, when it's clear almost no one would be interested in forging them? Because, the argument goes, it allowed North Korea to obtain OVI supplies. The colour it ordered was a mix of green and magenta. This was then subsequently tweaked to resemble the green–black mix on the big-heads.[26]

Such counterfeiting work would have been a complex and expensive operation to pull together, and it seems unthinkable that in the high-surveillance state of North Korea it could have been done without the leaders' knowledge. Defectors told journalists the state was behind it all: 'The counterfeiting was all done at government level. We had a special plant for doing it in Pyŏngsŏng. We bought the best of everything, the best equipment and the best ink, but we also had the very best people, people who had real expertise and knowledge in the field.'[27]

It may have started as an elite operation, but it seems it didn't stay that way. Pretty soon the superdollars would wind up in the hands of some very surprising (and much less skilled) people. They would massively expand the superdollars operation. But their greed would end up garnering even more attention from law enforcement, ultimately exposing a whole new edifice of North Korean activity.

The security-camera footage is filmed in a run-of-the-mill travel agency in Stafford, in central England. It's 1.50 p.m., on 30 October

1998. A man arrives wearing jeans and a dark jacket, balding, in his mid-forties. He goes to the currency-exchange desk and hands the employee a stack of $100 bills. He hovers for a while as the teller counts the money and changes it for pounds sterling. The camera stutters. Then he walks away with the cash.

It all takes place in less than two minutes, but this would be the moment British police found themselves pulled into the superdollars story – a chase that would lead to Russia and, eventually, Pyongyang.

The notes the man had exchanged in Stafford were identified as superdollars as they passed through the banking system. US authorities tipped off the UK's National Crime Squad, which assigned two undercover officers under the codename Operation Mali to the case. Their mission: to befriend the man from the travel agency and work out where he'd got the dodgy cash.

Over pints of beer in the White Swan pub in Wythall, 50 miles south of Stafford, the undercover cops started to chat to the man about buying and selling cigarettes. But then he let them in on something better – fake cash.

'This is made on the same paper and the same ink, the same little coloured flecks in the paper,' he raved, unaware his boasts were being recorded by the undercover team. '[They've] had every test done on them you can think of. The people who handle them all the time would take . . . these ones for real ones.'[28]

The man introduced his new accomplices to the contact supplying him with these miraculous notes: Terence Silcock, described by one officer as 'a lifelong criminal who would turn his hand to any type of criminality'.[29] Silcock met them in a pub in Birmingham called the Dog. Things had come a long way from the tightly run, expert operation defectors had described in North Korea.

As police put him under surveillance, they found Silcock had an unusual habit. He would book a return flight from mainland Britain to Ireland, but would return home using the ferry rather than flying. It soon emerged why: he was carrying hundreds of thousands of dollars in superdollars back into Britain, and he believed security was weaker at the ferry terminal than at the airport.[30]

Silcock's Irish jaunts led police to the next link in the chain: a man who acted as courier, bringing the forged banknotes to Ireland from Moscow.

In another covertly taped conversation, the man described his fraught efforts to escape detection at Moscow's airport. 'I've got one hundred and eighty thousand fucking dollars. I had the fucking things stuffed down here . . . I have 'em fucking stuffed down here, stuffed down everywhere. I have [them] in my fucking pants, I can feel one slipping down the fucking inside of my fucking pants . . . put my bag through, walked straight through, not searched, end of fucking story. I'm gone.'[31]

What comes through loud and clear from the surveillance tapes – and what must have been painfully obvious to the watching police – was that these foul-mouthed chancers were petty crooks, not master criminals used to operating on a global scale. How on earth were they getting hold of some of the world's finest counterfeit currency? Clearly they didn't have the contacts to arrange all this. So who did?

Seán Garland was a larger-than-life figure in the Irish independence movement. He was also a committed communist. So when the Irish Republican Army split in 1969 he sided with the Marxist wing, which called itself the Official IRA.[32] He was also President of the Workers' Party of Ireland, the political wing of the OIRA. As such, he had carte blanche to travel the world meeting fellow communists. Investigators claim this became his cover as he developed a key role in the superdollars network.

Police had arrested one of the UK superdollars gang, who'd described buying tens of thousands of counterfeit $100 notes from Garland.[33] The source said Garland had walked into his hotel room, emptied a leather satchel containing 800 bills on to the bed and offered to sell them for $30,000. The deal happened at a hotel in Moscow. Clearly the Russian capital was a key link in the chain, and, if the police wanted to catch Garland red-handed, they'd need to go there. Next time Garland went to the Russian Federation, the police would be watching.

On 25 June 1999 Garland arrived in Moscow. For a committed communist he had expensive taste, checking in with his wife to the Metropol, a five-star hotel ten minutes' walk from the Kremlin.

For the US Secret Service, the idea of running a surveillance operation on Garland in the middle of Moscow probably brought them out in a cold sweat. So they approached the country's interior ministry, the MVD, to ask for help. Amazingly the Russians agreed to put Garland and his wife under 24-hour surveillance along with Silcock, who was also in the capital. It was a remarkable turn of events: here, in the birthplace of communism, officials were now willing to tail a leading Marxist figure, potentially taking American investigators to the door of one of Russia's oldest socialist allies, North Korea.

The MVD's report on Garland's movements was brief but revealing, according to a later account from a US legal representative: 'Garland and his wife were picked up at the Metropol Hotel by a sedan with diplomatic license plates registered to the Embassy of North Korea. The MVD followed the vehicle to the Embassy of North Korea. Garland and his wife were observed entering the embassy, where they remained for some two hours.'[34]

First, Garland's accomplices had incriminated him in the trade in superdollars, and now his former communist comrades had traced him to the embassy of the suspected source of fake money, whose diplomats had repeatedly been caught trying to foist off the fakes.

One North Korean defector told the BBC that Moscow was a hotspot for superdollars activity: 'Of all the North Korean embassies around the world, the biggest was in Moscow. Almost all North Koreans travelling abroad return via Moscow. People would go to the Treasury Department of the embassy. They would be given either real US dollars or counterfeit notes. Nobody knew what they were getting because you couldn't distinguish between the real money and the fake money. Only a very few people knew that the notes being given out were counterfeit.'[35]

Another defector, a former North Korean diplomat, says he found himself unknowingly carrying some of the fake bills: 'I was at a local bank in Thailand changing dollars in the bureau de change. They told me that the money I was giving them was counterfeit. I had fake notes mixed in with the real ones. It was confiscated but luckily for me they decided not to take it any further, I was released.'[36]

Meanwhile, the UK gang had learnt they were being watched while in Moscow. They had an accomplice, a former KGB officer who was involved in the superdollar criminal operation. It's believed his old contacts tipped him off about the MVD's surveillance of Garland and the others. The gang began to suspect a leak in their operation. The British police needed to act quickly before the suspects went to ground. They moved in to arrest Silcock, nabbing him in the same pub, the White Swan, where Operation Mali had started eighteen months before. In total, fourteen were arrested.

Garland, however, was not among those caught in the dragnet. He fled to the Irish Republic, where he spent years fighting American attempts to extradite him to face charges in connection with the superdollars plot (his colleagues labelled the extradition proceedings an 'attack at the hands of the bourgeois state').[37] He died in 2018, taking whatever secrets he knew to his grave. Despite the best efforts of law enforcement, Garland was never caught with superdollars in his hands. Neither did the operation reveal direct evidence linking North Korea with the trade in forgeries, let alone their manufacture.

The Americans now faced a much bigger problem, much closer to home. Superdollars were washing up on US shores. Millions of dollars' worth were being shipped in through ports. Counterfeiting overseas is bad enough, but, with the forgers now trying to infect domestic-currency supplies, the US response went into top gear. It would lead to an audacious undercover operation by the FBI – one that would make the British police's pub-based efforts pale by comparison.

*

Inasmuch as it's possible to imagine what an undercover FBI agent looks like, Bob Hamer really fits the bill. He's grizzled, stubbly and speaks in a gravelly, laconic drawl. 'I got into undercover work mainly because I watched too much television as a kid. It just seemed like undercover work would be the exciting way to go. After I had my first assignment, it was an adrenalin rush and I kind of chased that adrenalin drag the rest of my career,' he tells me.

In twenty-six years' service he had posed as a burglar, a drug dealer, an international weapons trader and even a contract killer. Now retired, he's carved out a career as a writer, penning novels with titles like *Blood in the Desert* and *Targets Down*.

Back in 2002, Bob's bosses came to him with a new undercover operation: he would be trying to infiltrate a gang smuggling knock-off cigarettes into the US. Bob was underwhelmed: 'It's kind of like "Man, why is the FBI working counterfeit cigarettes?" But I didn't care if it meant I could get out of the office.'[38]

So he took on the assignment of tracking the criminal syndicate behind the smuggling operation. At this point, all he knew was that they were a Chinese gang. So he came up with a cover story. 'I was an older white man. I had a warehouse in the Los Angeles area. I could store their contraband or whatever in my warehouse, and I could help them move it across the country.'

Soon the case expanded beyond counterfeit cigarettes. Hamer got into stolen cars, clothing, weapons and fake pharmaceuticals such as Viagra.

And the drugs didn't stop there. As Hamer earned the criminals' trust, they let him in on bigger and bigger schemes. Then one day they hit him with a jaw-dropping proposal – something which revealed that the criminal syndicate he was working with was closely linked to the Pyongyang regime. The gang wanted Hamer to set up a crystal-meth laboratory in North Korea. The idea was to produce 600 kilos of the drug. He was told the Chinese middlemen would keep one third, Hamer another and North Korea the final third.

'North Korea would ensure the successful production and the

successful exportation of the crystal meth out of the country,' says Hamer. 'And then we had to turn over the manufacturing plant to North Korea. It was going to be [turned into] a laundry-detergent factory. My case agent talked to a Drug Enforcement Administration official who said, yes, the same equipment that can make crystal meth could make laundry detergent. I didn't know that.'

Hamer was keen, but his bosses vetoed it – the idea of undercover US government involvement in crystal-meth manufacture was a stretch too far, it seems.

Besides, Hamer's bosses now had a more important assignment: the superdollars worth millions that had been discovered arriving into the US by boat. The prospect of fakes flooding the home market was deeply concerning. Could Hamer use his smuggling contacts to get hold of some of the notes, potentially giving US law enforcement a lead? Sure enough, Hamer's gangland connections obliged, providing him with samples. But when Hamer gave some of them to his FBI bosses, the response was unexpected. 'The analysts in LA said that this money was real,' Hamer tells me. 'I kind of laughed and I said, "Well, they're willing to sell me this 'real' money for 35 cents on the dollar. So if you're telling me that that this is real, I'm going to mortgage my house and I'm buying as much as they're willing to sell me!" '

The notes were returned to the headquarters in Washington DC for more analysis. This time, word came back: these were indeed superdollars. Now the challenge was to catch those importing them.

On the West Coast, where Hamer was based, an FBI sting was set up under the name Operation Smoking Dragon. On the East Coast, where superdollars had also been arriving, a parallel effort was called Operation Royal Charm.

Hamer arranges to buy a million dollars of the fakes, paying $350,000.[39] He's told the counterfeits will arrive in a shipping container filled with numbered rolls of fabric. Hamer is given the numbers of the rolls that will contain the dollars. The container is delivered, and, in the privacy of Hamer's warehouse, he and his FBI colleagues start to unpack the carpet rolls. But none of them match the numbers Hamer's expecting. He fears they've been ripped off. 'There had been some concern by the FBI that this was a sting [by the criminals],' he recalls.

Finally, right at the back of the container, they find the right rolls. 'We're all excited because we pull out the numbers that we're looking for. My case agent and I, we're down on the ground rolling out the fabric and we can't feel anything. And we're pushing the fabric, unrolling it, unrolling it, unrolling it. And eventually we feel, like, a knot and we keep pushing it a little bit further. And there it is, these bundles of the counterfeit bills that are taped on to the very end of the roll. And it was like a little kid at Christmas time. We had our million dollars.'

Now the FBI is in a position to make arrests. But with the suspects overseas, it needs a ruse to get them on to US soil. On the East Coast, two of the undercover FBI agents had been posing as boyfriend and girlfriend. Now they use their fake relationship as the hook – announcing their engagement and inviting their overseas counterfeit smuggling contacts along to a glitzy wedding in New Jersey. No effort or expense is spared. Invites are sent out on expensive-looking gold-trimmed notepaper. 'Hotel accommodation and transportation to the wedding will be provided,' the invites state – little did the guests know that the transportation would be into the criminal-justice system, and not to the nuptials.[40]

The four-carat-diamond engagement ring worn by 'Melissa Anderson', the bride-to-be, has been lent to her by the FBI, from its stores of seized criminal goods (just like the purple Porsche Carrera driven by one of her undercover colleagues).[41]

Across the other side of the country, Hamer sets up his own sting and takes the polar opposite tack when it comes to inventing a story. 'In my undercover capacity, I was married and I had a female FBI agent who was [posing as] my girlfriend. So I told the bad guys that my wife had found out about my girlfriend and she was filing for divorce. I told them that I was going to have a divorce party at the Playboy Mansion. I hadn't contacted [*Playboy*'s then Editor-in-Chief]

Hugh Hefner,' jokes Hamer. 'I hadn't made reservations at the mansion. But none of the bad guys followed up on it.'

The wedding is to be on Sunday, 21 August 2005, at 2 p.m., with Hamer's divorce party the following day. As the suspects arrive, the hammer falls. Fifty-nine people are arrested. Among them is a smuggler who was later sentenced to twenty-five years in jail for offering to import shoulder-to-air missile launchers.[42]

The dragnet snared culprits from China, Taiwan, Canada and the US – but none were from North Korea. By now the US government was unequivocal in its claims that not only were the notes distributed by North Korea but they 'emanated' from that country.[43] Yet, given the many years of work by US law enforcement and others, how come no North Korean had ever been convicted? For some there's a simple explanation: most North Koreans who are allowed to travel abroad are government workers, and they're protected by diplomatic immunity.

North Korean officials have their own explanation as to why their compatriots have been caught so often with counterfeit bills. A diplomat in Hong Kong told the *Wall Street Journal*: 'North Koreans have no choice but to carry large amounts of cash, as the US freezes us out of the global financial system.'[44] The suggestion is that this cash-based existence makes North Koreans more susceptible to ending up with counterfeit notes, an argument made by others sceptical of accusations of North Korea's involvement with superdollars. That may be true, but, given the relatively small number of counterfeit notes in circulation, you'd have to be damned unlucky to be caught repeatedly with thousands of them, as North Korea's officials have been.

But the conspicuous lack of North Korean convictions has led to scepticism among some about claims of the country's involvement in superdollars.

Some question the logistics of creating such a counterfeiting operation. Defectors may claim that they took $1 bills and bleached them to create authentic paper for $100, but experts dispute that this is possible with the newer bills. One former employee of the Bureau of Engraving and Printing told me that the value of the note is micro-printed on to the bill, and that this would survive the bleaching process, exposing any attempt to reprint the bill at a higher value. If true, it means the North Koreans would have to have acquired the right paper another way, or created it themselves.

As with many of the allegations made against it, North Korea sees the superdollars 'plot' as a stitch-up, an attempt by its enemies, notably the US, to smear it. Logically, however, this makes no sense. If America is trying to get one over on North Korea, doing so by deliberately jeopardizing trust in the dollar – a major factor in US global hegemony – would be an insane tactic.

Nonetheless, short of verifiable video footage, direct evidence of North Korea printing superdollars is lacking. Even in 2009 a Congressional Research Service report equivocated about 'whether the DPRK is responsible for the actual production or not'.[45]

What is certainly true, however, is that North Korean officials and those connected to them have repeatedly been caught passing on the world's highest-quality forged notes. And, so far as the US is concerned, this would give it a key bargaining chip in its dealings with North Korea, which have become even more fractious, and even more high-stakes.

That's because, despite the lack of North Korean arrests, the FBI's undercover sting operations Royal Charm and Smoking Dragon opened up a fresh line of inquiry, one that would lead investigators almost back to the beginning of the story – the tiny bank in Macau that had been one of the first to be embroiled in the superdollars plot.

From 2001 David Asher had been working for the State Department, trying to answer the question posed at the end of the last chapter: how was the North Korean economy staying on its feet, given the famine, the isolation and the country's parlous financial management?

'I mean where did they get the money? And I'm thinking there is only one source that I can see and that's crime,' he tells me.

In 2003 he'd helped to establish the Illicit Activities Initiative, aiming to gather evidence of North Korea's alleged criminal behaviour.[46] According to him, things went very well. 'We found billions of dollars in illicit funds being produced. It was like a separate economy. It was extremely well run. And what made it particularly interesting to me was that it came right under Kim Jong Il. He was the mob boss. He was the Tony Soprano. He was the Pablo Escobar. But he also was the head of state.'

To be clear: Asher is a 'hawk', an outspoken critic of the North Korean regime who believes hard words (and ideally hard action) are vital in reforming the country. And it's left him with some interesting mementos. As we speak, he rummages through the contents of his desk drawer: North Korean counterfeit cigarettes, birth-control pills, Viagra ('We asked [Viagra's manufacturer] Pfizer: does this work?' he tells me. 'And the answer that came back was "Yes, it does work", and, by some standards, it's much more potent and long lasting and there's side effects with that, which I don't want to elaborate on . . .').

The superdollars became part of Asher's investigation, and, as the FBI's undercover operations against the smugglers progressed, he says the money trail led back to Macau, and to Banco Delta Asia, the bank which had been caught selling superdollars from North Koreans back in 1994.[47] It seems the US Treasury agreed. In 2005 it announced its belief that Banco Delta Asia was a 'primary money-laundering concern'.[48]

The Banco Delta Asia crackdown would go on to have even greater ramifications. As part of the action against the bank, the Monetary Authority of Macau froze $25m that was held in North Korean-linked accounts at Banco Delta Asia. That money would now become a bargaining chip in a high-stakes game of poker, as North Korea pressed ahead with its ambitions to become a nuclear power, introducing a frightening new dimension to the dynamics that had previously driven relations between the country and the rest of the world.

As for the superdollars, around 2006 there was a change of tone from Pyongyang. The regime said it would prosecute counterfeiters (raising the outlandish suggestion that in rigidly controlled North Korea the forging could have been done by criminals without government knowledge and sanction).[49]

Perhaps North Korea had decided it didn't need the superdollars any more. After all, at this point in time there was a financial revolution under way. Online banking, retailing and investment were taking off. The world was being computerized, and money was no exception. And, according to security researchers, North Korea's leaders were embracing this new scene with gusto – not to take part in the democratizing tech revolution enjoyed by the rest of the world, of course, but as a new way to exert power on behalf of the regime. North Korea's military was going online – and the world would soon feel the consequences.

4

Dark Seoul

Wednesday, 20 March 2013, started like a normal day for Son Taek Wang. As the diplomatic correspondent for YTN, a 24-hour TV news station in South Korea, he'd arrived as usual at the studio, near a giant transmitter mast in the middle of the greenery of Namsan Park overlooking the capital, Seoul. But, just after lunch that day, something strange started to happen to the office computers. The usual, friendly Windows icons were gone – instead staff members were greeted by a black screen with the words 'Boot Device not found. Please install an operating system on your hard disk' in white text. For techies this is a heart-sinking message – it means something's gone badly wrong with the machine. Diagnosing and fixing it is a real headache.

But to Wang it didn't seem like a big deal. 'We'd had similar problems from time to time because of technical issues,' he tells me. 'And when that happened we had our own team to control it, they took care of it. On-site reporters, including myself, we did nothing. It's not my job, it's their job.'

Wang certainly didn't think it had anything to do with his area of journalistic expertise: he was a veteran reporter who'd covered North–South relations during the fractious decades outlined in the preceding chapters. 'At that moment I didn't recognize how big it was,' he says. Quite the contrary: thanks to the computer problems Wang was secretly relishing a bit of downtime. Besides, he could still write articles and get on air thanks to the back-up systems the company had installed.

It was only a few hours later, after YTN's engineers had pulled together some workarounds to get the computers up and running, that Wang realized this was no normal computer glitch. He'd started to discover that YTN wasn't the only company affected: computers had gone down at exactly the same time at two other major broadcasters, MBC and KBS, as well as two big banks, Shinhan and Nonghyup.[1]

While the TV companies managed to stay on air, reports were coming in that people were having trouble getting cash from ATMs because of the computer trouble at the banks. Far from an isolated IT outage, this was starting to look like a co-ordinated campaign with some serious consequences.

Then came the briefings from the South Korean government and National Intelligence Service. Hackers had infiltrated the banks' and broadcasters' networks, they said. One of the world's most technologically advanced nations was under digital attack. And it was not to be the last incident. Within months more key parts of the South's digital infrastructure would be taken down, apparently by the same cyber-attackers.

As YTN's long-serving diplomatic correspondent, Wang had observed the many physical incidents which had inflamed tensions between the two states. But now a new front was opening up in the conflict. North Korea's military had discovered the Internet, and things would never be quite the same again.

Just a couple of months before the March attacks, North Korea had opened its doors to an unusual and intriguing delegation. Stepping off the plane into the freezing January air of Pyongyang was one of the most powerful people in the tech industry (and therefore, arguably, one of the most powerful in the world).

Eric Schmidt was Chairman of Google. With him was Bill Richardson, former Governor of New Mexico, who'd visited Pyongyang several times over the years and had helped to broker the trip. With both of them was Jared Cohen, then thirty-two years old and head of Google Ideas, a think-tank set up within the online search giant.

Cohen and Schmidt were working on a book about the future of the Internet: 'trying to understand the worst pockets of the world in terms of censorship and cyber-attacks', Cohen told Jean H. Lee, my co-host for our BBC World Service podcast *The Lazarus Heist*. 'We were thinking about what countries would be interesting to go to as a way to give us additional context.'

When he learnt that Cohen had never been to South Korea, Schmidt suggested a visit. Cohen – a veteran of Internet censorship battles from Iran to Congo during his time at the US State Department – suggested North Korea might be 'more interesting'. He says that Schmidt jokingly responded: 'You just don't like stability.'

The trip was controversial. Cohen says there'd been pressure from some in the US government to postpone or cancel entirely. Richardson had to clarify that they were just private individuals taking a fact-finding trip, and not official representatives of the American government.[2] Although when an American ex-politician arrives in Pyongyang with two senior executives of one of the world's biggest companies, it's hard to ignore the political overtones.

North Korea had clearly weighed up the arguments and decided that the propaganda wins outweighed the downsides. It didn't matter that Schmidt and Cohen were calling out the country as an example of extreme online censorship: a tech titan was on North Korean soil, and that was the most important thing. And, as we'll see, the visit neatly tied in to a narrative the country's leaders had been carefully cultivating over the preceding years.

Meantime, however, Cohen was struggling with something that afflicts any savvy visitor to Pyongyang: the nagging sense that he couldn't trust anything he saw.

'At first you assume there are pockets of fake. [But] after spending a couple of days in Pyongyang, what you start to realize is the entire city seems to be fake, and you never quite figure out where the fake stops and the real starts. So you'll see kids playing in the snow as you're driving by a road. And after two days there, you look at that and you wonder: is that staged for us? Is this whole thing just kind of a *Truman Show*-type play that's being put on for us?' he says, referencing the 1998 movie in which Jim Carrey plays a man unaware that his whole life is being filmed for public consumption.

Remarkably, the answer to Cohen's questions might be 'yes'. Those who've fled North Korea have described how officials carefully prepare for foreign visitors, instructing citizens on what clothes to wear when reporters are in town, and giving them sample questions and answers to provide should the foreigners try to interact with them.[3]

But, unlike the film's eponymous character, Cohen was aware all along that the whole thing might be a set-up, and that quickly fostered in him the kind of fear induced in anyone living in such an intensively managed and monitored environment. He began to suspect (not unreasonably) that the hotel he was staying in was rigged with surveillance: 'the only time I've ever been to another country and made a conscious decision to shower in a bathing suit, I was in North Korea,' he recalls.

A key goal of Cohen and Schmidt's trip was to get a handle on North Korea's tech scene: 'What is the state of their infrastructure, and how many people have access to the benefits that come with that infrastructure?' asks Cohen. 'I think there was an element of curiosity: if we go to North Korea, what will conversations about the Internet even sound like?'

The answer is that it very much depends whom you ask, as Cohen found out on one of his guided excursions around the capital. 'You have these perfectly manicured traffic ladies with these big, puffy earmuffs all dolled up in makeup. And they're doing these acrobatic dances where they're directing traffic in very ceremonial ways on these ten-lane highways that have no cars on them,' recalls Cohen. Videos of the women had become a hit on YouTube, Google's video-sharing platform. 'I remember going up to one of them and telling her she was a YouTube sensation. And I had a translator with me and she kind of looked at me puzzled and I realized, not only does she not know what YouTube is, even if I was to explain that it was a video platform on the Internet, she wouldn't even know what the Internet was.'

The vast majority of North Koreans have no way of getting online. The mechanics of Internet communication that most of us take for granted – phoning up a broadband provider or mobile-phone company and getting hooked up – are simply not an option.

But not everyone in North Korea is shielded from digital life. Some sections of society have every bit as much technology at their disposal as Cohen and his peers, as he discovered when he visited the private train of Kim Jong Il.

'They had this massive train, and inside the train car it was outfitted for Kim Jong Il,' he recalls. 'And there was this beautiful silver MacBook.'

Here in the heart of anti-capitalist North Korea, in one of the inner sanctums of its avowedly socialist leader, was a gleaming icon of the American capitalist dream: an Apple laptop. Kim was not afraid of modern technology. Far from it: he'd been a major force in bringing North Korea into the digital age, albeit for his own very idiosyncratic reasons, as senior members of his administration had discovered.

Thae Yong Ho is one of the most high-profile defectors ever to leave North Korea. Before fleeing in the summer of 2016, he was Deputy Ambassador to the UK. One minute he was espousing Kim's policies and toeing the party line, the next he was exposing the regime's most intimate secrets. North Korea's reaction was predictably blunt: it made unsubstantiated accusations against him for a string of serious crimes and labelled him 'human scum'.[4] Thae is now a National Assembly member in South Korea.

He clearly recalls the moment when North Korea's leaders got switched on to tech: 'I entered North Korea's foreign ministry in 1988. And when I first entered, there was not even a single computer in my department, no computers at all. But entering into 1989 [and] the early 1990s, all of a sudden there was . . . a booming of connecting the offices of the foreign ministries up with computers. All of a sudden the leaders of the foreign ministry mentioned about the importance of using computers,' Thae told Jean H. Lee in an interview for *The Lazarus Heist* podcast.

Thae believes this networking boom was triggered by the

offspring of Kim Jong Il. The leader had been sending his children abroad for their education – mostly to Switzerland – and Thae believes they'd gone back to North Korea enthused about the digital revolution taking hold in the outside world. 'They were the ones who, I think, enlightened their father.'

It seems likely they were pushing at an open door. Kim Jong Il had long seen the potential of tech to solve many of his country's problems. He declared a 'technical revolution' in the early 1970s, hastening through modernization of factories, and, he promised, 'finally freeing all the working people from backbreaking labour' (although some believe his tech-development drive was actually a consequence of his increased militarization, which had stretched the labour force too thin and deprived the factories and farms of workers). By 1989, former North Korean citizens say, the regime was sending students to East Germany to learn about computers.[5] These modern devices were not just tools to increase factory output: the big revolution was in networking, allowing computers to communicate with each other. For a secretive, reclusive leader like Kim Jong Il, these networked computers were a godsend, because they allowed him to transmit orders to his minions without ever having to reveal his whereabouts. According to Thae Yong Ho: 'Kim Jong Il quickly caught the advantages of these computers and networking so that he [could] hide very easily where he stayed and worked, so he could have an even more efficient way to control the North Korean system. From that time on, it was very difficult to detect where Kim Jong Il stayed and where Kim Jong Il worked because . . . orders were delivered through the computers.'

But it wasn't just about hiding behind the screens. There was another reason Kim Jong Il was so keen on computerization – one that would have serious, lasting consequences for North Korea's people and their country's place in the world order. It would trap them in a terrifying cycle of military stand-offs that would, in turn, drive their country's leaders to escalating levels of crime.

*

It's October 2010, the 65th anniversary of the Workers' Party of Korea. A giant celebration is being held in Kim Il Sung Square, the favoured venue for North Korea's tightly choreographed displays of military might. If you've ever seen footage of the country's leaders staring out stoically as a parade of missile launchers rolls by, it was almost certainly filmed here.

But tonight things are different. Instead of parades of tanks and missiles, green disco laser lights illuminate the sky. Blaring music starts and thousands of young dancers flood across the square in a spandex phalanx. The men are clad in lurid lime-green bodysuits, the women in equally garish orange mini-dresses. As they execute a co-ordinated dance routine, they sing, and then the columns of dancers reel into formations, all caught on camera from above. It's the kind of mesmeric display that totalitarian regimes seem to pull off so well, 'the fascination of geometry', as some have called it.[6] As the song reaches its climax, the thousands of dancers merge seamlessly to spell out three letters, 'CNC', and, on giant screens on the surrounding buildings, there's an image of a rocket being launched into the sky.[7]

The letters stand for Computerized Numerical Control. As the Wikipedia entry helpfully explains: 'A CNC machine processes a piece of material (metal, plastic, wood, ceramic, or composite) to meet specifications by following a coded programmed instruction and without a manual operator directly controlling the machining operation.'[8] In other words, if you install a CNC system in a factory that makes widgets, the computer will take care of cutting the components to the right size and shape.

Why on earth is North Korea so hyped about CNC technology? Why compose an entire anthem dedicated to it (one which, whenever Kim Jong Il heard it, would make him 'shed tears as he recollected the arduous road he had travelled and the mental agony he had overcome while introducing CNC technology')?[9] Why is North Korea making, quite literally, such a big song-and-dance about it?

According to North Korea watchers, CNC wasn't just about letting computers control manufacturing. There was a much darker context behind it all: the computers were a key component in a power-grab that North Korea hoped would allow it to punch far above its weight on the world stage. With the collapse of the Soviet Union, China's shift towards capitalism and rising tension with the international community, North Korea's economic and strategic position had become increasingly precarious. Kim Jong Il had a plan to get his country back in the game: nuclear weapons.

The history of nukes on the Korean peninsula began around the end of the Korean War, and it's the Americans who started the ball rolling. In 1953 the US had hinted that it might use nuclear weapons to bring the war to an end.[10] After the conflict finished, as North Korea nestled into the Soviet bloc under an uneasy truce, the Americans sent missile units to South Korea in 1958.[11]

Within this context, North Korea almost certainly saw clear justification for developing its own nuclear programme, with both energy and military applications – the former being part of its policy of *Juche*, and the latter being self-defence against a nuclear aggressor it felt was frighteningly close.

With help from the Soviets, work began on a reactor complex at Nyongbyong in the 1960s. By 1979 the North was going it alone, with a reactor operational by the mid-1980s.[12] Rumours that the plant was being used for weapons development began spilling out a few years later, despite the fact that North Korea had signed the Treaty on Non-Proliferation of Nuclear Weapons (NPT) the year before the reactor went online.

In 1991 then-US President George Bush announced his country would withdraw its nuclear weapons from overseas bases, including South Korea. If the North's argument for developing weapons was the proximity of American missiles in the South, it was now on thin ice.

What followed was a grim, decade-long tick-tock of diplomacy and denial, cajoling and compromise, as the international community desperately tried to steer Kim away from his weapons programme. Ultimately, it failed.

On 9 October 2006 North Korea conducted its first nuclear test. Just a few months earlier it had test-fired a ballistic missile, raising fears the two technologies could eventually be combined to stage a long-range nuclear attack.[13]

None of this could have been achieved without those Computerized Numerical Control systems. The awesome atomic forces unleashed by nuclear power and rockets (whether for civil or military use) can be contained only within extremely high-precision components, and they can be machined only using technology like CNC. This is why North Korea trained thousands of young dancers to sing CNC's praises that night in 2010, accompanied by footage of missile launchers. It wasn't just a way to bring North Korea's factories into the twenty-first century; it was also the country's ticket to the nuclear-weapons club.[14]

Kim may have told his people that the nuclear-weapons programme was essential to counter an existential threat facing their country. But it also fulfilled a second purpose: Kim believed he could use nukes to buy a seat at the international table. And it worked.

North Korea's withdrawal from the NPT in 2003 had led to six-way talks between North and South Korea, Japan, Russia, China and the US. Which meant that tiny North Korea now sat opposite some of the world's superpowers. As far as Kim was concerned, it was a coup. He had dragged his long-sworn enemy, the US, to the negotiating table, and could now use the nuclear threat to extract some concessions. One thing he was determined to include on the agenda was the unfreezing of the $25m in North Korean accounts that had been blocked when the US took action against Banco Delta Asia. He got his wish. In return for agreeing to shut down the main reactor at Nyongbyong and allowing inspections by the International Atomic Energy Agency, Kim duly got back the $25m.[15] The detente didn't last. It seemed that, for Kim, the negotiations were simply a poker game. By 2009 North Korea had pulled out of the six-party talks, and in May of that year carried out another nuclear test, creating a detonation many times bigger than its first.[16]

Sanctions followed. Within a week of the first nuclear test the UN had passed Resolution 1718, banning UN member states from supplying North Korea with military supplies and luxury goods.[17]

And so a pattern emerged. Each nuclear test (and the missile launches that were interspersed between them) led to fresh sanctions from the international community. North Korea's reaction was to keep up the nuclear programme, pile on the pressure and follow its military ambition unswervingly.

Kim Jong Il's thirst for nuclear weapons and the power they conferred had now locked North Korea and its people into a trajectory similar to that of his rockets: dangerous, and ultimately doomed to failure. Once again North Korea's leaders would not back down, but nor could they win. Each military advance and resultant sanction pushed the country's economy further towards the brink and cemented its reputation as a pariah state, which in turn pushed its leaders to pursue more missile and nuclear technology to use as political leverage. Kim Jong Il had trapped his country into yet another ruinous ratchet effect.

Arguably, it was his last major act as leader. On 17 December 2011 Kim died, aged sixty-nine.[18]

Now came the difficult question of succession. Whereas the leadership had spent decades grooming Kim Jong Il for power by carefully introducing him to the public, curating his backstory and allowing him ever-greater roles in governing the country, they'd had a far shorter timeline with his heirs. As Kim Jong Il's health deteriorated in the years leading up to his death, they began the fraught task of preparing the next generation of the Kim Dynasty.

Kim Jong Un was the child of Kim Jong Il's second mistress (the older man reportedly had two wives and three mistresses). By 2009 it was obvious even to outsiders that, among his father's three sons, he was a prime candidate for the top spot. And, sure enough, as the dancers sang of their love for CNC back in 2010, it was Kim Jong Un who was seen clapping along at his father's side, a clear indication of his standing in the pecking order.[19]

Kim Jong Un assumed power aged barely thirty, even younger than his grandfather had been when he became leader (exactly how old he was is a tricky question – there's speculation that his official birthday may have been fabricated by the North Korean authorities to make it a more auspicious date).[20] The apparatchiks who surrounded Kim now faced a problem: how to quickly bolster the reputation of a baby-faced man who clearly had neither the military kudos of his grandfather nor the governmental experience of his father.

Their solution was canny: they pitched Kim Jong Un as the millennial leader. He was painted as a vibrant character with his finger on the pulse who would embrace tech to take his country forward.

North Koreans (if they can afford it) can now buy basic mobile phones and tablet computers, usually imported from China. Some former citizens have even described owning a laptop computer – although, thanks to the country's sketchy electricity supply, they also described having to power it up using a petrol-driven generator.[21] But the influx of these devices presented a big headache for the new leader, as Google exec Jared Cohen realized during his trip to Pyongyang: 'It's a control issue. There's such a such a fine line for the leadership. They want to open up. They know that they need information. They know they need outside help. But with that comes the possible loss of control over the flow of information. And I think that's a really tricky line that Kim Jong Un is walking, and trying to figure out how he can maintain totalitarian control, while still allowing in enough of that information to help his country develop economically.'

Kim's solution was a strict system of control over who could access the Internet. First up: the elites.

'The 0.1 per cent of North Korea, the most senior leaders in the military, the political establishment and their families do have regular access to the global Internet,' says Priscilla Moriuchi. She now works for Apple's threat-intelligence unit, but previously spent more than a decade studying and reporting on North Korea for America's National Security Agency, after which she helped to compile a report for a tech-security firm which shed an intriguing light on the online lives of the country's rich and powerful.[22] Because of the Internet's open architecture they were able to analyse online traffic heading in and out of North Korea, even working out what type of websites they were visiting. 'We do know that the senior leadership are regular Internet users. They check social media, they look at global news, they stream video normally, like the rest of us,' says Moriuchi.

Such unrestricted access is of course strictly controlled within the country, and is a perk reserved only for the very top tier, as Thae Yong Ho discovered while he was still Deputy Ambassador to the UK. One day he was given a somewhat unusual assignment: 'I was with Kim Jong Chul, the brother of Kim Jong Un, for three and a half days when he travelled to London to watch Eric Clapton.' It turns out the new leader's older brother was a big fan of the British guitar legend, and travelled the world to see his concerts. No sooner had he landed in London in 2015 than he was surfing the Internet. 'He was just a genius using the network,' remembers Thae, 'because as soon as he arrived at a hotel, he searched the Internet to track all the recent records of Eric Clapton's performances. So I was surprised the man from Pyongyang was much, much better than me at using the Internet.'

Kim Jong Chul's entourage eschewed the hotel Internet connection and used more than a dozen 'burner' Wi-Fi dongles, swapping them every two hours or so. 'I was shocked,' says Thae. 'The people from Pyongyang were much, much better educated and much more talented in using these instruments.'

The second group of North Koreans afforded Internet access are clustered in the highly controlled education system. Under strict supervision, students are allowed to surf websites. Foreign teachers who've witnessed this set-up describe the youngsters as using the Internet like a library: they're told which website to visit and what information to retrieve.[23] They do so, and that's that. There's no sense that they might click more links and explore further. It's not just that such behaviour would be instantly spotted and shut down by their teachers; it's that generations of surveillance and censorship have created a society in which the students just don't feel the same curiosity that to the rest of us seems an innate facet of youth.

On their trip in 2013 Jared Cohen's group were told they would get to see North Korea's educational tech set-up first hand, during a visit to the library of one of North Korea's most prestigious institutions, Kim Il Sung University. But when they arrived, once again Cohen had a feeling everything was not as it seemed. 'I went over to this one computer and there was a bunch of code written on the screen. And I was thinking, "Oh, this student is coding." And all he was doing was just moving his mouse up and down. So at some of these workstations, they're just kind of there pretending to work and performing a routine function over and over. You see the sort of fake students that they put in front of you and you conclude they're fake because whatever is in front of them on the screen, they don't seem to understand it.'

Cohen was also suspicious that his minders allowed him to ask the 'students' anything – he even got one of them to pull up photos of New York City on Wikipedia. It seems highly unlikely the authorities would have allowed such free and easy interaction with anyone but the most vetted individuals. Cohen wasn't allowed to chat to normal students, and as a result he would never have got anywhere near those who would go on to join North Korea's 'cyber-army'.

According to defectors, the country has a well-honed system for recruiting hackers. North Korea needs such a system because, unlike in more developed countries, it can't rely on a culture where hackers are often self-taught, refining their skills on laptops in their bedrooms, says Martyn Williams, a former journalist who runs the website North Korea Tech.[24] 'You can't do that in North Korea because homes don't have computers or Internet access, so it's all done through the school system,' says Williams. 'Right at the primary-school level, they'll initially identify kids that have an aptitude for mathematics, and they'll be given additional exposure to computers. At the high-school level they now have an annual programming contest. And that's at city, provincial and national level, so you get the best of the best selected that way. Then the best of those will go off to the specialist universities. A certain amount will go to military hacking schools. There's a system to find the best of the best.'

Remember Jihyun Park from Chapter 2, the woman who escaped North Korea and who's now a Conservative Party candidate? This was the path her tech-savvy sister was on before the family's 'hostile' social status stymied her chances. For such gifted students, there are generally two options: they will end up working either on the nuclear programme or on government hacking projects. Experts on North Korea like Priscilla Moriuchi see similarities between the two activities: 'The North Korean strategy is about utilizing its asymmetric strengths, being able to find tools of national power that they can use to level the playing field against their much stronger adversaries in the West. The ballistic missile and nuclear programme was one of those asymmetric tools. It's this kind of "moon shot" [that enables] them to level the playing field. The cyber-operational programme is along those same lines. You can put a relatively small amount of resource into a cyber-operations programme and have a much more outsized impact.'

Jared Cohen and Eric Schmidt, of course, hadn't been shown any of this capability. North Korea's hidden hacker army – reckoned by some to number around 6,000[25] – was operating far from the gaze of any foreign visitors (in the same way, to be fair, that government hackers in countries including the UK and US operate under a blanket of secrecy).

As Cohen and his colleagues packed their bags and left windswept Pyongyang in January 2013, North Korea's hackers were already gearing up for a strike which, investigators say, would make their enemy in the South a testing range for a new and dangerous form of cyber-war. The days of Dark Seoul were about to begin.

By 2013 North Korean-attributed cyber-attacks against South Korean targets were nothing new. From the Caucasus to Kashmir, most global conflict zones were seeing an uptick in online attacks commensurate with the rise of tablets and phones as a ubiquitous part of daily life. Such cyber-campaigns had become simply another tool in the armoury of states desperate to take any kind of pot-shot at their enemies, and the Korean peninsula was no exception.

Many of these strikes took the most basic form: the Distributed Denial of Service attack. Here's how it works: when you visit a website, the components (the photos, text and so on) are stored on a computer out on the Internet called a server. Your browser (be it Chrome, Firefox, Safari, etc.) sends a message via the Internet to the server, summoning the components and assembling them to form the website you see in front of you.

Servers are set up to deal with a certain volume of requests. If they get too many, they're unable to fulfil the demand and the server shuts down, effectively disabling the website for everyone. This is a Distributed Denial of Service (or DDoS) attack. It's likened by some to a digital sit-in, and among some tech-security folks it barely even counts as hacking.

This was the form that suspected North Korean cyber-attacks had mostly taken in the lead-up to 2013. Some of the South's government and large organizations' websites had been taken offline. Occasionally they would be defaced with a mocking message. For the most part, it was a short-lived irritant: once the attack abated, the website server would recover. The activity in March 2013 was very different. This was a co-ordinated day of digital strikes, and, rather than taking a few websites offline, the assailants set out to show South Korea that they could destroy the computer networks of key institutions from the inside.

Their viruses targeted the heart of each computer they infected by hitting a thing called the Master Boot Record (MBR). When you turn your machine on, it's the MBR that tells it what to do, and where to find the operating system (Microsoft Windows, for example), which in turn makes everything else tick. Running the MBR is akin to turning on the light switch when you walk into a dark room. No MBR effectively means no computer. The hack spread like wildfire. At 2 p.m., on Wednesday, 20 March 2013, 32,000 computers in two of South Korea's major banks and its three largest TV stations were plunged into digital darkness.[26]

As the banks struggled to get their systems back online, ATMs and Internet-banking services were disrupted.[27] The TV stations managed to stay on air: as Son Taek Wang discovered at his employer YTN, the kit that ran their broadcasting ability was separate from the computers hit by the virus. But it still took days for them fully to restore their systems to normal. Ultimately, however, the attack was survivable and for most people not too disruptive. Life went back to normal. Even when the South Korean government accused the North of being behind the attack, it sent only limited shockwaves through the population. As Wang points out, they saw it in the context of other incidents which may well have seemed more pressing. A few years earlier North and South had actually exchanged fire in a flare-up over a South Korean island, and four South Koreans had been killed.[28]

But what concerned tech-security experts about the March 2013 cyber-attacks was the sudden escalation in tactics and the co-ordinated nature of the hit.

In military circles they talk about the 'five D's' – the series of strategies an aggressor can use against an enemy: deny, degrade, disrupt, deceive and destroy.[29] In the 2013 attacks those targeting South Korea had jumped right to the top of the chain: this was no longer about the irritating experience of a website being unavailable for a few hours, as in a DDoS attack. Staff in the affected organizations had sat, bewildered, as their screens turned black. Their computers' software had to be painstakingly rebuilt, machine by machine.

At exactly the same time the banks' and TV stations' internal systems were being attacked, the website of South Korean mobile-phone company LG Uplus was also being hit.[30] Its front page was replaced by a bizarre, shlocky image of skulls with red eyes, under a banner proclaiming 'Hacked by Whois Team'.[31] The name had never been used by a hacking group before (and hasn't been seen since).

The following day an online message appeared, claiming responsibility for the bank and TV station attacks. It read (*sic*): 'Hi, Dear Friends, We are very happy to inform you the following news. We, NewRomantic Cyber Army Team, verified our #OPFuckKorea2003. We have now a great deal of personal information in our hands.'[32]

No one had ever heard of the NewRomantic Cyber Army Team either. It seemed beyond coincidence that the attacks had happened simultaneously. Were the two hacking groups connected? Adding to the confusion was the fact that during this period hackers from the Anonymous group were rampaging around the Internet. The Guy Fawkes-mask-clad renegades delighted in taking websites offline using DDoS attacks and defacing their front pages with mocking messages. Perhaps the LG Uplus incident was an unrelated strike by Anonymous?

In fact, the two curiously named hacking groups were not only linked but were one and the same. Later investigations would discover that the Lazarus Group, North Korea's government hacking unit, was hiding behind these masks of online anonymity – a tactic it would use again and again in a bid to outfox its pursuers.

But at this point the investigators in South Korea were still in the dark. They started trying to unpick the attack and work out who was behind it. They found links in the code between Whois Team and NewRomantic Cyber Army Team.

South Korea's intelligence agencies found another lead in the code – something they claim pointed firmly towards their old enemy north of the border: North Korean IP addresses.

An IP address is your computer's doorway to the Internet. It's the unique number your machine uses to identify itself online, so that websites' servers know where to send the components of the web page, for example. Different countries are assigned different blocks of IP addresses, and analysing them is one way of working out where an attack came from.

It's not a slam-dunk piece of evidence, of course. It's possible for people to change or spoof IP addresses, so that their Internet traffic appears to be coming from a different country (as will be familiar to anyone who's used a Virtual Private Network, or VPN, to illicitly watch TV programmes that are available only in certain territories).

But spoofing North Korean IP addresses isn't easy. For example, many VPN providers allow you to choose which country to make your computer's Internet connection appear to come from. You'll notice North Korea isn't among the options. While other countries might be okay with bouncing your Internet connection through their computer networks, North Korea's paranoid, secretive regime would baulk at the idea (as would many VPN providers).

Tech-security analysts studying the March 2013 incident were also uncovering more evidence that pointed to a nation-state attack. They traced the viruses used and discovered they'd been deployed in South Korea as far back as 2009. The same tools, they said, had been used to create 'a sophisticated encrypted network designed to gather intelligence on military networks'. In other words, whoever hacked the banks and TV stations had also been snooping on South Korea's armed forces. Chillingly, the researchers found that the hackers could have used the same tactics levelled against the banks and TV stations in 2013, overwriting the MBR of the infected machines and rendering them useless.[33] Whoever hacked South Korea's forces had the power to wreak havoc on its military, but they stopped short – perhaps to avoid being discovered, or perhaps for fear of the real-world consequences such a hit could have unleashed.

As far as the South was concerned, the case against North Korea was compelling. And it got more so on 25 June 2013, when there was another outbreak of attacks, nicknamed 'Dark Seoul'. They used the same hacking tools as those employed in the March attacks, but this time the aims were less destructive: the online assailants went back to the old DDoS tactics, taking down dozens of websites.[34]

The targets included government departments, among them the presidential office, known as the Blue House. To analysts, the targeting of national institutions suggested a state-led attack. The date also seemed to put North Korea in the frame: 25 June was the 63rd anniversary of the beginning of the Korean War.

But, while those in Seoul fretted and fought to comprehend the new threat, outside the Korean peninsula these incidents didn't really make waves. Perhaps people saw them as just a minor technological skirmish in the decades-old spat between two avowed enemies.

They were wrong.

In the space of a few months, hackers had successfully struck at South Korea's banks, TV stations and government. Finance, media and governmental institutions are among the foundations of any functioning modern democracy. From behind their computer keyboards the hackers had done serious damage to all three. South Korea was among the most advanced societies in the world, and now the very tech that had underpinned its emergence as an economic powerhouse was being used against it. Remember Priscilla Moriuchi's comment about asymmetric cyber-warfare? This is what it looks like on the frontline. And for those who dismissed the Dark Seoul incidents as a geeky, computerized row in a faraway land, that frontline was about to get much, much closer.

Perhaps people should have paid more attention to the lurid green text of the online message left by Whois Team, the group that hacked the website of LG Uplus. Underneath the image of the red-eyed skulls, the text read (*sic*): 'This is the Beginning of Our Movement. We'll be back Soon.'

5

Hacking Hollywood

For many people, 'Hollywood' simply means the place in the US where movies get made. They might have a vague sense that it's somewhere around Los Angeles – probably right underneath that big white sign proclaiming its name.

Strictly speaking, however, Hollywood is a specific neighbourhood in LA, and it's a good few hours' meandering walk uphill to those iconic letters. And Hollywood isn't the be-all-and-end-all of film-making in the city, nor has it ever been. Movie production happens in other areas dotted across LA – among them Culver City, a few miles south-west of its more famous counterpart. Culver was the site of the old MGM film lot, where they put together classics like *Gone with the Wind* and *Ben-Hur*. MGM is long gone, but the site is still there and behind the giant white entrance gates they do their best to keep the buzz of Tinseltown going strong. There's an enormous rainbow sculpture, a tribute to *The Wizard of Oz*, along with movie-themed funfair rides. They also still make TV programmes on the lot, and there are public tours for rubbernecking tourists hoping to glimpse a celebrity or two.

But, away from the glitz and glamour, the MGM lot is a workplace like any other, and home to the HQ of Sony Pictures Entertainment. Hundreds of the company's employees are based there, carrying out all the back-office functions that make a modern media giant tick.

Among them was Celina Chavanette, a chatty and gregarious young woman who'd worked for various movie companies over the years before making her way to Sony in 2014. She wouldn't describe her job as glamorous ('it's really just being in the cubicle, just a lot of computer work and spreadsheets', she tells me), but the perks are pretty sweet: 'On your breaks or at lunchtime, you get to go walk around and you could see productions. I'm very social, so I would talk to everybody and then try to get on to the sets. I got on the *Jeopardy* set. I go places until people tell me "No".'

Chavanette was enjoying her access-all-areas lifestyle until one day, on Monday, 24 November 2014, something strange happened: her security badge stopped working. To get into the office she had to get signed in by the guards. It may not seem like a big deal, but, because of Sony's high-tech set-up, it soon turned into a real headache for Chavanette. 'They networked everything, so your badge was basically your key to get anywhere,' says Chavanette. 'So you had to scan your badge driving into the lot. You had to scan it to get into the building, scan it to get into the rooms.'

Chavanette soon discovered she wasn't the only one affected, and it wasn't just the badges that were out of action. 'No computers were on. Everybody that was in the office was just talking to each other, trying to figure out what was going on.' Unknown to her and her colleagues, Chavanette's organization was now the target of a meticulously planned digital assault with one aim: annihilate Sony Pictures Entertainment.

A few days before her pass stopped working, senior executives at Sony had received a very strange email from someone calling himself 'Frank David', which read (*sic*): 'We've got great damage by Sony Pictures. The compensation for it, monetary compensations we want. Pay the damage, or Sony Pictures will be bombarded as a whole. You know us very well. We never wait long. You'd better behave wisely.'[1]

With its vague threats issued in dodgy English, it sounded like a classic spam email. But the threat was real – someone was about to do Sony very great damage indeed. Unknown to the firm's executives, a computer virus had been sweeping through its network, disabling computer after computer. The eventual target on each machine was the MBR, which the virus wiped.[2] Three days later, when Sony employees logged in to their machines, they were greeted by a bizarre sight. One by one, a horror-film image of a blood-red skeleton with claws, fangs and glaring eyes took over their screens. 'Hacked by #GOP' read the message alongside the image – later revealed as an abbreviation for Guardians of Peace, an as-yet-unknown hacking group.

Is any of this sounding familiar? The skeleton graphics, the MBR-wiper, the claim of responsibility from an unheard-of group? Anyone who'd witnessed the Dark Seoul campaign the previous year would have instantly recognized the modus operandi. But, outside the world of tech-security folks and Korean conflict experts, few people had really studied the incident, so, when Sony came under attack, the connections weren't immediately obvious to many.

This time the hackers would go even further, adopting a new and frightening tactic that would have serious consequences for Sony and eventually its employees, including Chavanette. Below the skeleton graphics (which now came with sound effects: six gunshots and a scream) was a message written in neon-green text which read (*sic*): 'We've already warned you, and this is just a beginning. We continue till our request be met. We've obtained all your internal data including your secrets and top secrets. If you don't obey us, we'll release data shown below to the world.'[3]

The 'data' consisted of five links. Clicking on them brought up images that would have turned Sony studio executives' blood cold: screenshots of folders apparently containing incredibly sensitive information, such as executives' salaries, confidential internal emails, insider gossip – the kind of embarrassing dirty laundry that no company wants out in public. There were also details of as-yet-unreleased films. The folders themselves couldn't be downloaded in order to verify what was inside. But the message was clear: whoever sent it was claiming they had swathes of Sony's most private data, and they were threatening to leak the lot.

For staff at the studio, the skeleton graphics, cheesy sound effects and over-the-top threats may have made the whole thing look like some kind of prank. But this attack was deadly serious. It was the opening salvo in a battle to destroy Sony Pictures.

In the end, half of Sony's global digital network would be wiped out, some of the most powerful players in Hollywood would lose their jobs, and the digital break-in would trigger an international incident.

Remarkably, what sparked it all off was a goofball movie.

Dan Sterling is a comedy writer who's worked on some of the most contentious programmes around, from *King of the Hill* to *The Daily Show*. He's the kind of person you imagine will always say the thing everyone else is thinking, even if it means being thrown out of the party. 'I come from a long line of feather-ruffling people and writers and activists,' he tells me. 'The things that most interest me are political in nature, and it's only fun if it's provocative.' It was a character trait that would upend his life in 2014.

Sterling had been working with writer–actor Seth Rogen and writer–producer Evan Goldberg, who between them were behind a string of comedies including *Knocked Up* and *Sausage Party*. In the late 2000s Sterling says that Rogen and Goldberg came to him with an idea. 'This was when Osama bin Laden was still alive, I think. The logline was "What if you were a journalist and you got an interview with Osama bin Laden, would you kill him during the interview?" '

Sterling loved the idea but was aware that there was already a comedy in development featuring a Middle Eastern leader called *The Dictator*, starring Sacha Baron Cohen.

'So I started kicking around for ideas. If it's not bin Laden, who is epic enough? And then I had a drink with a friend. He's like, "Oh, it's got to be North Korea." And I was like, "Oh, yes, of course it does." '

But Sterling says that he initially stopped short of using the North Korean leader's real name. 'I just made up a name that sounded like his and it was obviously a stand-in for him. But it wasn't till much later that I was sitting in a trailer with Seth and Evan and some executives and they said, "We just want to try this: what would happen if you changed it from your fictitious name to Kim Jong Un?" And as soon as they said it I thought, "Of course, that is so much edgier." It's just much more provocative and much more titillating to take a swat at the real person. And why not? It did not seem very controversial at the time to mock one of the world's most dastardly living people.'

The movie went into development, but shortly before shooting started Sterling says that Sony (which by now had bought the rights to make the film) began to feel that portraying the real Kim might be 'too provocative'. Sterling says Rogen and Goldberg were keen. 'They pushed back,' he says. And so the plot of the film, now called *The Interview*, started to take shape.

Actor James Franco plays a shallow, narcissistic TV host; Seth Rogen plays his producer. They discover Kim Jong Un is a massive fan of their vacuous chat show, and manage to secure an appearance by the dictator, played by Randall Park as a bashful, vulnerable man in awe of the American journalists who arrive to interview him. The TV team are then approached by CIA agents who recruit them into a plot to assassinate Kim during their visit to Pyongyang.

After much slapstick messing around, the pair carry out their mission. To the strains of 'Firework' by Katy Perry, Kim is shown dying in a fireball. The movie's CGI team really went to town, portraying the gory details in unflinching slow motion.

It's one of only a tiny number of fiction films ever to portray the killing of a sitting head of state,[4] and Sony knew it would be controversial. Despite Kim's dire international standing, the depiction of his demise might still be seen by some as unnecessarily provocative. So they asked for advice from Bruce Bennett, a North Korean specialist and senior defence analyst at the RAND Corporation, a long-standing American think-tank. Bennett immediately understood why Sony had ended the movie the way it had: 'They painted [Kim Jong Un] throughout the film as an incredible villain. And so you're not going to just walk away and say, "Yes, we let him continue to live, he's a great guy, we support him." The ending was a natural part of what the plot had built towards.

'Did I think that North Korea was going to cause hundreds of millions of dollars [of damage] to Sony? No. Did I think they would try to hack Sony? Probably.'

But Bennett also saw a bigger geopolitical picture. A much, much bigger picture: regime change.

'Did I think that there would be some value of the film that might influence events in both South and North Korea? The answer was, I was hopeful that that might be one of the effects of the film. Certainly many in North Korea would be just furious about the ending. But some would view it and think: "Is this a guy we don't want to have and could get rid of?" So I guess I was of two minds: that it's a risk, but also it might be useful in information warfare that ought to be going on with North Korea.'

Based partly on advice like this, Sony toned down the ending but pushed ahead with the release. By the summer of 2014 the advertising campaign started, and teaser trailers were aired which left potential viewers in no doubt as to the film's plot and the fate it held for the dramatized Kim Jong Un. Inevitably, the regime in Pyongyang found out, and its reaction was predictably robust. In a letter sent to the UN in June 2014, North Korea's Ambassador wrote: 'To allow the production and distribution of such a film on the assassination of an incumbent Head of a sovereign State should be regarded as the most undisguised sponsoring of terrorism as well as an act of war. The United States authorities should take immediate and appropriate actions to ban the production and distribution of the aforementioned film; otherwise, it will be fully responsible for encouraging and sponsoring terrorism.'[5]

For years the US had included North Korea in the club of terrorism-sponsoring states. Now Kim's Ambassador was trying to turn the tables and use the same argument on its old enemy.

The Kim regime wasn't the only one in Pyongyang that had concerns about *The Interview*. Jean H. Lee, my co-host for *The Lazarus Heist*, was covering North Korea for the Associated Press news agency when she heard about it. Foreign journalists face an uphill battle in a society inimically opposed to free speech, in which they're constantly under surveillance and suspicion. She feared the movie would add to her problems. 'My first reaction was "Great, just what I need: another movie that reinforces the impression that American journalists are working for the CIA." When you're in Pyongyang, you don't take suspicions of espionage lightly because it's always a risk for any of us working in North Korea. And the consequences of being accused of espionage are very high. After all, I was an American working in a country that considers the United States its arch-enemy.' Just a few years earlier two American journalists had been accused of unspecified 'hostile acts' and sentenced to twelve years' hard labour. It had taken months of negotiations and a visit to North Korea by former US President Bill Clinton to secure their release.[6]

Sony clearly felt differently and pressed ahead with the film's release. Meanwhile, the hackers went to work with a plan to make it regret its decision.

As marketing for *The Interview* went into high gear, some of the cast and crew started to see an unusual message posted on their public Facebook accounts. 'Nude photos of many A-list celebrities!' said the post, which came from a user calling himself Andoson David. The message might not have seemed so unusual at the time: only a few months before, intimate photos of a slew of celebrities had been leaked online in an incident known as 'The Fappening'. Anyone downloading the material from Andoson David's links would indeed have received a screensaver with some photos of a female model, but they would also have unwittingly contracted a computer virus.[7]

It doesn't seem that any of the cast and crew on *The Interview* fell for this ruse, but that didn't matter. The fake Facebook messages were just one part of a concerted, multi-pronged campaign being waged by hackers desperate to penetrate Sony's systems.

On 15 October 2014 a Sony employee received a politely worded email from a woman calling herself Christina Karsten entitled (*sic*) 'Getting Recruited by Sony Pictures Entertainment'. Christina wrote: 'I'm a sophomore at the University of Southern California and am very interested in graphic design of digital productions,' giving the name of the person who'd suggested she get in contact.

The email included a link to download her résumé and portfolio.[8] Once again, it was a trick – the online CV was laced with a computer virus.

It's unclear why this email was sent, because, according to later investigations, the hackers had already broken into Sony several weeks before. On 25 September someone calling themselves Nathan Gonsalez had sent a message to a Sony employee with what looked like a link to download some video files for an advertising campaign. Once again the links contained a virus, and this time it worked. Someone downloaded the files and inadvertently installed the malicious software. The hackers were now inside Sony's computer networks and would spend many more weeks there, carefully moving from computer to computer to avoid detection, stealing data and planting more viruses as they geared up for their big finale. Then, on 24 November 2014, they let the hammer fall.

Tatiana Siegel is Executive Film Editor at the *Hollywood Reporter*, which details the latest twists and turns in the film and TV industry. She's covered all the big stories and interviewed many of the stars. But back in late November 2014 she was looking forward to a bit of downtime. It was Thanksgiving and, like many Americans, she was heading away from the office for the holidays. Then the phone started to ring – reports were coming in of something very bad happening on the MGM lot. 'There was chaos,' recalls Siegel.

The cyber-attackers had triggered the viruses they'd spent the last two months secreting in Sony's network, reducing the firm's computer systems to digital rubble. Eight thousand machines had to be disconnected to contain the outbreak.[9] The 'blast radius' of damage stretched surprisingly far and went way beyond just the computer terminals. 'The phones didn't work,' says Siegel. 'There was a Coffee Bean [café] on the studio lot, and they still couldn't take credit cards six weeks after the hack.' A source close to the investigation also told me that employees of Sony had to queue up in the car park to receive their pay cheques in person because the company's financial systems were so badly affected.[10]

Siegel's vacation was quickly put on hold – she remembers her desk piling up with newspaper clippings about the hack as she tried to pull it all together.

And then things got even worse for Sony thanks to a remarkable turn of events.

In the original email sent by Frank David, the hackers had demanded payment, but they received nothing. So on 26 November at least four senior Sony Pictures Entertainment execs received an email stating (*sic*): 'We began to release data because Sony Pictures refused our demand . . . You are to collapse surely. Damn to gruel and reckless Sony Pictures!'[11]

It may have sounded like a badly worded, over-the-top threat, but once again the attackers followed through unflinchingly.

> Hi, I am the boss of G.O.P. A few days ago, we told you the fact that we had released Sony Pictures films including *Annie*, *Fury* and *Still Alice* to the Web.
>
> Those can be easily obtained through Internet search.
>
> For this time, we are about to release Sony Pictures data to the Web. The volume of the data is under 100 Terabytes.

This was the curious email that began to arrive in the inboxes of various American reporters on the morning of Saturday, 29 November 2014. The hackers were now anonymously emailing journalists with links to data they'd stolen from the company's servers, and then exhorting them to write stories about it.

Siegel was one of those on their mailing list.[12] She was rightly cautious. 'The first time they contacted me and said that they had this information that I might find interesting, you had to click on a link to get the hacked information,' says Siegel. 'I remember I forwarded it to my IT Department and said, "I'm not clicking on this link without you telling me it's safe first."'

Having been given the okay, Siegel clicked, and was stunned at what she found. 'It was kind of a "Holy cow" moment. *This* is what they've stolen, followed by eight more days of that, where what was being revealed got more and more dramatic.'

During their two months lurking inside Sony's networks, the hackers had pilfered an estimated 38 million files and now set about organizing them into chunks, which were released in eight stages to the media (and then to the general public) at set intervals.[13] What was incredible about this exercise was the acumen that the hackers exhibited. It was a concerted and well-planned campaign of anti-PR.

Initially they leaked some unreleased movies, including a remake of *Annie*, and *Fury*, a Brad Pitt vehicle. For the general public, this raised awareness of the Sony hack – no longer was it just about a few studio execs struggling to get their emails; this story now had celebrity appeal and the chance of seeing some illicitly released films.

Next, the hackers started leaking data from inside Sony, exposing its salaries and showbiz contracts, guaranteed to have some journalists salivating. 'Huge data dumps of corporate information,' recalls Siegel. 'Studio information, how much they were paying actors and actresses, how much they were paying their executives, things that were just very damaging to have out there in the ether.'

The ruinous drip feed of headlines began: 'Hacked Documents Reveal a Hollywood Studio's Stunning Gender and Race Gap' was one of them.[14] It was above a story written by Kevin Roose, one of the journalists who, like Siegel, had received direct communication from the hackers.[15] At the time Roose was Senior Editor for a website called Fusion.net. You could be forgiven for not having heard of it; the site was not exactly a news behemoth. What it did do, however, was focus on juicy stories that might not be covered elsewhere and turn them into spiky, compelling coverage. It was the same with the other outlets the hackers contacted: Gawker, BuzzFeed, The Verge and, to a certain extent, the *Hollywood Reporter* – they're not the biggest of publications, but they know their audience, and they're hungry for scoops.[16] The hackers seemed to be demonstrating an impressive grasp of the media landscape. Thanks to the smaller publications' coverage, the story of the Sony hack soon ended up on the front pages and the big TV networks' programmes. The glamour of Hollywood and the intrigue of computer crime proved irresistible.

It's fair to say that even some of those reporting on the stories felt a sense of unease about receiving stolen data direct from the hackers. As Siegel says: 'You're corresponding with somebody who is doing something hugely destructive in the industry you're reporting on. It's a very weird position to be in when you're covering hackers, that you're doing the bidding of a criminal enterprise or a criminal person. It's uncomfortable.'

Others, however, were less circumspect, as summed up in Gawker's comment: 'We're taking this opportunity to enthusiastically dig through Sony's cyber-trash.'[17]

But the hackers weren't just aiming to damage the corporation by generating a slew of negative headlines. Things were about to get personal. Having got the attention of the media and the public, the Guardians of Peace now set out to stage the very public destruction of two of the most powerful figures in Hollywood.

Among the data stolen from inside Sony were thousands upon thousands of emails sent to and from its employees. Every bit of office gossip, every ill-considered comment, every off-colour joke – all of it was now in the hackers' hands, including those from its most senior execs.

On 8 December the Guardians of Peace leaked 5,000 emails from Sony Pictures Entertainment's Co-Chairperson Amy Pascal, one of the most powerful people in Hollywood. For the journalists who'd been circling Sony, this was the motherlode. Like many of us, Pascal was a prolific email communicator, and now her every word was up for scrutiny. It didn't take the media long to find the dirt. She'd been part of a conversation in which actress Angelina Jolie had been described as a 'minimally talented spoiled brat'. She joked about the movies then-President Barack Obama might like, including *12 Years a Slave* and *The Butler*.[18]

For months Pascal had been moving further and further into the limelight as she fought to limit the damage. The hackers had watched her take centre stage, knowing the trapdoor of damaging information they had on her, and on 8 December they let her drop.

The Guardians of Peace warmed to their task, and began hyping up their forthcoming releases of data. They had all the emails of Pascal's Co-Chairperson Michael Lynton, who was also CEO, and gleefully promised a 'Christmas gift' containing his most private communications.[19]

Meanwhile Dan Sterling, *The Interview*'s screenwriter, was watching all of this with dismay. 'I felt so bad for all these very famous and powerful people impacted by that,' he recalls. 'The executives that had supported this all the way through at Sony were under huge fire. And it started to become a pretty heavy burden.'

He was also discovering that the old adage 'There's no such thing as bad publicity' has its limits. 'At a certain point, I think the feeling of guilt and responsibility started to overtake the feeling of excitement and wonder at having your first movie be so talked about.'

But, through it all, Sony was still intending to open the film on Christmas Day of 2014.[20] The release seemed to be running on rails despite the controversy. So, on the night of the premiere, Sterling put on a smart blue suit and a crisp white shirt and headed to the United Artists theatre in Los Angeles. It wasn't quite what he was expecting. 'It was a rather depressing event. Some of my friends texted me on the way over to the premiere saying that their publicists had told them not to come because it was likely to get blown up. When I saw one of the high-level executives from Sony in their seat, they were weeping . . . which is a bummer.'

Nonetheless, some were starting to feel a sense of confidence that the movie might yet be able to ride out the furore and emerge as a success. Ben Waisbren was one of the film's Executive Producers; he helped to raise the money to make it. He says the test screenings had been very encouraging: 'The scores were higher than [Sony's earlier 2014 action comedy] *22 Jump Street*, which was a $200m domestic box-office performer.'

But, just five days after the premiere, all dreams of box-office success came to a crashing halt. On 16 December the Sony hackers published a chilling new message on the Internet (*sic*): 'Warning. We will clearly show it to you at the very time and places "The Interview" be shown, including the premiere, how bitter fate those who seek fun in terror should be doomed to . . . Remember the 11th of September 2001. We recommend you to keep yourself distant from the places at that time. (If your house is nearby, you'd better leave.)'[21]

Suddenly this wasn't just about damaged computers and trashed reputations – traumatic as those had been for the people involved – it now appeared the movie might be the cause of physical harm.

Sony had a big dilemma on its hands. Pull the movie and risk being accused of self-censorship in the face of a dictator's demands? Or press ahead and risk potential violence? In the end the studio's hand was forced, when the major cinema chains refused to screen the film.[22]

Feeding into the calculus was the fact that, only a couple of years before, a gunman had opened fire at a midnight screening of *The Dark Knight Rises*, killing twelve and injuring scores more. 'They didn't want people just to go, "Oh, I can't go to the movies because there's going to be a shooting,"' says Waisbren. But, even though he understood the arguments for cancelling the film, he was left with significant concerns about a situation in which anonymous hackers could bully the media into a climbdown. Pressure from studios led to pressure from cinemas which led to pressure on Sony: 'So you see the domino effect of chill, and that . . . should be a big concern in a free society,' he says.

A few small cinemas screened the film, however, and it was later released online, where it seems the controversy did indeed raise its profile. It made $15m in its first four days – coincidentally the same amount Sony initially set aside for remediating the hack.[23]

Meanwhile, suspicion was swirling around who was behind the attack. Fingers were already being pointed at North Korea. In addition to the similarities to the Dark Seoul incident, ever since the hack first went public some in the media had been referencing *The Interview*'s mocking portrayal of Kim Jong Un and speculating that North Korea might have carried out the hack as revenge.[24] But

North Korea denied having anything to do with it. Through a spokesman, the regime suggested it might be 'the righteous deed of the supporters and sympathizers of North Korea who are joining its efforts to put an end to US imperialism'. But, without more evidence, many were doubtful about blaming the attack on Pyongyang – including one of the film's creators, Seth Rogen. At this stage the investigators had given out precious little detail to back up any attribution. And there were other good reasons to be sceptical of North Korean involvement: if the hack was in revenge for *The Interview*, why did the Guardians of Peace start to talk about the film only weeks after journalists had first mentioned it? Why did they initially demand money from Sony? (North Korea might be short of funds, but surely not desperate enough to try to blackmail a few studio execs?) And why was North Korea suddenly interested in leaking movie bosses' private emails? On top of all this, in 2014 most people (even including those in government and the intelligence community) perceived North Korea as a technologically backward nation. Was it really capable of carrying out such a well-planned digital assault?

But for the moment these questions would need to take a back seat, because the attackers who'd destroyed Sony's computer networks were about to switch gears and unleash a new and deeply damaging tactic. Sony's rank-and-file employees were about to be thrust into the spotlight, and, for some, their lives would be changed forever.

6

Fallout

December 2014 may have been a busy time for the Sony executives, FBI investigators and showbiz journalists frantically following the twists and turns of the hack on the studio. But, for lower-level employees like Celina Chavanette, whom we met in the previous chapter, the chaos had created a strangely becalmed office environment. Although she and her colleagues were still told to turn up to work, it was hard for her bosses to find them things to do, as large parts of the computer network remained out of action.

'Basically, they wanted us to do "busy work",' she recalls. 'They made us come into the office every day and they're like, "How about we clean out this office over here? Let's go through some files and throw some stuff away."'

Anyone who's had to look busy to satisfy the boss knows it's actually more exhausting than doing genuine work. Chavanette says having a smartphone was a godsend. 'I watched all the seasons of *Breaking Bad* and *Sons of Anarchy* at work on my phone. So I wasn't doing anything, but I had to show up.'

Then one day her phone threw up something far less entertaining: private data about herself and her colleagues.

'I was doing research, googling myself, and then I found my stuff online, and then I found some work friends' stuff online. And I asked them, "Hey, did they tell you your stuff was stolen?" And then I started getting mad.'

What Chavanette had just discovered was that the hackers who broke into Sony weren't just leaking pirated copies of movies, celebs' details and the messages of senior execs. They were now exposing everything they'd stolen – including private staff emails, confidential documents, personnel records and more.

'I found my offer letter, how much I was getting paid, my Social Security number,' remembers Chavanette. 'I was just lucky that I wasn't there for very long, so they didn't have any medical records.'

Suddenly, the spotlight that had been shone on Sony Co-Chairperson Amy Pascal with such disastrous consequences was being beamed even wider, and hundreds of employees were dragged in, along with anyone they'd been emailing outside the company.

The impact of these data leaks got a huge boost thanks to a website that's been a prime mover in some of the biggest stories of the last decade: WikiLeaks. In April 2015 it published a giant trove of documents and emails stolen from Sony.

Founded by Julian Assange and launched in 2007, WikiLeaks had a track record for carrying data that revealed lies and unscrupulous behaviour by governments and corporations. However, this didn't seem to be the case for Sony: unlike many of WikiLeaks' targets, there was no prima facie suggestion the company was involved in corruption or duplicity. As justification, WikiLeaks stated that the documents offered 'a rare insight into the inner workings of a large, secretive multinational corporation' and that 'behind the scenes this is an influential corporation, with ties to the White House . . . with an ability to impact laws and policies, and with connections to the US military-industrial complex.'[1] In other words, as far as Wiki-Leaks was concerned, Sony was fair game.

WikiLeaks makes a point of not editorializing the data it publishes. The entire lot went online, and is still searchable today: 30,287 documents and 173,132 emails. Part of what makes WikiLeaks such a powerful force is the search-engine technology it brings to bear on these huge data stores. Unlike the raw dumps of information that hackers often leak online, WikiLeaks' website makes trawling the data as easy and instant as a Google search. For one Sony employee that would have life-changing consequences.

Amy Heller was Vice-President of Global Sales at Sony Pictures Entertainment, but, along with others, she was laid off in a big restructure seven months before the hack hit the headlines. Having gone back to finish an MBA degree, she was now looking for work. With an impressive track record in the entertainment industry, she was confident she'd land a job soon. But then one day everything changed.

Like Celina Chavanette's private data, Heller's was now spewing out online for anyone to see. And, in Heller's case, that looked very bad indeed, because one of the first things that appeared when she searched her name was a document marked 'Incident Report. Property Crimes – Civil/Missing Property'.

'I still remember my legs getting numb. I'm like, "What? This is crazy," ' she tells me.

It turned out that when Heller left Sony back in March the company had cleared out her office and found that an ergonomic computer mouse was missing. In the way of big bureaucracies Sony had filed an internal company report marking it as a 'property crime', but it didn't go to the police and it had all been ironed out. But that's not how it looked from the document that was now online among the Sony leaks. Heller's name was inextricably linked with a crime report.

'I was interviewing at a level where people google you,' she says. She feared recruiters would find the document and decline to put her forward for jobs, and that, even if she did get an interview, it would be a serious distraction.

'This was horrible for me, because I'm needing to get a job, but how does this fit into the narrative of interviewing?'

She believes she lost out on roles as a result and says she even tried for more junior posts without success. All because of a $90 computer mouse that went missing.

Heller was starting to worry about what kind of damage the leaked information was doing to her career prospects and her future earnings. So she took legal action against Sony for negligence. But the decision had disastrous effects.

'It backfired on me,' says Heller. 'The newspaper got a hold of my filing.' Suddenly her 'legal spat' with Sony was headline news.

Heller was now publicly identified not only as someone connected with a property crime but as someone who was trying to sue her former employer.

'So now I'm in a situation where I've sort of exacerbated the very issue I wanted hidden. Once my industry knew I had filed a lawsuit against Sony, I became untouchable. It was over for me,' says Heller.

Between the leaks and her attempts to battle the effects, Heller's dreams of Hollywood success were killed off. 'That part of my career ended. I had no choice but to reinvent myself,' she says.

She's since settled her case with Sony, which provided her with a letter confirming she didn't commit any property crime. And there is a silver lining. The incident has given Heller a new purpose: she enrolled in law school with a plan to advocate for people who've had similar experiences.

'It started as this passion for . . . basic protections for data and privacy. But it morphed into more of a human-rights endeavour, because I think technology is well ahead of us. There's so many questions that we haven't addressed. And then there's just the danger of what a hack could do. I saw what it did to a company. It's unimaginable what it could do to a world.'

Heller isn't the only one whose life and outlook were permanently changed by the Sony hack. Celina Chavanette switched career and became an emergency-medical technician. But she's still haunted by the leaks of her personal information. She's set up alerts to warn her when her data appears online. 'Almost every other week, I would say, I get a little ping saying that my email address has been exposed or my Social Security [number] or my passwords. Everything about me has been exposed. I filed reports with the Federal Trade Commission for identity theft, and I put a seven-year freeze on all my credit reports. If someone asks to check my credit, they have to call me first to prove that it's them. But it's too late. All my stuff is out there and there's nothing I can really do about it. I'm paying for it forever.'

Chavanette and Heller aren't alone. Thousands of former and

current Sony employees have had their personal information exposed online – and to this day are living with the consequences. They filed a class-action lawsuit against Sony Pictures for failing to protect confidential employee records. The company eventually settled the case, promising its staff up to $8m for identity-theft protection and creating a compensation fund.[2] All of which came on top of the millions of dollars the company had already paid out in IT repairs and loss of business. The damages just kept on mounting for Sony – and so did the pressure to bring the hackers to justice. On that front, some very experienced people were already on the case.

During her listless days on the MGM film lot in late 2014, when the computers were down and they were scratching around for work, Celina Chavanette had started to notice some new people turning up. 'Geeks in suits' was how she described them. In fact, they were FBI officers. The Sony hack was now being investigated at the highest levels of US law enforcement. But identifying a culprit was not going to be easy.

Ever since the hack went public, speculation had been mounting over who might be behind it. While some suspected North Korean involvement, there were a number of competing theories.

Some believed it was an inside job. In the months leading up to the attack, there had been a number of layoffs (Amy Heller was among those let go during that time), and some speculated that the hit may have been carried out by a disgruntled former employee or group of employees. This theory was bolstered when someone claiming to be part of the Guardians of Peace hacking group gave an interview indicating they had had help from staff within the company.[3] One cyber-security firm also claimed it was 'very confident' that insiders were key to the takedown.[4] Even Seth Rogen, one of the stars of the *The Interview*, has his doubts about North Korean involvement, mainly because he and his co-director Evan Goldberg had not been directly targeted.[5] Some media reported claims that the real culprit was actually Russia.[6]

All of this was happening very publicly across the febrile world of the Internet. However, the best clues and therefore the best chance of finding the hackers would come from inside Sony. Its computer systems held the breadcrumb trails that might lead to the identity of the person or group who'd brought the company to its knees, digitally speaking. It was here, away from the public gaze, that a painstaking investigation was under way.

Sony had initially called in FireEye, a vastly experienced tech-security firm which has dealt with some of the biggest hacks around. As its investigators trawled through the evidence, they found worrying signs among the technical traces that showed this wasn't just the work of a few bedroom hackers. The FBI got involved, and they soon reached the same conclusion.

'It quickly became apparent that it was national-security related. And when I say that, I mean that there may have been a foreign government behind it,' says Tony Lewis. He's now in private practice, but at the time of the hack Lewis was Assistant US Attorney for the Central District of California. The FBI is in charge of handling investigations, but ultimately it's the Attorney's Office that will have to take charge of prosecuting the culprits – if they can be found.

Lewis didn't know it yet, but the Sony case and the subsequent fallout would go on to occupy him for years. He'd become a key part of the team racing to keep up, as this hacking group marauded across the online world. But for the moment he had his hands full understanding how the criminals had inflicted so much damage on Sony.

As they pieced together the evidence, Lewis says FBI investigators found signs of just how much effort the hackers had put into the attack. The viruses had been tweaked specifically for this one target, with the aim of doing as much damage as possible. Investigators found thousands of different Sony computer IDs written into the code. 'So, in other words, they'd been able to crawl through the network and identify all these different computers and then programmed them into the malware they were going to use to make it work more effectively,' says Lewis.

The investigators also started to look more closely at the Facebook personas that had been used to send temptingly salacious messages to the cast and crew of *The Interview* to try to trick them into downloading viruses. They began to uncover an entire network of fake social media accounts. The hackers behind these accounts would steal legitimate users' profile photos to use as their own. Then they would create connections and friendship links between the accounts to make them appear more realistic. As a result, when they sent the phishing links, it would seem as though they'd come from genuine sources – a process called 'catfishing'.

All of which threw up some very handy lines of inquiry for the FBI. The social media companies, including Facebook and Twitter, are of course based in the US. That meant the FBI could apply for court orders for information from those companies. It transpired that the accounts had often been set up using Gmail addresses provided by Google, which in turn allowed for more warrants by the FBI. By the end, US investigators would submit around 100 search warrants for roughly 1,000 email and social media accounts.[7] Poring through this trove of data, they began to piece together the network behind the catfishing accounts. Part of what they obtained was the IP addresses of the computers the hackers had used. As we learnt in Chapter 4, such IP addresses are the machine's doorway to the Internet and can often be used to trace the physical location of the computer. While it's possible to cheat the system to fake an IP address, this is far from easy in the case of North Korea.

And it was North Korean IP addresses that the FBI claimed had been used to set up the Facebook accounts that were, in turn, used to message the cast and crew of *The Interview*. Those same IP addresses had also been used to access the computer server that held the virus hidden behind those 'nude celebs' photos'; they were spotted scanning Sony's website in the months leading up to the attack; and they'd been used to set up the accounts which sent phishing emails to cinemas that had promised to screen *The Interview*. What's more, the FBI alleged the email address used to log in to the catfishing Facebook accounts had also been linked to a North Korean front company in China.

More and more traces, according to the FBI, led straight back to North Korea. And that wasn't all. Tony Lewis's FBI colleagues had analysed the viruses used on Sony and found tell-tale links to other cybercrime campaigns attributed to North Korean hackers, including the previous year's Dark Seoul attacks.

The Bureau was fast coming to the conclusion that the hacker handles under which all the attacks had been carried out – Guardians of Peace, Whois Team, NewRomantic Cyber Army Team – were just cover names for the same bunch of North Korean cyber-operators. From now on, most people would come to know them by one name: the Lazarus Group.

It's 19 December 2014, the briefing room of the White House. Barack Obama enters, almost six years in power by this point, his hair peppered with grey. He makes his way to the podium and turns to the assembled reporters. 'All I want for Christmas is to take your questions,' he jokes. The first one is about the Sony hack. The movie studio had just confirmed *The Interview* would not get a mainstream cinema release: did the company make the right decision?

'I think they made a mistake,' says Obama. 'We cannot have a society in which some dictator someplace can start imposing censorship here in the United States. Because if somebody is able to intimidate folks out of releasing a satirical movie, imagine what they start doing when they see a documentary that they don't like or news reports that they don't like. Or, even worse, imagine if producers and distributors and others start engaging in self-censorship because they don't want to offend the sensibilities of somebody whose sensibilities probably need to be offended. That's not who we are. That's not what America is about.'

Obama then goes on to state what Tony Lewis and the other investigators had known for some time: the US is convinced North Korea has carried out the attack. It is an unprecedented move: never has a major world leader been so quick to publicly blame another country for a specific cyber-attack.

But, when it comes to the motivations behind it, Obama is

somewhat sniffy. 'I think it says something interesting about North Korea that they decided to have the state mount an all-out assault on a movie studio because of a satirical movie starring Seth Rogen and James Franco,' quips Obama, to laughter from the assembled press corps. 'I love Seth. And I love James. But the notion that that was a threat to them, I think gives you some sense of the kind of regime we're talking about here.'[8]

This may have raised a chuckle from reporters, but many North Korea experts might have bristled at Obama's joke, which seemed to indicate a worrying misapprehension of the threat. Those with a deep understanding of the country and its capricious leaders would have had no problem comprehending (though not endorsing) North Korea's reaction to *The Interview*.

That's because inside North Korea forces were at play of which, arguably, Sony could never have known. In taking a pop at Kim Jong Un the studio could not have chosen a worse target to pick at a worse time.

North Korea has a profound relationship with cinema. Not only is it one of the few genuinely hedonistic pastimes for the mass of its people, but its leaders also consider film a key element in the propaganda battle being waged both internally and externally.

One of the first jobs occupied by Kim Jong Un's father, Kim Jong Il, was to oversee North Korea's artistic output. He embraced the task with fervour and gave films top priority, sometimes personally overseeing the shoots. He did this partly because it helped him to solve a conundrum faced by many a socialist country: how do you incentivize workers to go the extra mile when financial inducements are not allowed (officially, at least)? Kim Jong Il's solution was to use the power of film. As journalist Bradley Martin writes: 'With material rewards ideologically frowned upon, positive motivation meant propaganda and mass mobilization.'[9] When he wanted to boost production at a truck-manufacturing plant, for example, Kim Jong Il drafted in a contingent of artistic types and effectively turned the place into a film set, replaying the patriotic themes of the movies he'd overseen in an effort to inspire the workers to hit their targets.[10]

It wasn't just in domestic propaganda that Kim Jong Il saw the influence of celluloid. He believed it could be used to bolster the country's reputation on the world stage, and he would go to incredible lengths to make that happen. In 1978 he kidnapped South Korea's most famous movie couple – director Shin Sang-ok and actor Choi Eun-hee – smuggled them to North Korea and coerced them into making movies for him which he hoped would win international awards. They eventually escaped and smuggled out covertly recorded cassette tapes demonstrating Kim Jong Il's passion for movies. He talked at length about his plans for the industry, had a projector installed in every house and spent most of his evenings watching films.[11]

All of which goes to explain why North Korea's leadership is obsessed with film. But it doesn't explain the reaction to *The Interview*. Why, according to investigators, did North Korea launch such an aggressive attack on its producers?

Part of the answer is the image cult surrounding the Kim family. It's hard to overstate just how seriously this is taken. Images of the Kims are everywhere – many North Koreans wear a pin badge of them over their left breast, closest to their heart. There are official portraits in almost every building, issued by the government along with a special cloth to clean them with. Newspapers cannot be shoved in the rubbish, because they will almost certainly contain the Kims' images, and crumpling them up would be considered a crime. In this context the gruesome portrayal of Kim Jong Un's death in *The Interview* would have been unimaginably offensive to him and the many North Koreans taught to idolize him.

But even that doesn't explain the reaction to Sony's film. After all, Kim Jong Un's father had been depicted meeting an equally grisly demise in the 2004 film *Team America: World Police*, and, in that case, as far as we're aware, the film-makers weren't hit with a massive retaliation.[12] So why did Kim Jong Un go on the warpath? For that, you have to understand his rise to power and the precarious position in which it left him.

When *The Interview* was released, Kim Jong Un had been in office just a few years. Not only was he newly installed, he had a series of disadvantages that his father hadn't had to cope with. North Korea's governing class had had decades in which to groom Kim Jong Il for power and introduce him to the citizens as the next, inevitable Great Leader. Kim Jong Un had had no such run-up. For many in North Korea, the first time they really heard of him was practically the moment he took power. As a result, Kim Jong Un's succession to the top job was even more insecure than his father's.

Just two years after he took office, Kim Jong Un would give the world an insight into how paranoid and vulnerable he felt, and the vicious measures he was prepared to take to secure his position. He oversaw the execution of one of his most senior colleagues, a man who sat at almost the very top of North Korea's hierarchy. But what made the death of Jang Song Thaek even more shocking was that he was Kim Jong Un's uncle. As Jang was a close relative and confidant, many in the country's elite had assumed he was untouchable. They were wrong. By killing off such a prominent figure, Kim Jong Un, the baby-faced new leader, was sending out a clear message: 'Don't fuck with me.'

This is the final piece of the puzzle behind North Korea's aggressive response to *The Interview*, with its grisly depiction of Kim Jong Un's death. By making the movie, Sony was (knowingly or not) taking direct aim at a nation steeped in the power of film, whose leaders were obsessed with their image, and whose new ruler would tolerate absolutely no assault on his authority. For Sony, it was a fatal combination.

Judging by his press conference, President Obama seemed unaware of the internal North Korean dynamics driving the Sony hack, but he wasn't alone. Many in the intelligence community also perceived it to be a bizarre overreaction to a stupid movie, and this led them to ignore or downplay the threat from North Korea, according to former US National Security Agency analyst Priscilla Moriuchi.

Instead, it should have led to a deep reappraisal of the country's cyber-skills and outlook, she says: 'The [Sony] leaks demonstrated an awareness, an understanding of American popular culture and the news cycle that we hadn't really attributed to North Korea, especially its cyber-operators, before. What would make news in the US ... were embarrassing personal emails back and forth between movie-studio executives and celebrities. That was quite an adept move on their part. What's really stuck out to me as I've done my research is that North Korean cyber-operators are much more technically adept and aware and plugged into contemporary Internet society and media culture than they ever really get credit for.'

It also raised the question of what the US would do about the incident. At this point nation-state cyber-attacks were still a very new phenomenon, and the rules of engagement were unclear. Added to which, this was an attack on a private company, not a public entity. What should the government do? In the end, the US opted for the sanctions route, targeting North Korean government officials and departments.[13]

North Korea responded by accusing the US of 'groundlessly stirring up bad blood' against it. It went on to say the sanctions would 'only harden its will and resolution to defend the sovereignty of the country'.[14] According to investigators, that short statement contained a significant hint as to what might happen next. They claim that, even as the US was announcing the sanctions, the Lazarus Group's hackers were already on to their next target. This time, the motivation was not political point-scoring but cold, hard cash. The hackers were going to knock over a bank. And not just any bank – they would go after the national institution at the heart of a country where every dollar is desperately needed. The heist was on.

7

Casing the Joint

Zubair Bin Huda could be forgiven for not wanting to be at work on Friday, 5 February 2016. As Duty Manager for Bangladesh Bank, he'd worked until after 8 p.m. the previous evening, and was now coming back to the office before 9 a.m. to start all over again.

To make matters worse, he was working the weekend (which in Bangladesh runs from Friday to Saturday).

As Bin Huda passed the security gates at the bank's grey twelve-storey HQ, the morning traffic was already churning round the roundabout outside, its centre dominated by a giant statue of a water-lily blossom, the national flower of Bangladesh.

Bin Huda made his way up to the tenth floor, home to some of the most restricted areas of the bank and accessible only to senior members of the team. He settled into the morning's tasks. But then a colleague threw him a curveball: he told Bin Huda he'd been to retrieve some messages from one of the printers but found it wasn't working. Bin Huda went with him to take a look and the pair tried a few fixes but to no avail. The printer's power was on, but the expected pages weren't forthcoming.

It's the kind of workplace headache many of us have endured on countless occasions, and Bin Huda and his colleagues at Bangladesh Bank thought the same thing most of us do: no big deal, just another office glitch to sort out.

But this wasn't just any printer and it wasn't just any bank.

Bangladesh Bank is the country's central financial institution, headquartered in the capital, Dhaka, and responsible for overseeing the precious currency reserves of a country where millions live in poverty. And the printer played a key role within the bank. It was located inside a highly secure room on the tenth floor. Its job was to print out records of the multimillion-dollar transfers flowing in and out of the bank.

This malfunction was not simply an IT glitch: it was the first sign that something was going very badly wrong within the bank. But at this stage neither Bin Huda nor his colleagues knew this.

For most Bangladeshis, the weekend was already in full swing. It's a predominantly Muslim country, and Friday prayers were about to begin. Bin Huda told his colleagues to keep him updated on the printer situation, and he left the bank around 11.15 a.m. His co-workers stayed for a little while longer, trying to fix the printer, but in the end they decided to try again the following day, and they left the office just after noon. The hours drifted by, Friday night came and went. Behind the scenes, deep inside the bank's computers, among the streams of ones and zeros that now control so much of our world, an audacious crime was taking place. Yet outwardly all was calm, just a blinking printer light in a windowless room high above the busy streets.

The next day, Saturday, Bin Huda was back in the office around 9 a.m. to have another crack at the troublesome printer. But this time he discovered a new problem. Now a pivotal piece of software was also malfunctioning. 'Whenever I tried to switch on the software, [there was] an automated message saying, "A file is missing or changed",' Bin Huda later told police. This anodyne warning could have been caused by any number of things – a badly installed update, a tech-support error, a systems change. In fact, it was another indication of the chaos that was raging inside Bangladesh Bank's computer network.

Nervous now, Bin Huda went to two senior colleagues and got the okay to try a different method to restart the printer. It worked. Messages began spewing on to the tray. But any sense of relief was painfully short-lived. As they looked through the printouts, Bin Huda and his colleagues discovered urgent requests for clarification from the Federal Reserve Bank of New York, nicknamed the 'Fed', where Bangladesh Bank kept a US dollar account (so if they wanted to pay someone in dollars, they could transfer the money straight from the Fed account).

The Fed's employees were deeply concerned. They'd received instructions, apparently from inside Bangladesh Bank, to drain the entire account: almost a billion dollars. As the printer sprang to life, message after message appeared from the Fed, querying dozens of transfer requests that had seemingly been sent by Bangladesh. The Fed had first started to send queries at around 10.30 a.m. the previous day, Friday. But, with the printer out of action, Bangladesh Bank's staff saw them only at 12.30 p.m., on Saturday.[1] The delay would have catastrophic consequences, and the bank's battle against time was only going to get worse.

At this stage Bangladesh Bank's staff didn't know what had happened, but there was one thing they were sure of: they had absolutely not requested that their billion-dollar account be emptied, and they needed the transfers stopped immediately. They scrambled to contact the New York Federal Reserve. They tried to phone the numbers on the Fed's website, but, because it was a Saturday, the Fed wasn't picking up on the numbers they tried. They sent faxes and emails too, but again received no response. Time was ebbing away, and so was the money.

They didn't know it yet, but Bangladesh Bank was in the middle of the most daring cyber-theft ever attempted. The Lazarus Group – the elite team of North Korean hackers the FBI were investigating over the Sony raid – had been inside the bank's systems for more than a year, carefully planning for this moment. They would now bring to bear all of the skill and acumen they'd honed during their previous years of hacking in an attempt to carry out the heist of a lifetime. To spirit the money away they'd use fake bank accounts, charities, casinos and a network of accomplices across three continents.

It was like something from a film – almost as though a bunch of hackers had watched a thrilling Hollywood heist movie and thought to themselves, 'We could do that.' But for the victims of the crime – Bangladesh Bank and the many others that would come after – there was nothing entertaining about what was unfolding. The bank was in trouble and it needed help.

Rakesh Asthana was on his way back from a cyber-security conference and driving to Washington DC on 18 February when he got the call from Bangladesh. 'The phone rang and the Governor of the Central Bank was on the line and requesting urgent assistance on a delicate matter,' he remembers. Asthana, understandably, asked the Governor for more details. 'And he said, "I'm sorry, I can't tell you on the phone and can't send you an email. Just get on the plane and come and join. We need you."'

It was a cryptic call, and in some ways Asthana was an odd recipient for it. He'd only created his company, World Informatix Cyber Security, a couple of years before, after decades working at the World Bank. His firm was hardly a household name when it came to tech security, and wouldn't be on everyone's list to call in the event of a computer emergency. But what Asthana lacked in corporate profile he made up for in connections. He'd worked with Bangladesh Bank during his time at the World Bank and got to know the Governor, Atiur Rahman. Now Rahman was urgently requesting Asthana's help as the scale of the incident became clear. Asthana was keen but immediately thought of the logistics. 'I did tell him, "Look, I need to get my visa. I need to book my ticket." He says, "Oh, don't worry about the visa, that's already arranged at the Bangladesh Embassy. Just go there and get it and travel."'

Within a week, Asthana was on the ground in Dhaka and escorted into the bank. But instead of heading for the twelve-storey tower where the printer was, he was directed to a smaller building and taken up to the third floor. This was where the Governor and his executive team were based, and Asthana says he and his fellow investigators were given a room right next door to his offices.

As he started to learn more about the situation, Asthana realized the enormity of the attack. A billion dollars represented 0.45 per cent of Bangladesh's GDP – losses of that scale would push Bangladesh's economy 'to the brink', he says.[2] He also began to discern the reasons behind his mysterious invite to Dhaka, and why he was being placed so close to the bank's top tier.[3] 'I think when the incident happened, the Governor and the team were quite perplexed,' he tells me. 'They didn't quite know what to make of the incident. And they wanted somebody they could trust, and somebody that could be discreet because he had not made this information public, which in hindsight you will see was not a good thing to do.'

So secret was the incident that almost no one in the bank knew about it. 'The bulk of the Central Bank had no clue what had happened,' says Asthana. 'They were hearing murmuring and seeing people come in and out. But nobody knew.'

It wasn't just the wider bank it was kept secret from. The Governor decided not to tell the government either. A billion-dollar hole had potentially appeared in the nation's finances, but no one in power was any the wiser. It soon became clear to Asthana why the bosses had kept it secret – at this stage, they still believed they could sort it all out without any fuss. 'The Governor . . . thought that a mistake had been made and some transactions had gone to the wrong bank or the wrong account, and we would get it back. The money would be there.'

It wasn't an outlandish conclusion. According to Asthana, such mistakes do happen and can usually be corrected and the money returned. But in the Bangladesh Bank case it quickly became clear this was not a mistaken transaction. Someone, somehow, had deliberately commanded the transfer of the billion dollars, and had messaged the Federal Reserve Bank in New York to make it happen.

The Bangladeshis began to suspect it might be an inside job. Maybe someone sneaked into the computer room overnight and made the transfers? So Asthana sat down and watched the security tapes – all eight hours of them. At one point, he paused the tape and peered at the screen: a shadow appeared in the frame. Could this be a rogue employee arriving at the scene of the crime? Sadly not. 'It was a cleaner outside the room,' says Asthana. 'There was nobody in the room for this whole eight-hour period.'

A locked room, no one goes in or out, and yet a billion dollars gets transferred. How?

Asthana began to switch his focus: if someone had managed to make international transfers from inside the bank, they must have done so using the same system the bank itself used – a piece of software relatively unknown outside finance circles but which connects the world's largest institutions and holds the key to trillions of dollars: SWIFT.

As we learnt in Chapter 1, SWIFT is the mechanism by which financial institutions send and receive requests for money transfers. The software is available only to the likes of banks and major organizations. That's a large part of the trust that exists in SWIFT – you can usually use it only if you're inside one of those institutions' computer networks, and the assumption is that this includes no one but legitimate employees. But what if a hacker managed to break into the network and pose as an employee?

This was the scenario Asthana was now confronted with. The transfer requests sent to the New York Fed had been issued using SWIFT. Someone had sent thirty-five requests, totalling $951m – almost the entire contents of Bangladesh Bank's account at the Fed.[4] What's more, whoever had hacked into Bangladesh Bank appeared to be well versed in using SWIFT. One investigator told me that 'it was like they were sitting at that machine and made the transfers as if they were the bank teller.' SWIFT isn't the kind of computer program most people have experience with, but these hackers knew their way around it like old hands. Clearly the bank had been raided by some very professional operators. And they'd planned the heist with great care: Asthana and his fellow investigators began to realize that the timing of the SWIFT transfers was no coincidence. The hackers had executed the entire raid meticulously, exploiting international time zones to give themselves the maximum getaway window, leaving those chasing them in the dust. These crooks were working to a schedule.

In the movies, the bank robbers typically time their heist for an opportune moment: a long weekend, perhaps, especially one where there'll be lots of celebration to cover the noise as they drill into the safe. In the Bangladesh Bank case, the hackers went way further.

The SWIFT transfers started at 8.36 p.m., on Thursday, 4 February, in Dhaka, exactly thirty-three minutes after Zubair Bin Huda left the building. But here's the trick: the account in which Bangladesh Bank's US dollars were actually held was of course at the New York Federal Reserve Bank, thousands of miles from Bangladesh, where, thanks to the time difference, it was 9.36 a.m., leaving plenty of time for the Fed to unwittingly act out the hackers' wishes. The hackers continued making transfers overnight while the Bangladesh office was empty, when all the while New York was awake and ready for action.

And there was something else playing into the hackers' hands. As noted above, in Bangladesh the weekend runs from Friday to Saturday, not Saturday to Sunday, as in many other countries. So, as the New York Fed was busy transferring the money, Bangladesh Bank's HQ in Dhaka was winding down for the weekend, with Bin Huda and his colleagues forming only a skeleton staff.

'So you see the elegance of the attack,' says Asthana. 'When [on] Friday New York is working, Bangladesh Bank is off. By the time Bangladesh Bank comes back online, the Federal Reserve Bank is off. So it delayed the whole discovery by almost three days.'

And the hackers had yet another trick up their sleeves to buy more time. Once they transferred the money out of the New York Fed, they needed to send it somewhere. So they wired it to accounts they'd set up at a bank in Manila, the capital of the Philippines. Like everything else in this story, the choice of country was no coincidence. Monday, 8 February 2016, in the Philippines was the first day of the Lunar New Year – a huge national holiday across Asia. So when Bangladesh Bank tried to contact the bank in the Philippines asking them to block the transactions at their end, most staff were absent, and the transfers went through.

By juggling the time differences in Bangladesh, the US and the Philippines, the hackers had engineered a clear five-day run to spirit the money away. Thanks to weekends and holidays, the different banks' schedules were all at odds with each another. So even when they discovered the hack, they struggled to communicate quickly enough to stop it.

By this point in the investigation, it became clear to the Bangladesh Bank officials that the transactions couldn't simply be reversed. The money had actually been transferred to the Philippines, and, to get it back, they'd have to get that country's help. The Philippine authorities requested that they obtain a court order to begin the process of reclaiming the money. Court orders are public documents, and so the cat was suddenly out of the bag regarding Bangladesh Bank's lost money. As soon as it filed its case on 29 February, the story went public, and quickly exploded worldwide.

Rakesh Asthana remembers leaving the bank's HQ one day and being mobbed by hundreds of reporters and TV crews. They were not the only ones suddenly alerted to the bank's losses: the Bangladesh government also found out, and, according to Asthana: 'The Finance Minister was furious, and he actually told the Governor, "How dare you not inform me? Because this is of national importance."'

It wasn't just in Bangladesh where the story of the heist was making headlines. The news also made its way to the US, where it captured the attention of Congresswoman Carolyn Maloney. 'I was leaving Congress and going to the airport and reading about the heist. And it was fascinating, shocking,' she recalls. Congresswoman Maloney represents New York's 12th District, an area that covers most of the East Side of Manhattan – including the world's largest central business district and the corporate headquarters of major media, entertainment and finance firms. She's also on the Congressional committee that deals with financial services and had been tracking the emerging cyber-threat. She quickly understood the significance of the attack on Bangladesh Bank. Her thinking took her way ahead of the immediate damage, towards the future ramifications for the entire industry. It quickly led her to a very dark place indeed. 'If you can't trust the SWIFT system, then the whole financial system breaks down,' she says. 'Markets run more on trust than capital. And this undermined the trust in international payments and the ability for banks to swiftly transfer money. And if you can't trust the security of international payments, then international commerce would absolutely stop and that would be catastrophic. It would undermine the entire world economy.'

The Congresswoman also had some big questions for the New York Federal Reserve Bank, which is 'usually so careful', she says. How did these transactions get through?

As she quizzed the Fed, Maloney discovered that it *had* spotted the suspect transactions and moved to stop them. It was the first of a series of setbacks for the criminals. They had been so close to getting their hands on almost a billion dollars, having created a meticulous plot which, until that point, had gone like clockwork. But, as in the best heist movies, they had made a slip-up. The heist was about to go sideways.

Making a SWIFT transfer isn't as easy as simply stating 'Please send a billion dollars to Geoff White, account number 123456789, at Acme Bank.' First, you have to check whether the bank you're sending the funds from has a relationship with the bank you're sending them to. If not, you have to route the transfer via an intermediary bank that has a relationship with both.

This was the first mistake the hackers made. When trying to transfer the $951m from the New York Fed, they failed to specify an intermediary bank, and all but one of the thirty-five transactions were declined. They quickly managed to correct their work, however, and resubmitted the other thirty-four requests.

But now another tiny detail would derail them. The bank where the hackers had lined up accounts to receive the money was at a branch located in Jupiter Street. There are hundreds of other banks in Manila that the hackers could have used, but they chose this one. And, by pure coincidence, that decision would cost them hundreds of millions of dollars.

As Congresswoman Maloney explains, '"Jupiter" is also the name of a sanctioned Iranian shipping vessel.' Just the mention of the word 'Jupiter' was enough to set alarm bells ringing in the Fed's automated computer systems. 'The red flag caused the Fed to review the entire batch of payment orders. And a quick-thinking New York Fed staffer noticed that something about these payment orders didn't look right,' says Maloney.

Thanks to that one word, the heist started to grind to a halt. The New York Fed stopped most of the thirty-four transactions. But not all. Four transactions got through. Including the first successful transfer, that made five in total, worth just over $101m. Not what the hackers were aiming for, but still a huge blow for Bangladesh. Its Ambassador to the Philippines, John Gomes, summed up a lot of his compatriots' feelings: 'I'm terribly shocked that this money earned by our hard-working farmers and our workers [was stolen]. It's their money. It's the poor people's money. It's the workers' money. That's why it hurts more.'[5]

This is the bit you don't often get to see in the glamorous heist movies: the real-world impact of the crime. The money that's been stolen doesn't belong to some rich bankers or wealthy companies – it's the government's own funds. And they're vital in a country like Bangladesh, where more than a tenth of the population lives in poverty.[6]

Now the country had a hole in its finances of $101m, money which was winging its way to a bunch of computer hackers who'd never even had to visit Bangladesh, let alone the bank's HQ in Dhaka. Instead, they'd staged their heist from behind the safety of their computer keyboards. What's even more remarkable, as investigators would later discover, is that they'd been patiently sitting inside the bank for more than a year, waiting for exactly the right moment to strike.

On 29 January 2015, just over a year before the billion-dollar-theft attempt, employees at Bangladesh Bank and several other big financial institutions in Dhaka had received a politely worded email from a job hunter, using the email address yardgen@gmail.com, who wrote (*sic*):

I am Rasel Ahlam, I am extremely excited about the idea of becoming a part of your company and am hoping that you will give me an opportunity to present my case in further detail in a personal interview. Here is my resume and cover letter. Thank you in advance for your time and consideration.[7]

Ahlam included a link to a website whence his CV could be downloaded. Anyone who did so, however, would also find themselves unwittingly downloading a virus.[8] The email from Ahlam was a phishing attack, of exactly the kind that had worked so effectively against Sony Pictures Entertainment and countless other cyber-crime victims. If their computers weren't properly protected, the malicious download would open up victims to the hackers. At least one Bangladesh Bank employee fell for the ruse and downloaded the virus. So an instant jackpot for the hackers? Not quite.

They now faced a number of challenges before they could even think about stealing any money. First, what if the person whose computer they'd just infected turned their machine off and on again? The virus code would stop running, shutting the hackers out. So they planted on the victim's computer a program called NESTEGG – the first of a series of esoterically named packages that would be used to break open Bangladesh Bank.[9] NESTEGG gave the hackers what techies call 'persistent access' – it didn't matter if the victim rebooted their machine, the virus would still be there, stealthily running in the background.

Now they turned to the next challenge.

In all likelihood the computer the hackers had just compromised belonged to someone in human resources, the most obvious target for a phishing email framed to look as though it had come from a prospective employee. But HR staff generally don't have access to the vaults. So, to steal the money, the hackers would somehow have to navigate their way across Bangladesh Bank's computer network to get to the machines controlling the funds.

To do so they used a piece of software that investigators would christen SIERRACHARLIE. Its job was to scan for other computers connected to the same network and try to connect to them too. This allowed the hackers to fan out through the bank's systems, hopping their way from machine to machine to reach their goal.

The final challenge was to do all this without being spotted by the bank's IT team. For this the hackers deployed yet another tool, named MACKTRUCK. Its job was to create an encrypted online-communication channel to and from each of the infected computers. Now the hackers could send in commands to their slave machines and pull data out of the bank, all hidden behind encryption, which prevented staff from spotting what was happening.

The way I've described it, these steps may sound like something relatively straightforward for an experienced techie, but that's far from the case. There's a myth among some of the public that hackers have God-like powers of omnipotence, and can instantly comprehend an organization's computer network and attack it at will. The reality is often very different. Most of the time hackers are breaking into an environment they don't know, and they have to move their way around carefully, all the while at high risk of getting caught. It's like being a burglar dropped into the middle of a dark house with a weak torch. At any moment you could bash into something and raise the alarm. It's tense.

'The biggest risk is obviously being found out. So they try to be as stealthy as possible, and try not to be uncovered,' says Eric Chien. And he should know, because he's one of the world's most renowned security researchers.

Chien cut his teeth working on a virus called Stuxnet, a frighteningly intricate piece of software that's often referred to as the world's first 'cyberweapon'. Stuxnet had been unleashed on the computer network of a uranium-refinement facility in Iran, which many outsiders believed was being used to develop material for nuclear weapons. The virus had skilfully caused havoc among the plant's centrifuges – a central part of the enrichment process – seriously damaging its output.

Chien, working for the Broadcom subsidiary Symantec, had been one of a core team that picked apart Stuxnet, revealing that it had been created to target this one specific nuclear plant with the aim of covertly sabotaging its machinery (many media reports attributed the cyber-attack to Iran's long-time enemies, the US and Israel – claims unconfirmed by either country).[10]

Now Chien turned his attention to the Bangladesh Bank hack, and began to piece together how the hackers had penetrated so deeply into its computer systems, with such catastrophic consequences.

He started to understand how, having hacked one computer, they'd use it to leapfrog their way through the network: 'They have access to a machine, and they basically dig on that machine for additional credentials: other usernames and passwords. They then use those credentials to [ask the computer]: "Hey, what machines are connected to this machine?" And they just try those credentials and try to jump from one machine to another. And they repeat and replay that over and over again.'

As soon as they've hopped from a less important computer to a more important one, they no longer need access to the first. So they wipe their viruses from it, making their progress harder to track, says Chien. 'Even though over time they might have infected dozens or even a hundred different machines, at any given time they might only actively be on a couple. The Bangladesh Bank information security team may have seen that a machine was infected, but then they might have thought, "Oh, it's cleaned up now," not realizing the attackers are actually still in their network.'

The attackers' goal was the computers that controlled SWIFT – the keys to the safe, effectively – allowing them to make requests to transfer huge sums of money. By 29 January 2016, exactly a year after sending their first phishing email, they hit the jackpot, finally accessing the SWIFT terminal. The bank's billion dollars were tantalizingly close. But there was a problem. The hackers realized that Bangladesh Bank records all of its SWIFT transactions on its computer system. That's a big issue, because, as Chien points out, 'if [a bank employee] noticed that these international transfers were taking place, they could potentially block them or reverse them. They could send SWIFT messages to tell the other bank, "Cancel this transaction, revert the funds, please." ' That was a risk the hackers didn't want to take, obviously. So they had to delete the digital records so there was no trace of them at Bangladesh Bank. That meant hacking into the SWIFT software on the bank's system and changing the code. This may sound complicated, but ultimately it was surprisingly straightforward, and the way they went about it is an incredibly elegant example of the art of computer hacking.

So elegant, in fact, that it's worth looking at the code close up (and if you've never seen computer code before, don't worry, I'll walk you through it). Here's how it looks:

```
85 C0                   test eax, eax
75 04                   jnz  failed
33 c0                   xor  eax, eax
eb 17                   jmp  exit
                        failed:
B8 01 00 00 00          mov eax, 111
```

If you're not a techie, this probably looks like a jumble of meaningless letters and numbers. But if you take it line by line it starts to make sense. Here's what each line means:

```
85 C0                   test eax, eax
```

This line is some kind of important check – did you enter the right password? Are you using the right computer? Are you logging in from the right network?

```
75 04                   jnz failed
```

If you fail the above check, go to the line marked 'failed' at the bottom If not, go to the next line.

```
33 c0                   xor eax, eax
```

You passed the check – success!

```
eb 17                   jmp exit
```

The check is complete, so go ahead and start using SWIFT.

```
                        failed:
B8 01 00 00 00          mov eax, 1
```

You failed the check, so you can't use SWIFT, sorry.

So the key line is that second one, right? The one that says if you fail the check, go to the 'failed' line. If we can get round that, we'll go straight to the success line and we'll be able to start using SWIFT. This is precisely what the Bangladesh Bank hackers did. They changed the code to look like this:

```
85 C0                   test eax, eax
90                      nop
90                      nop
eb 17                   jmp exit
                        failed:
B8 01 00 00 00          mov eax, 1
```

It may not look that different to you. The changes are small, but very, very significant. Because now here's what the code means:

```
85 C0                   test eax, eax
```

This line is some kind of important check – did you enter the right password? Are you using the right computer? Are you logging in from the right network?

```
90                      nop
```

Do nothing.

```
90                      nop
```

Do nothing.

```
33 c0                   xor eax, eax
```

You passed the check – success!

```
eb 17                   jmp exit
```

The check is complete, so go ahead and start using SWIFT.

```
                        failed:
B8 01 00 00 00          mov eax, 1
```

You failed the check, so you can't use SWIFT, sorry.

The 'failure' line is still there at the bottom of the code, but guess what? We'll never reach it because the line telling us to go there has disappeared.

It was the tiniest of changes, just a few characters in the code. But it changed a computerized 'no' into a 'yes' and swung open the digital doors to a billion-dollar bank vault. This is the beauty of computer code: just a few letters and numbers can wield immense power. It's like the knife of a sushi chef: understanding how to wield it efficiently can take years, but once mastered just a few strokes are all you need.

The hackers now had access to the SWIFT database and could erase all traces of their transfer requests, and the bank would be none the wiser.

Well, actually, not quite . . . The hackers faced one final hurdle. You know how there are people who don't trust computers? The people who always like to have a printed paper copy to make themselves feel a little bit more secure? Bangladesh Bank was no exception. They had a backup for the digital record of SWIFT transfers: the computer printer inside the office on the tenth floor. Its job was to churn out paper confirmations of every SWIFT transfer.

'The attackers needed to bypass all the printed-out copies of the transactions,' says Eric Chien. So they broke into the part of the SWIFT software that sends commands to the printer. 'Every time it tried to send a printout to the printer, they would simply over-write with zeros those files that contained the content to print. So nothing would print. Instead, there was all this blank paper in the printer.'

In the heist movies, there's often a sequence in which the thieves take over the surveillance cameras and alter the footage to make it look as though the vault is empty while the gang goes to work. This was the hacker version.

The printer malfunction that Bin Huda and his colleagues thought was an everyday glitch was actually the final stage in a care-fully executed digital break-in that had been a year in the planning.

With the traces covered, the heist was set to go. By now the hack-ers had discovered Bangladesh Bank's billion-dollar account at the New York Fed, and they used their access to SWIFT to send trans-fer requests. But when the Fed received the requests, it got suspicious. 'Nobody sends a billion dollars in a day,' says Rakesh Asthana. 'And they sought clarification from Bangladesh Bank by sending these SWIFT messages asking, "What is all this?"'

But of course the printer that was supposed to print out those SWIFT messages from the Fed had been taken out by the hackers, and all it was printing were blank pages. So the Fed's urgent appeals didn't get seen by the bank staff until Saturday, when they finally fixed the printer.

'And lo and behold, they started seeing all these clarification mes-sages that had come from Federal Reserve Bank of New York. And they were asking them, "Why did you send these billion-dollar transactions?"' says Asthana.

But, as we have seen, by that time, the Bangladesh Bank staff couldn't reach the Fed – it was the weekend in New York and their contact numbers didn't work.

As the scale and intricacy of the hack became clear, even veteran researchers like Eric Chien were astonished. 'We had never seen an attack like this, transferring so many millions of dollars. This was a huge first. No one in their right mind, no cybercriminal we had ever seen before, had tried to transfer one billion dollars from a bank. It was astounding.'

It wasn't just bank insiders and security researchers who were sitting up and taking notice. Inevitably the hack also grabbed the attention of the FBI. It particularly caught the eye of the team which, since late 2014, had been researching the Sony Pictures Entertainment break-in and data leak. Something about the bank heist was ringing a lot of bells with the investigators in Los Angeles.

'There were some accounts that were used to both target Sony Pictures and conduct reconnaissance and target Bangladesh Bank,' says Tony Lewis. As Assistant US Attorney for the Central District of California, he had been working on the Sony Pictures Entertainment case ever since late 2014. Now he and his colleagues started to look into the Bangladesh Bank case too.

Detail-minded readers will remember that the address used to send the initial spear-phishing email to Bangladesh Bank was yardgen@gmail.com. Lewis and his FBI colleagues began to look back through their leads from the Sony case and found that the same address had come up multiple times in the investigation.[12] It had been used prior to the hack to carry out Internet searches about one of the actors from the movie *The Interview*, which, according to the US authorities, had been the trigger for the Sony hack. But that's not a crime, is it? Maybe whoever owned the yardgen Gmail address was a big fan of celebs, and did a bit of multimillion-dollar bank hacking on the side?

So the FBI dug deeper. It managed to get access to the address book attached to the yardgen Gmail account (almost certainly as a result of the search warrants the Bureau submitted to the likes of

Google). According to the FBI, the address book contained something intriguing: email addresses that corresponded to the names of three actors from the movie, spelt seventeen different ways. Okay, so maybe whoever owned the account *really* liked celebs and was trying to contact them by guessing their email addresses?

Then the FBI says it found in the yardgen account a spear-phishing email mocked up to look like a Facebook alert, addressed to one of the actors from the film. Then it found links to the Facebook account of Andoson David, the persona who'd tried to trick *The Interview* actors into downloading virus-laden photos of nude celebrities. Then it found the same Gmail address had been used to search online for computer-hacking methods.

The more it looked, the more links the FBI found between the heist at Bangladesh Bank and the various email and social media accounts used to carry out the Sony hack. 'There were connections between accounts used for each of those things, but there were also some accounts that were used to target both of those victims,' says Lewis.

There were similarities in the virus code used too. To carry out the Bangladesh Bank attack, the hackers had wrapped their communications inside a layer of encryption using MACKTRUCK. The FBI found a table inside the virus code containing three IP addresses used to make that encryption happen. They found the same table with the same IP addresses among the viruses used to hack Sony.

Sure, cybercriminals might copy each other's code from time to time, but they generally don't share IP addresses – if they did, all of their juicy hacked data might end up in the hands of another cyber-crime gang using the same IP address. It makes no sense. For the FBI, that the same addresses were used in both attacks was further evidence the same gang was behind them.

The FBI now believed the Lazarus Group carried out the raids on both Sony and Bangladesh Bank. It was a stunning turn of events. North Korea's elite hacking team had successfully inflicted significant damage on one of America's largest corporations, and was now stealing hundreds of millions of dollars from national banks that were supposed to be impregnable. All within the space of a couple of years.

But this wasn't the only revelation awaiting the FBI's investigators. As they dug deeper into the trove of email and social media accounts used to carry out the two attacks, they would discover something incredible. So far the Lazarus Group's hackers had been anonymous, shadowy figures, using fake personas to wage their digital war. That was about to change. According to the FBI, the evidence would bring them face to (virtual) face with a key member of the Lazarus Group. And his story, as told in the Bureau's legal case against him, would shed light on the intricate and fascinating evolution of North Korea's hacker army, and its growing links with organized crime. Lazarus was about to be unmasked.

8

Cyber-slaves

For Park Jin Hyok, life in 2011 was pretty busy. He'd been born in North Korea thirty-six years earlier, but, unlike the vast majority of his fellow citizens, he'd been able to leave the country and was now experiencing just how different life in the outside world could be. It was all down to his sought-after skills.

Park was an IT whizz, fluent in several programming languages. He'd attended the prestigious Kim Chaek University of Technology in Pyongyang – a hot spot for ambitious young techies – and had worked his way into a hallowed career. Park was now a computer expert working for the North Korean government. In a hierarchical society like North Korea, such prestige could transform not only his life but the lives of his family too.

Sure enough, he was eventually rewarded with one of the most exciting perks the regime can bestow: a trip abroad. He was dispatched to the Chinese city of Dalian, a couple of hundred miles from the North Korean border. As a long-standing ally of North Korea, China is a fairly common destination for the tiny few chosen by the regime for overseas duties. Nonetheless, for Park it must have been a massive culture shock. In Dalian he would have found Costa Coffee outlets, about a dozen McDonald's eateries and even a Tesco supermarket.[1] All a far cry from Pyongyang's wide-but-empty streets and the limited pickings most citizens find in its shops.

Ostensibly, he worked for a company making online games, setting up email accounts, configuring computer servers, researching tech vulnerabilities – it was all in a day's work for someone like Park. According to investigators, however, he was living a double life, using these computer skills for something that was very far from a game.

But back in 2011 Park had other things on his mind. In September he was due to return to North Korea to marry his fiancée (whom he referred to as 'comrade'). He'd then return to China to continue working, and after that – who knows? If he served the regime well, he might be rewarded with a decent-sized apartment in Pyongyang. Nice furniture. A big TV. Just the ticket for a man starting out on family life.

But, first, Park would have to pay back the regime for his years of training and his plum overseas assignment. He would be using his skills to help carry out some of the world's most destructive cyberattacks, according to investigators who claim to have traced his online movements. Their attempts to track him down led them on a twisting path through the digital undergrowth. But, no matter how good Park was at covering his footprints, he wouldn't be able to hide his secret life forever.

For prosecutors, cyber-investigation is all about building a chain of evidence that leads from the crime to the person they suspect committed it, and trying to eliminate any opportunities along the way for that person to wriggle out of responsibility. In a physical crime, things like fingerprints, DNA and clothing fibres are all compelling pieces of evidence potentially tying the culprit to the scene of the offence. By contrast, it's no easy feat to link a cybercrime to the pair of hands on the keyboard that carried it out. Imagine you receive a dodgy email from me, and as a result you fall foul of a scam. You then try to prosecute me. There are many ways I could argue that I had nothing to do with it. Perhaps my account was hacked? Maybe I'd shared my email password with someone else, who logged in and sent the offending message? How can you prove it was absolutely, irrefutably me who scammed you?

This was the challenge facing Tony Lewis in the US Attorney General's Office and his FBI colleagues in 2016 as they investigated the hacking of Sony Pictures Entertainment and Bangladesh Bank.

Blaming the attacks on the Lazarus Group wasn't enough. They couldn't lay criminal charges against a shadowy hacker gang. They needed names. What they had to do was to identify the individuals behind the hack.

So they went back through the data and looked for a place to start the chain of evidence – a single thread that, when pulled, might unravel the case and lead to the individual hackers' identities.

Remember yardgen@gmail.com, the email address used to hack into both victims? Thanks to the legal warrants they'd executed on the tech companies, the FBI had accumulated a wealth of data about this and other email accounts, including the IDs of the computers used to log in to them, and the IP addresses those computers were using to get online. They discovered that, on 6 September 2014, the same computer using the same IP address had accessed both yardgen and another email account, tty198410@gmail.com. This implied that both accounts were being used by the same person or people. Messages had been sent back and forth between the two email addresses. And not just any messages – they were exactly the same type of scam Facebook messages that would later be used to target the cast and crew of *The Interview*. The implication was clear: whoever owned these two email accounts had been using them to craft phishing messages in the weeks leading up to the hack. Clearly, tty198410@gmail.com was part of the network of online accounts used to hack Sony.

It turned out that this wasn't the only link between tty198410@gmail.com and the attack. The same email address had been used to set up the Facebook account in the name of Andoson David, the persona who'd been messaging *The Interview*'s stars and exhorting them to download photos of nude celebrities that concealed a computer virus. It was just one of a series of connections between the email account and the hacks.[2]

The FBI dug deeper into the tty198410@gmail.com account and discovered it had been used as the backup address for yet another Gmail account: watsonhenny@gmail.com. This rang alarm bells, because the watsonhenny account had multiple links to both hacks:

its contacts book contained thirty-seven different email addresses for staff at Bangladesh Bank, and it had been used to send phishing messages to a British TV production company that was making a drama about North Korea. The company was targeted by the hackers at the same time as Sony. It was clear the watsonhenny@gmail.com address was another key part of the attack network.

As they started investigating the watsonhenny account, the FBI investigators came across a stunning lead. They discovered messages sent from the account in April and May 2015 by someone claiming to be a representative of the North Korean government. The person was corresponding with a contact in Australia, discussing deals for coal and metal. In the conversation, the Australian contact claimed to be a major figure in North Korea's overseas business empire, whose reports went directly to Kim Jong Un, the country's leader.[3]

As a result of their warrants in the Sony case, the FBI team had suddenly found themselves eavesdropping on a conversation apparently taking place between North Korea's political and commercial operations. If there was any doubt in their minds that North Korea was behind the hacks, this almost certainly helped to dispel them.

(The Australian contact was real. He turned out to be 62-year-old Chan Han Choi, who was arrested in Sydney in 2017 and sentenced to more than three years in prison for attempting to sell North Korean missile parts to Indonesia in contravention of UN sanctions.[4])

Now the FBI investigators went back to the tty198410@gmail.com address, the one which had been used to hack into Sony. If they could work out who was behind it, maybe they'd find their suspect. Sure enough, they began to reveal a network of other email, Facebook and Twitter accounts, all set up in the name of 'Kim Hyon Woo'. More and more links emerged: of the twenty email and social media accounts that were used to attack Sony and Bangladesh Bank, half had links to the mysterious Kim Hyon Woo.

So was this the true identity of the hacker? No. As the investigators pulled apart the leads, it became clear Kim was simply another puppet persona created by the cybercriminals. Like a Russian matry-oshka doll, whoever hacked Sony and Bangladesh Bank had embedded themselves within layer upon layer of fakery – a digital smokescreen to throw pursuers off the scent. But the Kim persona threw up an intriguing lead, and this time, instead of a blind alley, it would provide a remarkable window into the hackers' true lives.

Several of Kim Hyon Woo's accounts had links to an email account named surigaemind@hotmail.com. As the FBI discovered, it was created on 23 September 2010 under the name Jin Hyok Park. Then a couple of months later it was used to set up a Facebook account in the same name. Then it was used to set up a Twitter account with the handle @ttypkj, under the name Park Jin Hyok. ('Park' is the equivalent of a Western surname like 'Smith', but Koreans vary in whether they put it at the beginning or the end of their name.[5]) Usefully for the FBI investigators, they also found that the owner of the surigaemind address had sent themselves an email on 29 April 2011 entitled 'My Current Location'. The GPS co-ordinates led to an anonymous-looking set of buildings next to a flyover in the Chinese port city of Dalian, a couple of hundred miles from the North Korean border. The FBI was zeroing in on Park Jin Hyok. But, at this point, it couldn't be sure that it wasn't just another online persona masquerading under yet another fake name.

As the investigators continued to search the surigaemind email account, they found emails signed by 'Jin Hyok'. These were about projects he was working on for a company called Chosun Expo. It was based in Dalian, the same city that the email-account owner had given for their location. The trail was getting warmer – and the North Korean links kept coming. Chosun Expo was originally set up as an experimental joint venture between North and South Korea, a chance for the two countries to work on projects together, but, at some stage, the South had pulled out. An archived version of the company's website shows that a somewhat meandering corporate journey followed, from selling mushrooms and vases to offering bespoke computer-programming services.[6]

But was Chosun Expo really connected to the hacking? Maybe

there was an innocent explanation for the links between the company, Park Jin Hyok and the hacking attacks. Maybe Park was just a rogue employee, who worked for Chosun Expo on legitimate computer-programming projects, but had then used his surigae-mind email address to create the massive network of accounts used to hack Sony and Bangladesh Bank – all without his bosses' knowledge.

The FBI kept digging. It discovered logins to Chosun Expo's website that had come from the same North Korean IP addresses that had accessed the network of email accounts used by the hackers. This indicated that whoever ran the company's website was also taking part in the cyber-attacks. The FBI also claimed to have a witness who'd had first-hand dealings with Chosun Expo and told them that its employees were overseen by a North Korean political attaché, and that the bulk of their salaries was sent back to North Korea.[7] The more the FBI looked at Chosun Expo, the more links they found to North Korea and the Sony and Bangladesh hacks. They now believed the company was a front for North Korean computer hackers.[8]

Then the FBI hit the jackpot. It turned up a conversation between one of Chosun Expo's department heads and a customer of the company who used its programmers' services. In January 2011 the department boss wrote that a new developer was joining the team in Dalian, named 'Pak Jin Hek', an English-language variation of Park Jin Hyok. Attached was Park's résumé. It stated he'd joined Chosun Expo in 2002 as an 'online games developer' after graduating from Kim Chaek University of Technology. It listed his programming skills (including Visual C++, one of the languages used to create some of the malware deployed in the Lazarus Group's attacks).

For the investigators, it was an amazing result. Park Jin Hyok, they now believed, was not a shady online persona but flesh and blood. 'It had his name, where he went to school, what languages he spoke, what computer languages he was proficient in, his birthday. So the sort of biographical details that really showed this was a

person,' says Tony Lewis, the Assistant US Attorney who was helping the FBI team make the links between the Sony hack and the
Bangladesh Bank heist.

But the résumé contained something even more surprising: a
photo of Park Jin Hyok himself.

You can see it for yourself – just visit the FBI Cyber's 'Most
Wanted' list and there he is, staring out at you from a blue background.[9] He looks to be in his thirties, commensurate with the date
of birth given on his résumé: 15 August 1984. He's expressionless,
wearing a smart black-striped shirt and a brown jacket. You could
pass him in the street and forget him in seconds. Yet this, the FBI
claims, is the true face of all the pseudonyms used in the sprawling
campaign of cybercrime that took down Sony and robbed Bangladesh Bank of tens of millions of dollars: Rasel Ahlam, Andoson
David, Watson Henny, Kim Hyon Woo – they were all just parts
played by Park Jin Hyok as he manipulated his network of fake personas from behind his keyboard. The Lazarus Group was no longer
a faceless digital menace; it now had a name, a photo and a life story,
according to Lewis. 'It really put a face to all of the investigative
work that we had been doing.'

But, in some ways, the revelation simply prompts more questions:
how did Park end up working at a company in China? We've seen
how North Korea values mathematical skill among its youngsters
and how it uses this to identify and groom government hackers. But
why send them abroad, especially given North Korea's paranoid iso-
lationism? In fact, there are some very good reasons. Park Jin Hyok's
story is reflective of a much wider strategic approach. It explains
why so many of North Korea's hackers are sent outside the country's borders, and why they turn up in the strangest of locations.

Shenyang in China is one of the country's largest cities, with a population of just over 9 million. Close to the centre there's a hotel called
the Chilbosan. From the outside, it looks like a classic Asian business establishment, complete with stone tigers flanking the front
door.

It was here that an American called Mark found himself on a business trip in 2017 (I've changed his name: his company does a lot of work in China, where speaking to foreign journalists is frowned upon, and he doesn't want to jeopardize future work there). A colleague had organized his accommodation, so he knew nothing about the hotel before he arrived. His first impressions were positive. 'It was a beautiful lobby,' he says. 'All the staff were dressed well, very attentive to the people's needs coming in to check in.'

But, as he registered, he couldn't help but notice furtive glances from the staff. Things got worse when he got into the lift. 'We stopped at an intermediate floor. The door opened and some of the other hotel visitors looked very surprised. "Wow, who's this guy?" One of the people there took a step back, literally, and looked at me as if he was completely shocked. They got into the elevator and separated themselves a little bit off to the side. It was just dead silence.'

The hotel Mark had just checked into was owned and operated by North Korea – something that became increasingly clear as he settled down for his evening meal. 'I looked behind me at the TV set that was on the wall and they have these videos of the Korean War. It was very patriotic in nature and they're showing US tanks being shot at. I asked our employees who were with me, "What's this all about?" And they said, "What they're saying there on the screen, if you translate it, is how the North Koreans effectively fought off the US during the Korean War." I'm sitting here, having a dinner and watching this patriotic stuff about North Korea and how they won against the US.'

But it wasn't just the hotel's North Korean ownership that was getting Mark suspicious looks in the lift. According to FBI investigators, the Chilbosan hides a dark secret. In its investigations into the Sony hack, the Bureau had been tracking the IP addresses the attackers had used. Some of them traced directly back to the Chilbosan Hotel. It wasn't the first time it had turned up in cyber-attacks attributed to North Korea, according to Kyung Jin Kim, who led the FBI's office in the US Embassy in Seoul until 2019 and now works on cyber-security for FTI Consulting. 'The circumstantial evidence that we have, the intelligence that we gathered throughout many years, is that we suspect that [North Korean] cyber-hackers are operating out of that location.'

Back at the Chilbosan, Mark had started googling the hotel and came across the Internet gossip about its secret life. 'That's when I discovered that this was known as the "hacker hotel",' he says.

Nevertheless, by this time it was too late to find another place for his one-night stay, so Mark settled in for the night. But not before taking a wise precaution: he turned off his phone's Wi-Fi connection. (He also gave the hotel a four-star review online – because he genuinely thought it was good value: 'The rate was very reasonable. It was about $50, which is literally half the rate of probably any comparable hotel.')

Mark and the FBI weren't the only ones finding North Korean computer experts operating in China. Before fleeing North Korea, Hyun-Seung Lee was a successful businessman, well connected and definitely among the country's elite class. He was born in Pyongyang but spent years studying and working in Dalian, the same port city in which Chosun Expo was located and where his father was a high-level North Korean business official. He got friendly with some of the young North Korean techies in Dalian, hanging out with them on national holidays. As a result, he got a rare glimpse into their domestic lives, as he told Jean H. Lee, my co-host for the BBC World Service podcast *The Lazarus Heist*: 'I went to their apartment a few times to learn [about] computers. There were about twenty people living together in one space. Four to six people living in one room. They made the living room like an office: all the computers were in the living room.'

Lee asked what they did with all the computer kit that had taken over their lounge, and was told they were working on legitimate IT projects. 'They were making cell-phone games at the time, and they told me that they were selling these products to Japan and South Korea through brokers. And that they made about a million dollars a year. Just twenty people.'

It makes sense: there are plenty of companies around the world who don't mind turning a blind eye to employing North Korean workers (or remaining wilfully ignorant as to who's doing the work), especially if the rates are cheap enough. But it seems it's frighteningly easy for these legitimate programmers to cross the line into cybercrime to make illicit money for the regime. In 2011 South Korean police arrested five people who'd allegedly collaborated with North Korean hackers to steal millions of dollars via online gaming sites.[10] The scam reportedly revolved around a wildly popular video game called *Lineage*, a medieval fantasy adventure in which knights and princes slay monsters and lay siege to castles. Players can accrue in-game points, which they can then spend on special weapons and other goodies. As in many areas of the gaming community, there was a vibrant market of *Lineage* fans, who'd pay real-world money for points. So the hackers created an automated program that killed off monsters, winning points which they then sold to gamers for cash. You may well think that, compared to the Sony and Bangladesh Bank hacks, creating a program pretending to be an elf or a magician and running around bumping off ogres may seem small beer. Think again. According to the South Korean authorities, the scheme made around $6m.[11] If the police allegations are correct, much of that money would have made its way back to Pyongyang.

This is exactly the model the US authorities claim was being used by Chosun Expo. On the surface it was a legitimate computer-programming firm serving clients, as illustrated by the emails sent by Park Jin Hyok to his corporate customers. But behind the scenes the same company's infrastructure and staff were used to mount attacks on targets around the world.

'It's a methodology we've seen employed time and time again,' says Priscilla Moriuchi, the former NSA North Korea analyst now working for Apple. 'You send hackers abroad to work for ostensibly this front company. And then they use the infrastructure of that front company to conduct the cyber-operations themselves.'

But why send the hackers abroad at all? Why not conduct the attacks from inside North Korea (albeit hidden behind layers of online obfuscation)? There are some good technical reasons: as we've seen, North Korea has a very limited online window. Its Internet connection is provided by companies based in Russia and China,[12] and the entire country has only about a thousand IP addresses (compared to the many millions enjoyed by countries like the UK and the US).[13] And, inevitably, these are some of the most highly surveilled IP addresses in the world. If North Korea's hackers want to conduct their work away from prying eyes, it makes a lot of sense to hop over the border into China and hide among its millions of IP addresses.

As we've seen, however, this tactic isn't foolproof. If the FBI's analysis is correct, it seems the Lazarus Group's hacker colleagues back in the mother country still used North Korean IP addresses to access bits of their attack network. These became significant evidential links which allowed the Bureau to construct its legal case against Park Jin Hyok and his accomplices.

But there's another, more intriguing reason why North Korea might send its hackers over the border: it's also a chance for them to learn how the rest of the world thinks and communicates. If you're going to send effective phishing messages to trick your victims, you have to understand the culture they inhabit, and you can't do that from inside the tightly controlled information bubble of North Korea. 'Hacker dorms' like the one witnessed by Hyun-Seung Lee, with its messy living room full of laptops and cables, become training grounds for the country's hackers to learn how the rest of us live, and how we use the Internet to socialize, to network and to bank.

As Priscilla Moriuchi puts it, 'They live amongst each other, [leading] relatively secluded lives, but their jobs are to integrate into Internet society and culture, and to figure out how they can utilize it, whether it be from Internet gaming, Internet casinos, or the SWIFT inter-banking system, how those can be utilized, how they can be exploited to generate revenue for the [North Korean] state.'

For some, the cultural exposure that the hackers enjoy actually makes them among the most dangerous of all North Korea's military operatives. Unlike the vast majority of their compatriots, they've had access to the open Internet. While it's true to say that their access will be strictly monitored by their handlers (like the 'political attaché' assigned to workers at the Chosun Expo), they will inevitably be given more leeway to find information than would ever be afforded to those back home, even the university students whose tutors allow them to go online.

For example, if the FBI is right in saying that North Korean hackers sent messages to actors involved in *The Interview* urging them to download photos of nude celebrities, this implies that the hackers were aware of the leak a few months earlier of intimate photos from dozens of famous people's private accounts, including Rihanna and Jennifer Lawrence – the so-called 'Fappening' incident. For most people in North Korea's extremely conservative society, where even holding hands has traditionally been considered brazen, the idea of women sending naked photos of themselves would be unthinkably scandalous. The computer hackers would be among only a tiny minority of North Koreans ever to find out about such behaviour. It's just one example of the many, many insights into life beyond North Korea that the hackers must have gained as they worked out how the rest of the world functions and how to manipulate it to gain access to their targets.

Along the way, they would inevitably have found out about the lies the Pyongyang regime tells to its people, and the desperate poverty in which most of North Korean society lives relative to most of the world. Perhaps more than almost any other section of North Korean society, then, the hackers know of their government's hypocrisy, deceit and cruelty. Yet they keep going anyway. Why? There are multiple reasons, and it's a mix of carrots and sticks.

First, getting into computer hacking is a way to escape North Korea's rigid class system. As we learnt in Chapter 2, its society is divided into three tiers, based largely on each family's history and its relation to the country's founder, Kim Il Sung, and his heirs. Once assigned, these *songbun* classes are almost impossible to break out of. But, according to Thae Yong Ho, North Korea's former Deputy Ambassador to the UK, there are some ways to escape your fate. According to him, there are three golden tickets to a life of slightly better chances than you were born with. As he told Jean H. Lee for our podcast: 'First of all, the door for changing your class is open in sports areas. If you are a good football player . . . [or win] Olympic medals or whatever. The second way is music: pianists, dancers. And then the third one is computer science. If you are very good at mathematics, but you are living far from Pyongyang, from time to time there are mathematics competitions outside of Pyongyang. As a child of the low class, if you want to go to Pyongyang, if you want to upgrade your social class, then you have to study very hard in the field of mathematics. This is the field where true competition is available. And if you prove yourself very good, then you are chosen to go to very special schools.'

These gifted mathematicians, he says, can then take up computing. 'The schools' education for computer-science class starts at the age of eleven or twelve. North Korea has a very sophisticated education system for "cyber-warriors".'

With his education at Kim Chaek University of Technology, it's likely Park Jin Hyok would have come up via this route, mining his brainpower to forge a better life for himself and his family, upgrading their *songbun*.

There's another potential perk for those gifted in mathematics and computing: foreign travel. Even before they have the option of becoming state hackers, North Korea's maths whizz-kids can experience the outside world thanks to the country's participation in one of the most niche global contests: the International Mathematical Olympiad. Every year, national teams of high-school students from around the world gather to solve problems involving arcane concepts like 'convex quadrilaterals', 'circumcentres' and 'interior points'. Not only does North Korea enter a team, but its 'mathletes' frequently win a place in the top ten: a very impressive performance alongside vastly more populous and well-resourced countries like China and the US. (As ever with North Korea, however, there's a bizarre twist even in the dry world of mathematics: the country's been disqualified twice for suspected cheating.[14])

A North Korean participant in the competition who subsequently escaped the country described the wonder with which he first gazed upon the mass of streetlights and cars in the country in which he competed. Such experiences are normally reserved only for Pyongyang's elite class. The maths contests also seem to be a chance for the youngsters to let their hair down and socialize with people from across the world. One Internet forum described a North Korean team member as a 'party animal'.[15]

But, for the North Korean maths whizzes who go on to become hackers, such occasional privileges must be balanced against many hardships. These computer experts aren't like the techies we might see in the West, hanging out in artisanal coffee shops, wearing hoodies and tapping away on MacBooks. Most of North Korea's hackers are, like millions of their compatriots, part of the country's army, and they're treated as such.

As Thae Yong Ho said, 'If you are chosen as cyber-warriors, even though you receive better rations, the life there is very difficult because it's a military force. For instance, you have to get up at 6 a.m. You have to be very strong to work ten or fifteen or twenty hours without sleep. So that's why in this cyber-education field, North Korea chooses the best, talented young people.'

He also says that most government hackers work inside the country. 'Their whole life would be isolated from the rest of North Korea. They are working in closed areas so that they cannot easily travel out of the military installations.'

One former North Korean citizen who mixed with the country's hackers in China described them as 'cyber-slaves', and says they were tasked with earning at least $10,000 per year. The vast majority of that money would end up going back to the regime. As Hyun-Seung Lee says, 'They could get a salary of $300 a month, that's just for them, and then after that, all the money would go directly to the top people.'

In this way, the hackers are treated no differently from the hundreds of thousands of North Koreans who've been dispatched abroad by the regime to work. There's a long history of the country's workers cropping up everywhere, from construction sites in Siberia to North Korean restaurants in Myanmar.[16] These workers are kept on an even tighter leash than the hackers, and are sent overseas with one goal: to make cash for the regime and send as much of it home as possible. The US Mission to the UN claims Pyongyang raked in $500m a year from this practice.[17] Some see it as a clear case of state-backed slavery, and another desperate attempt by the regime to shore up its ailing economy. (The Pyongyang regime says allegations about human-rights violations such as forced labour are lies fabricated by the US.)

The good news for those worried about the conditions for North Korea's citizens overseas is that the practice should be coming to an end. A UN resolution passed in 2017 in the wake of North Korea's ongoing nuclear tests imposed a ban on the country's people being employed abroad, and numbers of officially declared overseas workers have plummeted – although some fear the practice is simply being pushed underground.[18]

But, for its hackers, North Korea may have found a clever way of getting round this ban. Because, as far as the outside world's concerned, they're not North Korean at all, as Thae Yong Ho explains: 'The majority of them do not use North Korean passports.'

He says North Korea's officials can purchase documents from other countries to give its hackers cover. 'The passports of Latin American countries can be very easily bought. [The hackers] are working like spies. So it is very difficult to track how many of them there are and where they are. If there is a cyber-unit in China, they are totally disconnected [from] the North Korean embassies.'

However, Park Jin Hyok, the hacker accused by the FBI of being a key player in the Lazarus Group, was using a North Korean passport, not one bought from another country. Nonetheless, given the level of subterfuge outlined by Thae, it's very possible that Park Jin Hyok is actually a fake name, given to him by his government as part of an undercover identity that he used while in China. And therefore perhaps I owe you an apology, because, when Park Jin Hyok was discussed earlier in this chapter, I made it seem as though his true identity had finally been revealed beneath all the layers of obfuscation. Yet it's very possible that the name 'Park Jin Hyok' is simply another lie, perhaps the final layer of the matryoshka doll.

For its part, North Korea's Ministry of Foreign Affairs states that 'the act of cybercrimes mentioned by the [US] Justice Department has nothing to do with us', and that Park Jin Hyok is a 'non-existent entity' (technically speaking, this could be true if the man we know as Park Jin Hyok was using a fake name).

If Thae Yong Ho is correct, and North Korea's hackers are flying under the radar on fake passports and outside the embassy system, this leaves them incredibly vulnerable. Unlike the North Korean diplomats suspected of trafficking the fake $100 superdollars, if the hackers are exposed they can't simply skip town under diplomatic cover.

So let's put ourselves in Park Jin Hyok's position for a moment. If his date of birth is even roughly accurate, he would have been an impressionable young boy as he witnessed the horrific famine that swept North Korea in the mid-1990s. He used his mathematical prowess to battle his way up against fierce competition for a place at a prestigious university, potentially transforming his family's fortunes as a result. Yet now he finds himself abroad, probably crammed into a dorm shared with his fellow hackers and strewn with computer equipment. His every move is monitored by government minders, and, like almost all North Koreans, he must undergo regular 'self-criticism' sessions in which he has to confess his own failings in following the regime's teachings, and incriminate his colleagues for theirs. He has access to the Internet, so he has more insight than he could ever have imagined into the outside world and how it compares with his homeland. He knows the lies the regime tells. He knows the standard of life in North Korea is way below what he would enjoy in many other places. He'll also have heard of defectors, and may even know the means by which some of them escaped. Why doesn't he join them?

This is where the sticks come in. In contrast to the carrots – the perks of foreign travel, more freedom and a potential *songbun* upgrade – North Korea's hackers are kept in check by a rigid system aimed at preventing any thought of escape.

For a start, if Park had tried to defect and was caught, he would face the horror of prison conditions back in North Korea. Potentially his family would be pulled in too. At the very least, they'd lose any perks and privileges his prestigious career had won for them.

In addition, although Park had been issued with a passport (an extremely rare event in the lives of most North Koreans), it would almost certainly be kept by his minders to restrict any possibility of escape.

But, beyond all this, there is a horrific disincentive that looms over any North Korean who dreams of fleeing, as Hyun-Seung Lee explained to Jean H. Lee: 'They always keep one person as a hostage inside of North Korea, one of the family members.'

In other words, would-be defectors know that a successful escape will see severe punishment meted out to their relatives back home.

Lee was lucky – he says the policy of keeping one family member in North Korea was briefly changed around the time he fled. His elite status allowed him to bring his close family to China with him, enabling them to flee together. Others are less fortunate, and must live with the knowledge that their vastly improved lives outside North Korea come at the cost of inflicting suffering on those closest to them back home. It's a traumatic trade-off: the price of freedom is enduring guilt.

In Park Jin Hyok's case, however, defection seemed far from his thoughts. In one of the messages allegedly seen by the FBI, he talked of 'looking for a way to return home permanently'.[19]

Why would anyone want to go back to North Korea, having experienced life overseas? Surely someone like Park would want to eke out his stay in Dalian as long as possible?

There are various reasons: for a start, as we've discovered, life in a hacker dorm isn't exactly luxurious. And, while they enjoy more freedoms and a little more money, they're still overseen by government staff. There are also perks waiting back home for anyone who's successfully served the government overseas: larger rations, bigger, better housing in a better area, the chance of promotion. And let's not discount homesickness: no matter how grim our view of North Korea might be, for those who grew up there it's still home. For Park, there was also a bride waiting for him.

And it seems Park eventually got his wish of returning home for good. An email sent to one of Chosun Expo's clients in February 2014 stated 'Pak' had been dismissed from the company.[20] As the Sony hack was going down, it seems he was back in North Korea. But the infrastructure he created was still very active indeed, and would go on to do tremendous damage.

According to the FBI, via his Kim Hyon Woo persona, Park had created a sprawling network of fake email and social media accounts, which had in turn been used to target Sony and Bangladesh Bank. The movie studio had been reduced to digital ruins and lost some of its most senior execs. The bank had lost $101m.

Investigators had now linked the two attacks and were furiously chasing down the culprits – and the money. So far the Lazarus Group, with the help of cunning hackers like Park, had managed to hack into Bangladesh Bank and transfer out the cash. But it wasn't out of the woods yet – far from it.

The heist on Bangladesh Bank started at the beginning of 2015. It was 29 January when those polite emails from 'Rasel Ahlam' began to arrive in bank employees' inboxes. Yet it was an entire year before the Lazarus Group's attackers finally struck, in 2016, creeping their way through the bank's systems to its SWIFT computers and attempting to transfer out a billion dollars. When you stop to think about it, this year-long wait was incredibly risky for the hackers: at any time, their work could have been uncovered by the bank, which would then have deleted their viruses and shut them out. Or, alternatively, as the months rolled by, Bangladesh Bank might simply have decided it was time for an IT upgrade, replacing its computers and unknowingly undoing all the hackers' efforts. Either way, sitting stealthily inside the bank's network for a year was a potentially fatal delay for the Lazarus Group's operatives. It would have taken nerves of steel to hold out this long. So why did they do it?

It turns out they had good reason to pause their cyber-operations. There was a lot of other work to do. The digital break-in was just one part of a complex global scheme aimed not only at stealing Bangladesh's money but also at spiriting it out in such a way that it could never, ever be clawed back. The Lazarus Group now needed to go beyond its computerized tactics into the very physical world of money laundering. It would take the story of the heist to some very unexpected destinations and take the investigators tracking it (myself included) on a journey across the world. The next stage of the heist would prove even more extraordinary, and reveal yet another side to North Korea's growing links with the criminal underworld.

9
The Getaway

At first sight, Jupiter Street doesn't look a likely setting for a multimillion-dollar criminal enterprise. It's around the corner from Manila's financial district: a busy little backstreet with the usual mix of shops, restaurants and cafés serving workers from the office blocks nearby. As you walk down the pavement under the mess of overhead power and phone cables, the units at No. 122 don't particularly strike you as unusual. On the top floor there's an eco-hotel and a dentist's surgery, and underneath them at street level is a branch of a big Philippine bank called RCBC. On the day I visited, standing behind its glass front door was something I saw a lot at prestigious offices and financial institutions in Manila: a bored-looking security guard with a frighteningly large pump-action shotgun. For me, this one image summed up the whole story – a story I'd travelled to Manila to get to the bottom of. It showed that the bank, like many other institutions, was ready for criminals entering via the front door and carrying out a traditional form of physical crime. What it was less prepared for – what so many businesses across the globe seem achingly unready for – was a digital crime being committed from within its own computer systems.

Because in February 2016 this little RCBC branch in Jupiter Street was to become a key part of the Lazarus Group's plans to vanish the money it had stolen from Bangladesh and evade the clutches of the various investigators now desperately trying to chase it down.

On 13 May 2015, a few months after the hackers first started to send phishing emails to Bangladesh Bank, five accounts had been set up at this small branch of RCBC, with help from its manager. In hindsight, there were suspicious signs right from the beginning about the way the accounts had been created: all five of the account holders claimed to have exactly the same job title and salary, even though they all gave different companies as their employers. And when the bank's manager sent welcome letters to the five new customers, they were returned unopened – clearly, they didn't live at the addresses they'd given.[1]

But no one seemed to notice these red flags, and in fairness at this point there was little reason for any suspicion. The accounts sat dormant for month after month, the initial deposit ($500 worth of the local peso currency) went untouched. Maybe the account holders left town and forgot about the accounts? Maybe they were just putting some money away for a rainy day?

But then, on Friday, 5 February 2016, four of the account holders instantly became multimillionaires: 'Michael Cruz' suddenly had $6,000,029.12. 'Jessie Lagrosas' got $30,000,028.79. 'Alfred Vegara' gained $19,999,990. And 'Enrico Vasquez' was sitting on $25,001,573.88.[2]

The money formed the bulk of the funds stolen by the Lazarus Group. It had come from Bangladesh Bank's account at the New York Federal Reserve. Of the $101m the hackers had stolen from this account, $81,001,662.16 was transferred to the four accounts at this backstreet RCBC branch in Manila.

If you're the kind of diligent reader who checks an author's sums, you'll notice that when you add up the amounts transferred to the four account holders above, we've already lost $40.37 of the total figure transferred from Bangladesh to the Philippines. I'm afraid you'll need to get used to it: thanks to the complexities of international finance, the obfuscation of the hackers and the wilful incompetence of some of the officials involved, the numbers rarely line up neatly.

You're also probably the kind of reader who's now wondering why the fifth account set up at the RCBC branch didn't receive any money. That's because, as we learnt in Chapter 7, the New York Fed had spotted the hackers' transactions and stopped most of them before they went through. The hackers' plan had been to wash almost all of Bangladesh's billion New York dollars through the five accounts at RCBC, transferring money to each of them in turn in chunks, most of which were around $30m.[3] But the Fed's intervention derailed thirty of those transfers, leaving only four payments that got through to Manila (as for the fifth payment, don't worry, that's an intriguing story we'll cover later on).

So did the account holders Cruz, Lagrosas, Vegara and Vasquez rush to the Jupiter Street branch to pick up their overnight fortunes? No, because they didn't exist. As a later investigation would find out, the accounts had been set up with forged documents. They were part of an intricate process created by the hackers' accomplices to launder the money. It wasn't the only revelation to emerge. The same investigation would unearth a huge amount of detail about what exactly happened at the Jupiter Street RCBC bank that weekend in February 2016. It would expose how a small branch became a vital link in the hackers' plot to steal Bangladesh's money. And, according to the FBI, it would reveal just how far North Korea's tentacles now stretched into the world of organized crime.

Five miles from the hustle and bustle of Jupiter Street is the Bayview Park Hotel, a plush, wood-panelled establishment looking out over Manila Bay. Inside is a large ballroom, and on 15 March 2016 it's packed and overheated. But it's not dancing and carousing that are filling the room. It's been taken over by the Philippines Senate for a series of special hearings. Why not use the Senate building itself? Because there's no available space, and these hearings are urgent: ten of the country's Senators have been assembled to get to the bottom of how Bangladesh's money ended up in Manila, and what happened to it next.

By this point, the Bangladeshis had already alerted the Philippine authorities to the fact that most of the stolen money had arrived there. Bangladeshi officials went to the country's courts to have the funds frozen, inadvertently alerting the world to the scale of the heist.

Now the Philippines itself wants answers. It won't be an easy process. The Senate's hearings are fractious, ill-tempered and, occasionally, darkly hilarious.

One of the most frustrating aspects is the testimony of RCBC bank officials. Its representatives repeatedly attempt to rely on secrecy laws to justify their failure to answer questions. The bank's lawyer at one stage argues that, even if the account holders are fictitious, their deposits are still covered by confidentiality laws. 'They have to protect the fake holders,' jokes one of the Senators huffily.

'I really, really want to help this committee,' replies Attorney Laurinda Rogero of RCBC's anti-money-laundering unit. 'If only we were not bound by Philippine laws on confidentiality, we would really love to tell you everything that we know. However, we also have a duty to the Senators who passed those laws.'

Whoops. Sadly for Rogero, she's chosen precisely the wrong person to pick this fight with. 'We were the ones who passed those laws,' snaps Committee Chairman Teofisto Guingona. 'I was the principal author, so don't give me that.'[4]

The bank's defensive response was a taste of things to come. What follows is a gruelling effort by the committee to prise the truth out of the various people involved, knowingly or not, in the plot to transfer and launder Bangladesh Bank's money through the Philippine financial system.

The first thing the committee establishes is that the four account holders themselves are not going to be turning up as witnesses. Its officials have tried to trace them via the driving licences used to set up the accounts and discovered that the documents are fake.

That throws up one of the first questions: how on earth did the accounts get set up in the first place? This is where we meet two of the characters who will come to dominate this section of the story: Kim Wong and Maia Santos Deguito.

Deguito was the manager of the RCBC branch in Jupiter Street: she oversaw the creation of the four accounts into which the stolen money was transferred, and she was in the bank for the key days surrounding the movement of funds.

Kim Wong was a Chinese man who organized gambling jaunts at Manila's thriving casinos. And it was in this glamorous world that the pair met and formed a business relationship, according to their testimony to the committee.

And that's about as much as they both agree on.

Deguito insists she met the account holders in person and checked the photos on their IDs. She says the four men were referred to her by Kim Wong, who then oversaw the deposits into the men's accounts, giving her instructions along the way as the 'authorized agent' for their affairs.[5]

Wong tells the committee that Deguito never met the men, and instead forged the creation of the bank accounts during a visit to his office at a casino. He says he just acted as a translator as Deguito set up the accounts with an accomplice.[6]

It's not clear who's telling the truth, but Deguito's credibility takes a knock when it turns out the photos used on two of the forged driving licences were actually pictures of her ex-colleagues – something she apparently failed to spot at the time.

RCBC officials also testify that Deguito was sent an email warning her that the welcome letters to the account holders had been returned unopened (Deguito denies receiving this).

Of course, none of this would have mattered if the accounts had just continued to sit dormant, as they had done for months after their creation in May 2015. But on Friday, 5 February 2016, huge sums of money suddenly flowed into the four accounts created under deeply suspicious circumstances – money we now know was stolen from Bangladesh Bank. What was happening in the branch at this time? How did the manager, Maia Santos Deguito, react? We may have an inkling, thanks to remarkable testimony from one of the bank's employees.

Romualdo Agarrado held the title of Reserve Officer at the Jupiter Street branch of RCBC, and Deguito was his boss. He is summoned to give evidence to the Philippine Senate Committee on 17 March. Dressed in a suit and tie, sitting awkwardly next to the RCBC officials, it seems clear that Agarrado is terrified by the whole experience. At one point the Chairman has to step in to calm him down. And, as Agarrado recounts what he witnessed, it soon becomes clear why he is so jumpy.

The Monday after the money arrived, 8 February, was meant to be a national holiday in the Philippines, but, according to Agarrado's testimony, there was an awful lot of activity in the Jupiter Street branch that day.

His boss, Deguito, was in the office, where concerns were already being raised about the massive sums of money suddenly flowing into the four accounts. RCBC claimed it operated a 'straight through' system, whereby any money transfers were deposited directly into the accounts without first being vetted. But that didn't mean that checks couldn't be carried out afterwards. Bank officials claim they queried the transactions with the branch's manager, Deguito, and she told them they were valid. Deguito disagrees: she tells the committee that no one had called her to query the transfers. Quite the contrary, she says: the bank sent an email to *her* stating that the transfers were okay.

RCBC also claims employees from its central office tried to phone Deguito about the incoming money but couldn't reach her. They spoke instead to Agarrado, the bank clerk. From this moment on, he's gradually pulled into the unfolding events, and the behaviour he claims to have witnessed is deeply troubling.

Agarrado says he went to his boss and told her about head office's attempts to freeze the money. Deguito just looked at him blankly. But it was what she said later on that really spooked him: 'I would rather do this than me being killed or my family.'[7]

As the day wore on, things got even more strange and troubling inside the branch. Agarrado says that 20m pesos (around $400,000) was ordered from the bank's cash centre and delivered to the Jupiter Street branch. The money was put into a cardboard box in Deguito's office. A little while later, a car pulled up at the bank and rolled down its window, and the box was loaded into the car. The bank's officials claim the car belonged to Deguito. There's a simple way to check this, of course: the bank's CCTV. Unfortunately, during this entire episode the camera system was out of action. The branch had reported a malfunction on Thursday, 4 February, the day before the multimillion-dollar transfers arrived, and thanks to the bank holiday it wasn't fixed until 2 p.m. on the following Tuesday.

The more testimony the Senate Committee hears, the more questions mount up around Maia Santos Deguito. She'd set up the accounts under unusual circumstances, and allowed Kim Wong, rather than the account holders, to control them. At one point she admits that she'd pretended to receive instructions from one of the fictitious account holders, in order to conceal Wong's name. Furthermore, if the bank officials are to be believed, she ignored warnings that the huge transfers were suspicious and should be stopped. And, if her colleague is to be believed, some of the cash was loaded into her car and driven away. All the while, her branch's CCTV was coincidentally out of action. It doesn't look good, does it?

Deguito herself did not want to be interviewed, but her lawyer, Ferdinand Topacio, agreed to speak to me. He's an idiosyncratic character, who was once interviewed in an office beneath a giant painted portrait of Adolf Hitler.[8]

His defence of his client is predictably robust. Deguito, he says, never received death threats. She also said it wasn't her job to check the IDs of the people setting up the accounts, that was for head office to do (she also denied the photos on the IDs were of her ex-colleagues). It was also head office's job, she said, to fix the CCTV – she had nothing to do with it. Topacio says that, even though she was the branch's manager, her job was less about day-to-day administration and more about schmoozing potential customers. A 'rain-maker', as he puts it.

Topacio again insists that Deguito was sent emails by the bank telling her that the transfers were legitimate. He offers to send me copies of the messages. (Despite repeated subsequent requests, he never did.)

Asked about cash being loaded into cars, Topacio suggests this was simply being helpful to a customer: 'You have to understand the culture of banking here,' he tells me. 'In cases of valued clients, the bank managers go over and above the call of duty to please them, with an eye always to the average daily balance.'

I point out that, in this case, going over and above the call of duty meant participating in a giant fraud.

'Ultimately, what happened was a fraud,' says Topacio. 'I'm not saying that my client is blameless. She was a victim of a confluence of events that made it appear that she was the only one here. She may have been negligent. She may have been too trusting. But something of this magnitude could not have been accomplished by a mere bank manager.'

It is the same argument Deguito herself uses in her appearance at the Senate Committee: 'I am but a pawn in a high-stakes chess game played by giants in international banking and high finance,' she tells the Chairman. 'If this committee is looking for the grand master, it is not me. In hindsight, I have unwittingly allowed myself to be set up as the scapegoat when all I wanted was to advance my career and, together with my husband, help provide for my family.'[9]

Throughout the proceedings, Deguito looks worn and racked with nerves. Dark rings surround her eyes; her forehead is creased with worry. She's right to be so fearful. In the end she was found guilty on seven money-laundering charges. She was sentenced to fifty-six years in prison and received a fine of $109m (which is more, of course, than the entire amount stolen from Bangladesh Bank).

Through her lawyer she's appealing against the conviction, and for his part Ferdinand Topacio is adamant that others have so far escaped justice. 'Here in this country, the law is like a spider's web,' he says. 'Only the small get caught. The big ones go right through.'

But, at the time of writing, Maia Santos Deguito is the only one to be convicted of any offence in the entire Bangladesh Bank case (and incidentally one of the very few women involved in the story).

RCBC didn't respond to requests for an interview, but it has previously insisted it followed all proper banking procedures. Nonetheless, its boss resigned in the wake of the scandal, and RCBC was fined a record $20m by the country's Central Bank.[10]

So . . . what happened to the money? Well, its journey was only just beginning.

From the four accounts, Deguito moved the $81m to a single account in the name of William Go, which was set up on the Friday, 5 February, just as the money transfers were arriving. Unlike the other account holders, William Go actually exists. He's another contact of Deguito's. But when the Senate Committee catches up with him, he claims his signature had been forged in order to set up the account.[11]

The use of Go's account is important, because, as RCBC's officials explain to the committee, the bank can only freeze funds in the accounts into which they're initially paid. So once the money left the four fictitious holders' accounts and moved to Go's account, RCBC would struggle to stop its onward movement.

In fact, it took the bank days to get round even to freezing the money in the initial four accounts it was transferred to. Apparently part of the delay was caused by the requirement for Suspicious Transaction Reports to be reviewed by a committee within the bank, which can take days. This seems a bizarre way to deal with financial fraud, in which, as we've seen, time is of the essence.

By the time RCBC got round to freezing the four accounts, all that was left of the original sum of approximately $81m was $68,335.63.[12] It was like a smattering of banknotes drifting in the wind after the safe has been blown open. The money was duly handed back to Bangladesh Bank. One can only imagine the reaction of the officials who received such a tiny cheque, having lost so many millions.

From the Go account the $81m was transferred to a Manila-based money-changing firm called Philrem. Its bosses were called in by the Senate Committee. When quizzed about why they accepted so much money from an unknown individual's account that was created so recently, they say they relied on assurances from the bank. This gets short shrift from one of the cross-examining Senators, Sergio Osmeña: 'If I sent you $10m and said it was owned by John D. Rockefeller, would you believe me?'[13]

But, as with all the stages of this process, the money wouldn't stay long at Philrem. From there, it was converted into cash in the local currency, pesos. Lots and lots of cash, in fact: $81m adds up to about half a billion pesos, and, as Rodolfo Quimbo, Director-General of the Philippine Senate Committee, helpfully explains: 'One million pesos equals about a kilogramme of bills. So half a billion pesos is about 500 kilogrammes.'

In other words, whoever was in charge of this part of the operation was dealing with a stack of cash the weight of a grand piano. What on earth were they going to do with it?

'It was picked up by two Chinese men with assistants who loaded the money,' says Quimbo. 'They had to have trucks. They had to have people who would carry those bills because 500 kilos is not capable of being carried by a single person. This was a big operation.'

Who were these Chinese men who picked up the cash? We know the identity of at least one of them, according to the Senate Committee. The people who ran the Philrem money-changing firm say they were told by Deguito to deliver $30m of the money to a Chinese man named Weikang Xu.

This met with more incredulity from Senator Osmeña. 'Do you know Weikang Xu?' he asks Deguito. 'No,' she replies. 'Next time can you deliver it to me?' jokes Osmeña.

So now a large chunk of the stolen Bangladesh Bank money is with Weikang Xu. Great. Perhaps he can help the committee get to the bottom of all the shenanigans in RCBC and Philrem? Sadly not. When the committee asks the country's money-laundering authority about him, they get the following response: 'We received information that Mr Weikang Xu probably has left the country via a private plane.'

To which Chairman Teofisto Guingona responds: 'I suppose if it is a private plane, you still have to go through immigration. What did the immigration [authority] say?' 'They don't have a record of his departure, Your Honor.'

In other words, whoever Weikang Xu is, he pocketed $30m of Bangladesh's stolen money, slipped out of the country and has never been heard from since.

There's a burning question that's been lurking in the background throughout most of this chapter: why did the crooks go to all this trouble? Why create so many accounts, and go to so much effort to whizz the money here and there, and then take it out via the money-changing firm Philrem?

It's time for a bit of money-laundering expertise, courtesy of Moyara Ruehsen, Director of the Financial Crime Management Programme at the Middlebury Institute of International Studies in Monterey, California. 'The money-laundering piece is the most challenging piece for criminals,' she says. 'Turning all of that criminal revenue into clean cash that they can then use.'

Key to the process, she says, is putting as many obstacles as you can in the way of the people trying to trace the loot. 'You want to make the money trail as muddy and obscure as possible,' says Ruehsen.

I'm not revealing any big secrets here, by the way: the general principles of money laundering are well known. And, besides, knowing the principles is a far cry from the effort of actually applying them, as we're discovering.

'The first stage is placing that dirty cash into the financial system. That is probably the most challenging stage for a criminal, because that is the stage at which investigators are most likely to red flag the suspicious activity,' says Ruehsen.

The Lazarus Group hackers who broke into Bangladesh Bank knew all about those red flags, because they'd already fallen foul of them. Their original plan to steal $951m by transferring it out of the Bangladeshi account at the Federal Reserve Bank of New York had been derailed when the Fed picked up on the word 'Jupiter' in the address of the bank to which the money was being transferred.

From that point on, the hackers didn't want any more red flags. They wanted to make sure that the money passed smoothly through the financial system. And, thanks to the groundwork that their accomplices had laid in Manila, they'd successfully moved $81m of the stolen money halfway around the world, washed it through a string of accounts and converted it into cash.

But they weren't finished yet. Even at this juncture, there was a slim chance the money could still be clawed back. After all, Bangladeshi officials were in town and scrambling to chase down the stolen funds. And now the Senate Committee was sniffing around too. The Senators had identified the bank accounts used to launder the money; they knew exactly how much went in and where it was moved to. Even having turned it into cash via the money-changing company might not have been enough to throw the pursuers off. The criminals still had to do more to get away scot-free with their loot. They had to break the link between the money and the crime.

It was time for the next stage of the laundering process: layering.

'The layering stage is the exciting part of money laundering,' says Moyara Ruehsen. It's all about swapping the money into something else so it can't be linked back to the original offence, she explains. 'There are a number of things that you can change. You can move it from dollars into cryptocurrency or dollars into British pounds, or gold or some other type of asset. You can move it into real estate or stocks, and then sell those.'

Forget real estate and stocks. In the Bangladesh Bank case, the criminals had a much more exciting option for layering the stolen money. The heist was about to enter its most dramatic phase – the final part of the getaway when the cash would vanish, leaving the pursuing investigators in the dust. It's not like the movies; there were no fast cars, no screaming tyres, no pumping soundtrack. But the process of escaping with the loot was going to be every bit as tense as in the films. And, like a good getaway driver, the criminals who raided Bangladesh Bank would need careful planning, nerves of steel and razor-sharp timing to make it all work.

10

Baccarat Binge

It's time to shift location again. This time we're heading down the coast on Manila Bay, to a casino called the Solaire. It sits right on the waterfront, prime real estate overlooking the bay. It's a gleaming white building, twelve storeys high, sticking up like a shark's tooth from the flatlands of the shoreline.

Up on the first floor, Tony Lau is in the middle of his shift.[1] He's a VIP host, and it's his job to look after the casino's richest customers. It's February 2016, the week after computer hackers set out to steal a billion dollars from Bangladesh Bank. But Lau doesn't know about any of that. He's just looking forward to a rest.

The last few days had been absolutely crazy. It was the Lunar New Year, one of Asia's biggest holidays and a hectic time for the casino. Lau's hoping things will start getting back to normal, when half a dozen men speaking Chinese walk into his VIP area. He's worked in the industry for years, and he instantly feels there's something off about these new customers.

'Their appearance was just really ordinary,' he remembers. 'The way they dressed didn't make them seem genuine. They just didn't look like people who had lots of money.'

Not like the kind of customers Lau's used to serving, with their fancy cars and designer clothes. He says that, once, a client pitched up with a deposit of 200m Philippine pesos – that's $10m. As you can imagine, when you're paying that kind of money, you expect top-quality service. It's Lau's job to roll it out.

'The VIP room is like a luxurious house,' he says. 'There's a lounge area, a dining table, a mini-bar with food and beverages on demand. They have their own bathroom. So everything feels really special.'

Such perks are reserved only for the casino's most valued customers. But that's the problem – Lau can't help feeling that the Chinese men who've walked into his VIP area just aren't . . . Very Important. But it turns out that his first impression is wrong. He soon starts to realize these guys are absolutely loaded. Behind the scenes in the VIP area is the 'cage' – a highly secure room where the customers' money is taken and changed into chips for gambling. After the men arrive, the cage starts to fill up.

'Suddenly the money they are here to gamble appears,' says Lau. 'And it's all in cash. It took them a while to count it all. There were stacks and stacks of cash, high like a mountain. And, as the host, I am thinking: "Wow, this group is very rich. Brilliant." '

Lau's impressed, but suspicious at the same time. The money doesn't seem right, because these men aren't regulars. 'Our VIP guests are usually high-profile people. So we would know their background. But who are these people? How come they have so much money? We have never heard of them.'

It's when the men start playing that Lau and his colleagues notice some really strange things. For a start they seem to treat gambling like a regular day job. 'Almost every day, they followed the same routine: they would play from 8.00 in the morning until 11.30. Then stop at lunchtime. Take their casino chips back to their hotel room. And the following day, the same thing,' says Lau.

But the thing that stands out the most is the men's reactions to the games they're playing. They don't seem to care if they win or lose. It's weird. 'People who gamble are usually quite tense,' Lau says. 'They're tense because they want to win. And when they lose, they look heartbroken. And when they win, delirious. But these people didn't seem to have any reaction either way. No enthusiasm.'

There's a good reason the men are behaving so strangely: they're hiding a secret. It's not their own money with which they're gambling. The cash in the cage belongs to Bangladesh Bank and has been brought to the Solaire for one reason: to make sure the bank can never get it back.

★

When last we heard of the $81m of stolen Bangladesh Bank money that arrived in the Philippines, it had been washed through a series of bank accounts and sent to a money-changing firm called Philrem. Around $30m was converted into cash and paid to the Chinese man called Weikang Xu, who disappeared with it. The remaining money was now split between two destinations. The first was the Solaire Casino, run by a firm called Bloomberry Resorts Corporation, which received around $30m. The second chunk, of $21m, went to a company called Eastern Hawaii Leisure, which was run by Kim Wong, the man who had allegedly helped to create the fake bank accounts at RCBC into which the stolen money was paid. This latter chunk was in turn sent to another casino, called the Midas. The casinos would form the next part of the money-laundering journey.

So it was to the casinos that I went too. So far on my trip to Manila I'd visited the RCBC branch into which the money was transferred. I'd gone to the Senate and interviewed those who organized the hearings and tried to get to the bottom of what happened. In the best traditions of investigative journalism I wanted to keep following the money, and the next stop on the itinerary was the Solaire.

To those who've never visited one, it's hard to convey the sheer over-the-top opulence of a high-end casino like the Solaire. Shopping options include Bulgari, Prada and Bang & Olufsen. At the time I visited, the theatre attached to the casino was staging a full-scale production of *The Phantom of the Opera*. The main reason the Solaire sticks in my mind is because it's the only place in the world I've ever been offered a 'bag stool'. I guess if you've just bought a Prada handbag you don't want to put it on the floor – but my rucksack looked pretty odd sitting on its own little chair.

In some ways, as I wandered round it became obvious to me why the criminals had brought their stolen funds here. Over the last decade, the Philippines has cultivated a thriving and lucrative casino scene that attracts throngs of wealthy gamblers, often from China, where gambling is illegal. The tens of millions stolen from Bangladesh wouldn't seem out of the ordinary in a place like this. A glitzy casino is the perfect location for people with a lot of cash to blend in, no matter the source of their money.

'You get the privacy, you get the service, you get the personalized attention that you feel you deserve,' says Muhammad Cohen, casino expert and Editor-at-Large of *Inside Asian Gaming* magazine. He's covered the industry for years and understands the kind of demands such high rollers make: 'I want a bottle of Hennessy X.O, and I want a mani-pedi for my wife, and I want somebody to take her shopping. Take her to see the sights in Manila, please, so she's not bored while I'm gambling. And make me my favourite dish when I'm hungry.' Amid such bacchanalian behaviour, multimillion-dollar fraudsters might well go unnoticed.

For the crooks who stole Bangladesh Bank's money, Manila's gambling scene offered several other vital advantages. First, at the time its casinos weren't covered by money-laundering regulations, vastly reducing the chances that anyone would ask awkward questions about the origin of the funds.[2] Second, the Lunar New Year timing was again working to the Lazarus Group's benefit: not only had it allowed the hackers extra time to wash the money through RCBC thanks to the bank holiday Monday, but now it would also help them to cover their tracks as they continued to move the cash. Because, as a result of the celebrations, Manila was awash with gamblers – and money. In this context the giant sums being sent to the Solaire and the Midas might have seemed less suspicious (although they clearly still caught the attention of Tony Lau).

Therefore in some ways it's no surprise that the money arrived in these big gambling establishments. But, despite all these advantages, I still couldn't figure out why the criminals had gone to the trouble of putting the money into casinos in the first place. They'd run it through various bank accounts and converted it to cash – wasn't that enough? Why bother with this extra step?

Money-laundering expert Moyara Ruehsen has an explanation: 'Imagine that I am a criminal with a lot of dirty cash. I turn that money into casino chips. I gamble a little bit. Try not to lose much money. And then, when I'm done gambling, I turn all of those chips back into a casino cheque. So now it looks like my winnings at a casino. Then I'm out the door. I deposit my winnings somewhere and nobody asks any questions.'

In other words, going to the casinos was the vital last step in the 'layering' stage of the money laundering. It was an attempt to break the chain of traceability, and to finally separate the money from the crime. If the crooks could gamble the proceeds through the Solaire and the Midas, their pursuers would struggle to link the cash with the hack, and would therefore be unable to claw it back.

But that still doesn't explain why they had to use casinos at all. After all, as the Senate Committee discovered, Weikang Xu just walked away with $30m of the money in cash – why didn't the gang do the same with the rest?

Here's why: put yourself in the position in which, investigators claim, the Lazarus Group's hackers found themselves back in 2015. You've successfully hacked into Bangladesh Bank and figured out that you can potentially transfer out a billion dollars. But you know you can't transfer it directly to your own bank accounts, because that will expose you as the perpetrator. So you need accomplices: middlemen who can receive and convey the money as part of the laundering process. What are you going to tell them? 'Hey, we're a group of North Korean hackers and we're going to steal a billion dollars from a bank in Bangladesh, would you like to help?' That's clearly not going to wash. You have to come up with some kind of explanation for why tens of millions of dollars are going to arrive in the Philippines and will need to be rinsed around. So you create a cover story about gambling, which then becomes the narrative under which everyone operates. This is what Kim Wong told the RCBC's manager Maia Santos Deguito the money would be used for. It's what the bosses of the Philrem money-changing company were told too. Usefully, it also created a means by which the various parties could be reimbursed for taking part – knowingly or unknowingly – in the heist. On the surface the commissions and payments they all received may have looked like reimbursement for a gambling scheme, but they were, in fact, pay-offs for taking part in the laundering.

Of course, some of those involved must have known the whole thing was dodgy. But, even if they suspected it, they didn't know the full scale of the crime and so they could convince themselves (and investigators) that they were just helping out some high-value gamblers.

The problem was, having invented this cover story and used it to organize the laundering network, the Lazarus Group's operatives had to go through with it. Once the money arrived in the RCBC branch, it had to be transferred to the casinos and at the very least a passable impression of gambling with it had to be undertaken. To do otherwise would have risked arousing suspicion. And, besides, the gambling ruse was the conduit through which the middlemen were to be paid – without these payments the accomplices wouldn't have moved the money along the chain.

So the Lazarus Group and its stooges now had to move $51m through the Solaire and the Midas. It's not as much fun as it sounds. The practicalities of trying to launder that much cash through a casino throw up considerable challenges – one of which was hinted at in Ruehsen's quote about gambling with the dirty cash: 'Try not to lose much money,' she said. I don't know about you, but that's never been my experience of visiting a casino. On the few occasions I've been, I seem to remember placing my chips on the table, something happening with dice or cards, and then my chips were gone. Clearly I'm no hustler. But, even if the people laundering the stolen Bangladesh Bank money were much better gamblers than me, how could they bet tens of millions of dollars without losing huge amounts of it? Well, there is a way of making it work . . .

Imagine you and I walk into a casino. We've each got $100, and we want to lose as little as possible. So we change our cash into chips and head for the big roulette wheel. I bet my $100 of chips that it will land on a red number. You bet your $100 that it'll land on black. It lands on black, so I lose my stake. But you win $100, so now you've got $200 of chips. And since we're such good friends, you give me half. We both go and change our chips back into cash, and walk out with $100 each, just as we had at the start.

There's a slim chance of course that the roulette ball will land on green – that's the casino's colour, and in that case we both lose. But there're only one or two green squares on the wheel (depending on where you play) so it's a fairly low probability. Most of the time, it's going to be either red or black, and so our little system runs just fine.

This whole scheme only works if we place polar opposites of each other's bets. The result is that we'll almost always break even, but neither one of us will ever profit. For most people, that completely destroys the point of going on a gambling trip: it's all about the fear of losing and the rush of winning.

But remember: in the Bangladesh Bank heist, the people who take the money to the casino aren't really going there for the buzz of gambling. They're playing a different game. They're going there to launder the money. So, for them, breaking even is absolutely fine. And that's why the men in Tony Lau's VIP room are so relaxed. If one of them loses, he knows that one of his accomplices will win. And vice versa. They're not concerned about making money from the games, because they're being paid by the launderers to wash their money through the system.

In order to make such a balanced method work, however, you ideally need a game that's fairly simple, with limited options and outcomes so you can keep an eye on what's happening. Usefully, one of the most popular games in Asia exactly fits this bill: baccarat. As casino expert Muhammad Cohen explains: 'Baccarat is a favourite game among Chinese gamblers. It has absolutely no skill involved. It's all pure luck. Some people feel like this is a contest between them and fate. They want to see if they can triumph over fate.' It's a card game in which players bet on two main outcomes: either the player winning or the banker winning.[3] The dealer deals two cards each to the banker and the player, and whoever's cards add up closest to the number nine wins. It's a pretty straightforward game, nice and fast, and therefore perfect for someone who wants to move a lot of money across the table in a controlled way – like a money launderer.

But there's a snag. What if you're playing baccarat and trying to run this kind of managed gambling system in order to minimize your losses, and some random stranger rocks up to the table and starts placing bets alongside you and your accomplices? That would completely ruin the balanced betting scheme you're trying to run. And you can't exactly turn around to them and start giving orders about how they should bet because, if you do, it will be obvious that you're up to something shady.

What the money launderers needed was a place away from prying eyes – somewhere private they could go where they could keep tabs on all the activity and control everyone involved. Luckily for them, this is exactly what the Solaire and Midas casinos gave them.

Whereas hoi polloi like you and me are gambling out on the floor of the casino, high rollers who bring in millions are given their own private room, of the kind overseen by Tony Lau, the VIP host. There's a name for these kinds of exclusive gambling rooms: 'junkets'. The one that Tony was working in was run by the Solaire itself, but in other cases the junkets are operated by outside companies. They have contacts with wealthy clients, and the host establishment is happy to rent out the private gambling rooms in exchange for a fee or commission. These junkets are effectively a casino within a casino. As Muhammad Cohen describes it: 'They have their own people staffing it. They have their own people staffing the cage. Somebody from the casino will be standing there to supervise it. But, basically, it's run by the junket, and they share the proceeds on some terms with the casino.'

Thanks to the immense amounts of money swirling around these junkets, there's now a whole industry of people connected to them. There are the junket operators who run the rented rooms, but there are also brokers who find high rollers and connect them with the junkets, taking a commission as a result. This was the world Kim Wong inhabited.[4] That he was such a casino veteran may also have helped to segue the stolen money into the Solaire and the Midas: his presence may have allayed some of the casinos' concerns. He'd been in before with high rollers, so they may well have thought that this was just another big-money weekend for him and his rich clients.

The funds stolen from Bangladesh Bank were pumped into exactly these kinds of junket rooms at both the Solaire and the Midas. They had exotic names like Gold Moon and Sun City. They offered the perfect place away from the public gaze for the hackers' accomplices to carry out the carefully balanced betting system that would help them to minimize their losses. But they came with a big disadvantage. The chips that are issued within these private junket rooms are called 'dead chips' – they can be used only for gambling, and they can't be changed back into cash (the reason for this is so that the junket organizer can keep a handle on what's happening, and work out its commission before everyone cashes out and leaves). That's no good for the money launderers: the whole point is to swap the dirty cash for chips, then swap the chips for clean cash and get out. However, the winnings that the gamblers receive in the junket rooms are paid out in regular chips that *can* be swapped for cash. So, having managed to get their $51m into the Solaire and Midas casinos, the money launderers must now – quite literally – play the game, placing bets using dead chips and winning back regular chips that they can exchange into money.

Usefully for them, baccarat has another key advantage in this respect: according to experts I spoke to, if you're good at the game you can get back about 90 per cent of the money you put in. For a money launderer, that's a fantastic return (on some underground cybercrime forums I've visited the percentage was as low as 60 per cent). But, of course, you can get this kind of return only if you play very carefully over a reasonably long period. If the money launderers had just gambled the whole $51m on their first game, they could have lost the lot. It therefore takes a long time to run this money-laundering system effectively. And it takes a team of people. As a result, the dozens of Chinese gamblers who'd been drawn into the scheme (but almost certainly didn't know the full scale of the fraud) were sitting in the junket rooms of the Midas and the Solaire for weeks, knocking back free drinks and placing bet after bet. This was the explanation for the confusing behaviour Tony Lau witnessed, in which the gamblers would turn up and depart at set times, as though the gaming were just a day job. Because for them, it was.

Perhaps the most remarkable aspect of all of this is to consider what would have happened had the hackers got away with the whole $951m from Bangladesh Bank, as they'd originally intended. As it was, just to launder $51m the criminals had to use four bank accounts, a corrupt branch manager, a money-changing firm, two Chinese couriers with a van and several dozen junket attendees; plus they'd handed over $30m to Weikang Xu, all of which had taken weeks. The idea that they were planning to carry out the same exercise with twenty times as much money is just jaw-dropping.

And the weeks of effort this whole casino process took throws up another question: what was Bangladesh Bank doing all this time? At this point its officials knew exactly what had gone on – they'd arrived in the Philippines, sat in the Senate Committee listening to the evidence and sussed out the scheme. What were they doing to catch up with their money?

Initially, as we saw, Bangladesh Bank's officials had kept the hack secret from their government, hoping they could sort out the problems and recover the money. But with the attack now very publicly exposed, the Bangladeshi government was on the case and furiously chasing down the stolen funds. It had been sending delegations of officials to the Philippines in the hope of clawing back the cash.

Ajmalul Hossain was among them. He's a barrister in England and the equivalent grade in Bangladesh: a senior advocate. He'd now been employed by the government to assist in recovering the money. The Bangladeshis were pulling in the legal big guns.

Hossain started to run into problems almost immediately. 'It was quite amazing,' he recalls. 'For the first several weeks, it was complete denial by everyone about third-party hackers being involved.' Hossain says the various other banks involved believed that the money transfers were legitimate. 'They were all treating [these] as genuine transactions. And so they needed to be persuaded about that.'

When it became clear that the money had ended up in the Philippines, Hossain made around half a dozen trips to the country, and says bank officials made many more. But they got short shrift there too. 'Complete denial. They were making assertions that the people in Bangladesh Bank were involved, and saying, "Well, this was all your problem." They really were not engaging with the fact that this was stolen money.'

But things began to change. It became clear that this was criminal activity, and more detail started to emerge about how the crooks had manipulated the money once it reached the Philippines. Bangladesh Bank was able to figure out its journey and its current location: the casinos.

Thanks to the lack of money-laundering regulations, that's as far as the Bangladeshis could go. As far as the casinos were concerned, the people who'd turned up with tens of millions of dollars were legitimate customers, and had every right to keep gambling their money. The casinos wouldn't do anything until it had been proved that the money was stolen, and that would take weeks of investigation. Meanwhile, the gamblers were free to keep spending.[5]

Bangladesh Bank's officials could almost see their money ebbing away over the casino tables, but were powerless to stop it.

They weren't the only ones bewildered by this state of affairs. Investigative journalist Alan Katz was Editor for Financial Investigations for Europe for Bloomberg News. The bank heist had caught his attention and now he was following the case very closely. 'The thing that struck me as soon as this hack happened was, "Okay, how are they going to get the money?" So tracking that part of the crime was what really interested me.'

When he discovered that the gamblers were still playing with Bangladesh's stolen cash in Manila, Katz could barely believe it. 'We were really surprised. Who the hell are these guys who sat in the casino for weeks? Everyone was aware of this story. Bloomberg wrote about it. Reuters wrote about it. The *New York Times* wrote about it. Obviously Philippine newspapers wrote about it. And these guys just sat there and played and played and played and no one bothered them, while the headlines swirled around them.'

As the Philippines Senate Committee hearings continued, this was one of the many twists it was trying to untangle. It had started hearing testimony from Kim Wong, the gambling junket promoter and business contact of Maia Santos Deguito. Wong insisted he knew nothing of the plot to rob Bangladesh Bank (he was charged, but the charges were later dropped). In addition, he handed back $16m of the $21m that had been sent to his company, Eastern Hawaii Leisure.

But Wong was still under pressure to explain to the committee how he'd ended up dragged into this whole mess in the first place.

That was when he dropped a couple of new names on the committee: Gao Shuhua and Ding Xixhe.[6] Two Chinese men who, he claimed, had played a pivotal part in the scheme.

Wong said he had a long history with Gao, a fellow gambling junket organizer. Gao had lost a huge amount of money at the Solaire Casino – a debt that somehow ended up being passed to Wong. Gao told Wong he'd be paid back with money that was going to arrive at RCBC. It was Gao, Wong claimed, who helped to create the dodgy accounts with the branch's manager that were set up to receive Bangladesh Bank's stolen money.

Gao then introduced him to Ding Xixhe, another gambling junket organizer, who, he said, would be part of the deal.

So the stage was set: between them, Wong, Gao and Ding would receive the tens of millions of dollars and feed them into the casino system, and Wong would have his debt paid off. But it was Gao and Ding, according to Wong, who were driving the whole scheme.

For investigative journalist Alan Katz, this was an intriguing lead. 'It seems odd, doesn't it?' he says. 'If you have an allegedly North Korean hacking group going after money in Bangladesh, moving it through the New York Fed to the Philippines, where did these Chinese guys come into this? What are they doing there and why?'

His attempts to answer those questions would lead Katz on a

wild journey as he dug to uncover the backstories of two men now accused of taking a key role in setting up the entire money-laundering scheme. There was another even more important question: if they were moving money for the Lazarus Group, what was their connection to the hackers and their alleged North Korean bosses?

Meanwhile, back at the Solaire Casino, Tony Lau was still at work, and found himself bumping into the Chinese high rollers who'd walked into his VIP room with their mountains of cash a few weeks before. This time, however, they didn't look so flush. 'They didn't have any money,' he recalls. In fact, it seems they didn't even have enough to buy a meal. They asked Lau to give them food and cigarettes on account, and he obliged as they were still technically his customers. What had happened to their millionaire lifestyle?

After watching the men's suspicious behaviour, Lau and his colleagues had reported their concerns to the management. The casino had finally moved in to stop the gang now suspected of helping to launder Bangladesh's money. The Solaire had gone to the men's hotel rooms (they were staying at the casino) and seized their gambling chips as well as their passport information. Casino staff managed to recover around $2m – mostly 'dead' chips the men hadn't yet managed to gamble for regular chips and exchange for cash.[7]

Amazingly one of the people in the room when the casino staff raided it was Gao Shuhua. The casino had just netted the man who, according to Kim Wong, had helped to engineer the entire money-laundering scheme. And then . . . they let him go. At this point he'd not been charged, there was no warrant, and the casino had no authority to arrest him. Along with the other gamblers, Gao simply drifted away.

The casino later handed the men's passport details to the Philippine authorities. They were almost all Chinese, so the Philippines went to the Chinese Embassy but received no help in trying to track the men down.

Gao and Ding had slipped the net. If Wong was right and they were the masterminds of the Philippines money-laundering plot, where had they vanished to? And how did they get involved in this whole scheme to start with? These were the questions now occupying Alan Katz as he set out to track down Gao and Ding and get some answers.

Also missing, of course, was the vast majority of the tens of millions of dollars stolen from Bangladesh Bank. What had happened to the money?

We'll come back to all of this later in the story. But first we have to clear up a loose end. You may remember the hackers transferred $101m out of Bangladesh Bank. So far we've followed the tangled tale of the $81m that went to the Philippines. Now we need to explore what happened to the other $20m. It's a story that takes us to another exotic location, and reveals yet another side to North Korea and its overseas criminal connections.

II

The Plot Unravels

In 2016 Shihar Aneez was working as an investigative journalist in Sri Lanka. Tired of seeing other reporters working on low-level articles – what he calls 'boy-scout stories' – he was looking for something more complex: a big, data-heavy tale that he could really sink his teeth into. He was about to get his wish.

In February of that year, he was working for the giant news agency Reuters in the capital, Colombo, when he got an unusual tip-off. A source of his who worked in a bank told him that a furious row had broken out between two people over tens of millions of dollars' worth of deposits. There were a couple of things about the story that piqued Aneez's interest. First, it was a huge amount of money, especially for a country like Sri Lanka. And, second, the fight was over a donation to a charity. If someone was making a good-natured contribution for philanthropic purposes, he wondered, how had the dispute become so acrimonious? It seemed odd.

He set about tapping up his other sources, trying to get to the bottom of the mysterious multimillion-dollar bust-up. He found out that one of the people involved in the argument over the money was called Shalika Perera. Aneez set out to track her down, and soon started to realize that what he was investigating was much, much bigger than a mere fight over a bank deposit.

He didn't know it yet, but Aneez had just stumbled on the Sri Lankan part of the Lazarus Group's money-laundering operation. The woman he was trying to find was at the centre of a tangled web of crime that stretched around the world – a web that was closing in on her fast.

*

Life had been rocky for Shalika Perera. A businesswoman in her late thirties, she had big dreams, and one day hoped to become a politician. Meantime she'd set up a string of companies in an array of industries including construction, car parts, publishing and catering. But none of them had really worked out. The losses from her publishing firm were apparently so bad she was forced to sell off all the computers.

So she changed tack and decided to go down the philanthropic route. In October 2014 she set up a charity in her own name, the Shalika Foundation, which she said would help to build houses for the poor and provide other social services.[1]

Perhaps she thought that this, finally, would be the enterprise that would change her life. It would – but in a way she could never have imagined.

She began working with a local Sri Lankan fixer who proved surprisingly adept at introducing her to people with masses of cash to invest. If the Shalika Foundation charity's website is to be believed, this proved to be a very lucrative collaboration. First, an Israeli donor gave $5m for a housing project. Then a Japanese donor named Tomiyama Takashi apparently handed over €30m for an electricity-generation scheme. Perera seemed to be on a roll. Thanks to her magic fixer, her charity was suddenly getting multimillion-dollar sums for her pet projects within just months of its creation.

But things were not as they seemed. For example, to the outside world Tomiyama Takashi may have looked like a wealthy Japanese benefactor, but a bit of investigation reveals he actually works for an industrial painting and decorating firm in Ibaraki Prefecture to the north of Tokyo. It appears Tomiyama Takashi isn't even his real name. It's unclear how this man ended up in Sri Lanka with tens of millions to throw around, and he didn't respond to requests for an explanation. Also unclear is how much of this was known to Shalika Perera herself. What was clear, however, was that the images being presented by the Shalika Foundation's website didn't match reality. And behind the scenes there were some even more worrying aspects to the mysterious benefactor who was suddenly beating a path to

Perera's door. 'Tomiyama Takashi' had attached some strings to his offer: according to a letter apparently signed by Perera, only half of the €30m contribution would actually go to Perera's charity itself; the rest would be paid into four other bank accounts in Singapore, Malaysia and Japan.[2] It was an unusual and deeply suspicious arrangement – the first indication that her charity was being used to move money on behalf of others. It should have rung alarm bells but apparently it didn't. Perera pushed on.

Her next key project was a dairy farm in Matale, a few hundred miles from her charity's base in the capital, Colombo. The plan was to create an operation that could not only supply local needs but export internationally too.[3] But the price tag was hefty, and Perera needed help.

Once again, her Sri Lankan fixer came to the rescue, introducing her in late 2014 to yet another Japanese donor with megabucks to spare (her fixer claimed to have lived in Japan, hence his connections in the country). Perera spoke no Japanese, so the negotiations all took place via the fixer, she says.

According to court documents, this donor, who called himself Tadashi Sasaki, was initially talking about bringing in an absolutely astonishing amount of money: €900bn, which he implied was being lined up by some kind of foreign sovereign-wealth fund, and would require assistance from the government in Sri Lanka in order to make the payment work.[4] Perera says she did her best to help but failed to swing the deal.

However, the parties kept talking, and Tadashi Sasaki kept promising big sums. By January 2016 he told Shalika Perera and her fixer that the transfer of a large donation was imminent. By now, the amount was $20m – significantly less than the hundreds of billions he'd first been mentioning, but still another massive boost for the Shalika Foundation.[5] Keen to receive the funding, Perera once again agreed that only some of the money would go to her charity, and the rest (around half) would go to her fixer's company account. She says Sasaki told her to set up an account to receive the money. These were yet more red flags: why not just use the charity's existing bank account? And why allow the charity to be used once again as a conduit for money to be transferred elsewhere? Perera appears to have ignored all these warning signs. On 26 January 2016 she opened an account at Pan Asia Bank in Colombo and emailed the details to Tadashi Sasaki, no doubt looking forward to the imminent arrival of the funds.

Reassuringly for Perera, her fixer then provided her with a letter which appeared to confirm that the donation was real, and was coming from a legitimate source.

The letter was on notepaper headed with a logo incorporating the letters JICA. The logo belonged to the Japan International Cooperation Agency, a government aid agency that invests in projects around the world. 'We are pleased to inform you that we are agreeable to donate funds towards the above mentioned project,' the letter stated, referring to the dairy farm that Perera had been trying to get off the ground.[6] On the surface it all seemed to make sense: Tadashi Sasaki was Japanese, he'd promised a $20m donation, and here was a big Japanese investor confirming the amount and linking it to one of Perera's projects.

With hindsight, there were some very obvious indications that the letter wasn't genuine. It referred to a 'rural electrification upgradation project', but the word 'electrification' was spelt incorrectly. And on page two of the document was a grainy generic image of a wad of banknotes tied up with a green ribbon – hardly commensurate with a multimillion-dollar donation from a sovereign-wealth fund. Once again, these warning signs passed Perera by.

Meanwhile, more good news had arrived from her fixer. There was to be another donation of $25m coming soon after. It was shaping up to be quite a week for Perera and her charity. On Thursday, 4 February, she went to Pan Asia Bank, informed them of the imminent arrival of the initial $20m donation and gave them instructions (including how much was to be paid into her savings account – about $7m).[7] The money arrived at the bank the following day. Everything appeared to be going to plan. Tadashi Sasaki, the Japanese donor, emailed the fixer with confirmation of the transfer.

But there was a problem. Staff at the bank became suspicious because it was such a large amount of money. They held up the transfer, and would not deposit it into the accounts until they'd done further checks.

By Saturday, 6 February, Perera was back at the Pan Asia Bank branch, this time with her fixer in tow; they demanded that the bank release the money and requested that $11m of it be paid into his account. But it was not to be. The bank had been poring over the transfer documents and discovered a tiny but worrying error. Instead of sending the money to the Shalika Foundation, the transfer had been made out to 'Shalika Fundation'. Alarm bells were now ringing in the Pan Asia Bank. It sent urgent queries both to Bangladesh Bank and to Deutsche Bank – the latter was the intermediary which had been handling the transaction. By Tuesday, 9 February, Bangladesh had sent an equally urgent reply, telling Pan Asia Bank not to release the money.[8] It was, of course, part of the $951m that the hackers had tried to transfer out of their New York Fed account. First they had been derailed when, by pure coincidence, the word 'Jupiter' saw their transfers being flagged as suspicious. Now a tiny spelling error had just cost them $20m. The Sri Lankans promptly returned the money to Bangladesh Bank.

Remarkably, according to police reports, Perera was back at the bank a fortnight later, giving them instructions as to how she wanted to carve up the $25m she was still expecting to receive – part of which was to be divided between two of her personal accounts.[9] It never happened, of course; by now it was obvious that Perera's charity had been used for money laundering, and, once this had been exposed, the multimillion-dollar donations came to a halt.

Sadly, charities are a common conduit for such criminal schemes, for a number of reasons. They often try to keep overheads down, and so cannot necessarily afford all of the legal-compliance infrastructure of a large institution. And, in addition, some charities are useful to money launderers because they regularly receive donations from different countries and send money overseas to fund their work. Years ago I visited a dark web financial crime forum on which an insider from a small Birmingham-based charity made exactly this pitch. He was offering money-laundering services, and reassured potential customers that, because of the volume of international transactions washing through the charity's accounts, he could send and receive laundered cash without fear of being noticed. Shalika Perera's charity had been lined up as an escape route for the hackers' stolen haul. The question was, how much had she known?

After hearing about her dispute with the bank, investigative journalist Shihar Aneez had been digging into the detail and finally tracked down Perera to get her side of the story. (It wasn't easy: when police turned up at the address given for her charity, they found a small house owned by her elder sister, who denied that the foundation was based there.[10]) Perera admitted meeting and working with the Japanese donor, Tadashi Sasaki, but said that because of the language barrier much of the negotiation was done via her fixer, who, she said, had been pressuring her not to ask too many questions about the donors. Looking back, there are some obvious weaknesses in her defence of her decision to accept the money: her own charity's website stated that the dairy farm would cost just under a million dollars to build, but she was happy to accept twenty times as much from the Japanese. It all looks extremely suspicious, but Perera denied breaking the law. 'We do not launder money. We have not done any such thing,' she told Aneez.

As more details emerged about what had happened at the Shalika Foundation, the Sri Lankan authorities confiscated Perera's passport, along with those of all the other directors of the charity and her fixer.[11] The Sri Lankan criminal investigation continues. At the time of writing Perera's fate is unknown. She's no longer responding to my messages. Shihar Aneez also tried to track her down but to no avail. One thing that's clear is that Shalika Perera's life has been irreversibly damaged.

From that perspective, her story is similar to that of Maia Santos Deguito, the manager of the RCBC branch in Manila through which $81m of the stolen money was laundered. Both made significant errors of judgement and failed to spot obvious warning signs, but both were caught up in a scheme that was almost certainly way bigger and more dangerous than they could ever have predicted. Both have had their lives turned upside down. Both are women. It's hard not to conclude that there is a gender dimension to those caught up in the gears of the Lazarus Group's global machinations.

There are other similarities between the Philippine and Sri Lankan operations too. On the SWIFT transfers that were used to send the $81m to Manila, the payments were disguised as donations for infrastructure projects from the Japan International Co-operation Agency, the same explanation used for the transfer to Colombo.[12] It turns out Bangladesh Bank has a long history with the agency, going back to 2012.[13] The Lazarus Group's hackers must have discovered this, because they used the JICA name as cover for their transfers to both countries. (To be clear: JICA says it had no idea its name was being used and is unconnected with the case.)

However, there are important differences between what happened in Sri Lanka and what happened in the Philippines. And, as you start to understand those differences, you'll start to appreciate how important it is to keep digging on the Sri Lankan end of this story.

You may remember that, in the hackers' rush to transfer out a billion dollars from Bangladesh Bank's account at the New York Fed, they had failed to specify the intermediary bank on almost all of the transactions. All except one: the transfer to the Shalika Foundation.

There's another intriguing distinction between the Sri Lankan and Philippine operations: the JICA projects listed on the Philippine money transfers were genuine schemes that had been backed by the agency in the past: engineering projects, bridge building, mass transit and so on. This implies that after the Lazarus Group hacked into Bangladesh Bank it went back through other transfers made by the bank, came across the JICA donations and copied the details to make the Philippine transfers seem more legitimate.

That's not the case in Sri Lanka. Here, the Lazarus Group hackers concocted a fictionalized JICA scheme, the dairy farm 'rural electrification up-gradation project' mentioned in the letter sent to Shalika Perera. Why? Because it was the project Perera was trying to get funding for. But how could the hackers have known about that? Think about it: they must have been told about the project by Shalika Perera, her fixer or the Japanese donor Tadashi Sasaki.

Another thing that sets the Sri Lankan incident apart is the timing. In the Philippine operation, it took a year of planning to set up the fraudulent bank accounts, line up the casino operators and recruit the network of middlemen. In the Sri Lankan case the turnaround was far quicker. From the time when Shalika Perera was told to set up the bank account to the time when the money arrived was just ten days. And, within that narrow time window, Perera is given the fake JICA letter. which is then used to make the transfer look legitimate. Whoever helped to line up this part of the money-laundering operation for the Lazarus Group, they had a much quicker, more direct line to the hackers than the network in the Philippines.

And, lastly, there's the difference in the amounts. Around $931m was originally destined for the Philippines but just $20m was sent to Sri Lanka. Why? Was it a pay-off? A mistake? A trial run?

If anyone can help answer these questions, it's Tadashi Sasaki, the Japanese donor who did so much to bring the money into the country. But, while Shalika Perera and her colleagues had their passports confiscated, trapping them in Sri Lanka, no such fate met Sasaki. He left the country and I assumed that would be the last we would hear from him. I was wrong. But, before we deal with that, we need to address a broader question: how might a Japanese man get caught up in North Korean activity in the first place? It turns out there are deep links between the two countries going back decades, and crime has long been woven into the relationship.

As we've already covered, the entire Korean peninsula was colonized by Japan from 1910 to 1945. Inevitably, many Koreans ended up living in Japan, either by choice or because they were shipped over as labourers. After the Second World War ended, many stayed in Japan. When Korea was permanently divided into North and South in 1953, it created a complex situation. Some ethnic Koreans in Japan sided with the North, some with the South, some vacillated from one to the other, and some just hoped reunification would bring the whole debate to a close. As relations between the two Koreas became ever-more fractious, divisions sometimes grew between these diaspora communities in Japan. The rulers of North and South Korea weren't averse to stirring the pot from time to time. In 1959 then-leader Kim Il Sung made a speech in which he offered perks to any Koreans in Japan who fancied returning home: free housing, free education, free medical treatment. One of those who took him up on the offer was a wrestler whose daughter eventually caught the eye of Kim Il Sung's son, Kim Jong Il. They in turn would go on to have three children, one of whom became North Korea's current ruler, Kim Jong Un. (Most North Koreans aren't told this, of course; as far as they're concerned, the entire Kim family was born and bred inside the country's borders.)

But, while North Korea's rulers promised returning ex-pats a life of perks in a socialist utopia, the reality turned out to be very different. Relatives from Japan who later went to see those who'd returned discovered what North Korea had been hiding from the outside world for years: food shortages, repression and isolation. Meanwhile, Japan was starting to emerge as a world-leading economy. Those in the country who were still sympathetic to North Korea started to support the regime, sending gifts and money to the country.

In Japan the hundreds of thousands of ethnic Koreans were still discriminated against, partly as a legacy of Japan's colonial past. They were labelled *zainichi*, 'foreigners', and struggled for acceptance in mainstream society. They came to inhabit a 'world within a world' in Japan, as one expert told my podcast co-host Jean H. Lee. Some ethnic Koreans attended special schools where classes and songs were in Korean, and they studied under the portraits of Kim Il Sung and Kim Jong Il. Those growing up in this environment have described how they were taught to be loyal to North Korea and show allegiance to the Kim family. The North Korean diaspora in Japan eventually became known as the Chongryon community.

According to experts, it has its own businesses, banks, schools, universities and publications – a 'self-completing bubble', as one academic puts it.[14]

As a result of their exclusion from mainstream Japanese society, some ethnic Koreans found themselves forced into the fringes, and for some that meant rubbing up against the criminal underworld.

Anyone who's been to the less glamorous parts of Tokyo will have come across pachinko parlours. They look like a Japanese version of slot-machine arcades. Rows and rows of people sit, seemingly entranced before the flashing lights and sounds of the machines, feeding tiny metal balls into something that looks a little like a pinball game, hoping to win back more balls. And so the ludic loop continues.[15] But there's a big difference between these mesmeric rooms and their Western equivalents, which explains why the gamblers are feeding in tiny metal balls and not shiny coins. Gambling for cash is illegal in Japan in most cases.[16] The players pay to hire trays of metal balls from the pachinko parlour, and then at the end of their session they return the balls, and, if they've done well, they're given a prize. It could be a pen, or a cigarette lighter, or a little gold trinket (Jean H. Lee, my co-host for *The Lazarus Heist* podcast, visited one such parlour and managed to win a slice of cake). It might not sound like the most lucrative gambling jaunt. But here's the twist: handily located around the corner is a little booth that will pay cash for exactly the prizes handed out by the pachinko parlour. What a coincidence! (Jean opted to eat her cake rather than attempt an exchange.)

It's a pretty transparent way to get around the law. It's also astonishingly lucrative. Quite how lucrative is a little difficult to assess, given the wilfully opaque business model.[17] Some estimate its revenues at $200bn per year, which would be thirty times the annual gambling take of Las Vegas and greater than the GDP of New Zealand.[18] If that seems unbelievable, consider a figure from a more verifiable source: Sega Sammy, which makes many of the pachinko machines, stated in its financial reports that it raked in $1bn from sales of the units in just nine months in 2017.[19] Whichever way you cut the cake (provided you haven't eaten it), pachinko is a massive business.

It's also operating on the very fringes of the law, and as a result pachinko parlours have long been associated with the criminal fraternity. Organized-crime gangs in Japan, the *yakuza*, have traditionally had a hand in pachinko operations (although the country's police have worked hard to crack down on this). And, because of their struggles to penetrate mainstream society, it's where some ethnic Koreans ended up too. Some estimate that four out of five pachinko parlours are owned by Koreans, of which about a third have ties to North Korea.[20] Given the amounts of money the industry generates, and the beneficence of some of Japan's ethnic Korean diaspora towards their homeland, it's possible these peculiar little gambling dens have generated many millions of dollars for the Kim regime.

They also helped to forge links between ethnic Koreans in Japan and the *yakuza* organized-crime gangs. A former officer of Japan's Public Security Intelligence Agency was filmed in 2006 revealing that a third of *yakuza* members are believed to be ethnic Koreans, of whom a third are allied with the North.[21] Media reports have also revealed close links between North Korea and ethnic Korean *yakuza* operatives, who have taken part in money-laundering operations in Japan on behalf of the Pyongyang regime.[22]

It must be stressed that this is not the fate of all ethnic Koreans in Japan, many of whom live perfectly law-abiding lives far away from the criminal underworld. But, given the close links fostered in Japan between organized crime and North Korea, it starts to make sense that a Japanese man may have ended up embroiled in a North Korean money-laundering scheme, just as Tadashi Sasaki seemed to have been in Sri Lanka. But what about Sasaki as an individual? What's his story? How did he get involved in it all?

Back in Sri Lanka in 2016, Sasaki had departed the country, but left behind one solitary lead which was our only chance to track him down. A business card. It had his name on it, of course, but that

wasn't much help. Tadashi Sasaki was described to me by a colleague as being an 'almost comically bland' name, like calling
oneself 'John Smith'. And, besides, it might not even be his real
name: as a result of the discrimination described above, ethnic
Koreans in Japan will sometimes take Japanese names in order to
try to fit in. I was convinced Tadashi Sasaki was a fake name, from
a fake ID, and that we'd never find the real man behind it all.

But the business card contained other details: phone numbers, a
website and email addresses – all of which are a goldmine for an
investigative journalist. So, with help from Sri Lankan reporter
Shihar Aneez and a Japanese BBC colleague, we set about following
the leads. Eventually it led us to a Facebook account which looked
genuine, with multiple photos of the same man in different locations at different times. As we scrolled back through his timeline,
there was a trip to Sri Lanka in August 2014, at exactly the time
when Sasaki was alleged to have been in the country being introduced to Shalika Perera via her fixer.

It wasn't conclusive evidence. Perhaps this was simply a Japanese
tourist visiting the country who happened to have the same name.
I dug further. He'd clearly gone on a road trip: his Facebook profile
photos showed a journey through some dusty locations, including
to a place called Tissamaharama, a town of a few tens of thousands
of people on the south of the island. The name rang a bell with
me. It was where Shalika Perera's fixer lived. A man with exactly the
right name turning up in exactly the right location at exactly the right
time? It was too much to be a coincidence. Sasaki was real.

So far, most of the characters we'd investigated in this story had
made strenuous efforts to hide themselves away, secreting themselves inside layer upon layer of fakery, like Park Jin Hyok, the
alleged Lazarus Group hacker. By contrast, Sasaki was proudly
posting selfies and updating his Facebook account. Yet, from what
we now know of the events in Sri Lanka, he was deeply embroiled
in a money-laundering plot and appeared to have a direct line to the
hackers who broke into Bangladesh Bank.

We'd made attempts to coax him into doing an interview but

they had fallen on deaf ears. He'd emailed to deny knowing anything about the incident. Then, to our amazement, after many requests, Sasaki agreed to talk.

It was a somewhat bizarre conversation, conducted online through an interpreter during the depths of the coronavirus pandemic with all its attendant technical complexities. But little by little Sasaki told his story – the first time he'd done so in an on-record interview. Back in Japan in 2014, he said, he was the Director of a company selling second-hand cars to Myanmar and doing some consulting. He was approached by a Japanese contact, who asked him if he knew anyone who could receive a large amount of money from a bank in Switzerland using a niche type of money-transfer system called a Depository Transfer Cheque. The amount that they were planning to transfer was around a billion euros, which is more than a billion dollars, of which Sasaki would get a 1 per cent fee.

(You may recall that in her initial conversations with Sasaki, charity boss Shalika Perera says he'd talked about transferring the giant sum of €900bn. In our conversation Sasaki never mentioned this amount, leading me to believe Perera may have been mistaken, possibly getting 900bn mixed up with 900m.)

Faced with such a tempting offer, Sasaki asked around, and another Japanese acquaintance put him in touch with a man in Sri Lanka who could help with the transfer. But when he got to Sri Lanka, Sasaki was told the money wasn't going directly to the recipient, but needed to go via a charity. The charity would keep 30 per cent and the recipient would get the rest, minus a 1 per cent fee for Sasaki and the others helping out. The charity, of course, was the Shalika Foundation.

Sasaki says he met Shalika Perera in Sri Lanka and even went to the bank with her. They were trying to get the bank to receive the billion euros via the Depository Transfer Cheque system, but Sasaki says the bank couldn't make it work. This isn't a surprise. I spoke to one financial expert who told me these Depository Transfer Cheques are a pretty old-fashioned way of transferring funds, and a big money-laundering concern. For example, unlike normal cheques, DTCs don't even carry a signature, making it hard for investigators to track who authorized them.

Sasaki says that, when he realized the transfer couldn't happen, he left Sri Lanka and that was that. But this contradicts Perera's story. She told police that he later contacted her about the transfer, which was now no longer a billion euros but the much smaller sum of $20m.

Sasaki's story threw up so many more questions. Who were these mysterious Japanese men who'd asked him to get involved in the scheme in the first place? They were both now dead, he said. And he'd lost touch with his Sri Lankan contact.

Didn't he think it was incredibly suspicious that someone wanted him, a used-car salesman, to broker a billion-euro transaction? No, he said, he just assumed the Swiss bank would handle all the compliance.

Did he even ask what the money was for? No. He was thinking of his pay-off. 'We all want money,' he tells me.

He denies any links to *yakuza* organized-crime gangs. Asked about the North Korean links, he says it seems like North Korea has been resorting to different ways to bring in hard currency in the face of economic sanctions, something Sasaki says he finds scary.

I'm an experienced journalist and I've interviewed everyone from slippery tech executives to online fraudsters, and I've had pretty good results. But talking to Sasaki was like trying to nail jelly to the wall. Every line I pursued with him went nowhere. All his contacts had conveniently disappeared, so there was no way of corroborating or contradicting his story. He'd asked no questions and had therefore remained wilfully ignorant of the circumstances surrounding the deal. What he was involved with was clearly deeply suspicious, but ignoring your suspicions isn't necessarily enough to get you prosecuted. And of course a large part of the problem with pinning anything on Sasaki is that the fraudulent transfer never actually happened. It was reversed before it ever entered the accounts.[23]

It seems I wasn't the only one to quiz Sasaki and wind up in a dead end. He says the CIA also interviewed him, but no further action was taken.

However, Sasaki's interview does throw up an interesting thought. He was originally told he'd be handling around a billion dollars – roughly the same amount the Bangladesh Bank hackers were going after. So maybe their initial plan had been to move the entire amount through Sri Lanka using the Depository Transfer Cheques? It certainly makes sense compared with the complexity of the operation in the Philippines, with all those fraudulent bank accounts and casino players. But, on the other hand, Sasaki was given that billion-dollar figure back in 2014, and the hackers apparently broke into Bangladesh Bank only early in 2015. Did they already know how much they were going after? Did they somehow know how much money Bangladesh had in its New York Fed account?

Ultimately there's limited use in ruminating on what could have been. We know what actually happened: $81m was eventually stolen from Bangladesh and washed through the Philippines casinos, vanishing along with Gao and Ding, the two Chinese men who allegedly organized the laundering operation. And, on that front, further interrogation of Sasaki threw up one final intriguing lead that puts us right back on the trail of the money. When Sri Lankan journalist Shihar Aneez asked Sasaki about his contacts, he discovered a common link among some of the names: 'They were in Macau,' says Aneez.

That's more than just a random connection. Sasaki's network is not the only link to Macau. As you'll see, a conspicuous number of threads of this story start to converge on this tiny enclave jutting off China's southern border. It turns out this little region is another vital foreign link for North Korea – one that's given rise to some truly grisly episodes.

12

The Las Vegas of the East

When last we left him, Bloomberg journalist Alan Katz had been trying to get to the bottom of the story of Gao Shuhua and Ding Xixhe, the two Chinese men who'd emerged as allegedly key players in the heist.

The pair had been in Manila when Bangladesh Bank's stolen money was laundered through the city's casinos, and, according to Kim Wong, the man whose company received some of the cash, they were the ones who set up the whole operation.

The Philippines Senate hearings had shed further light on what happened, and on the involvement of Gao and Ding. Of the $81m that was transferred to Manila, around $30m had disappeared with the mysterious Weikang Xu. A further $30m had been transferred to the Solaire Casino, run by Bloomberry Resorts Corporation. At the hearings Bloomberry's representative confirmed that this cash was used as 'front money' by Ding – meaning it was converted into casino chips and sent off for gambling in the private rooms run by the junket operators.[1] There were three junkets involved: Sun City, Gold Moon and, lastly, the Solaire's own in-house operation (this was the VIP room in which Tony Lau was working when his Chinese high rollers arrived). The Senate Committee was also told that Ding brought in eighteen players to gamble with the money.[2]

The rest of the cash, around $21m, was sent to Eastern Hawaii Leisure, the company run by Kim Wong, for gambling in the Midas Casino (Wong had handed back $16m of this money, which he claimed was all his company had been given). Wong had admitted knowing Gao Shuhua for many years, and claimed that he and Gao had negotiated the transfer of the money in order to settle a gambling debt.

That was Wong's story. But what about Gao and Ding? They hadn't given testimony to the committee. The Philippine authorities had tried to track them down but got little help at the Chinese Embassy. One of the Senators told Katz that the Philippines' immigration authorities had no trace of their departure. Like Weikang Xu, they seemed to vanish into thin air, taking the money with them. The allegation from the Senate hearings was clear: they'd been instrumental in setting up the scheme to launder tens of millions of stolen dollars. What was their story? And how had they managed to slip away so easily? With a colleague from Bloomberg News, Katz set out to track down the men. They spoke with family members, fished out legal documents and traced former colleagues, gradually building up a picture of the elusive pair.[3]

The first thing that emerged was that Gao and Ding were no cyber-geniuses. Gao's wife told Katz that her husband was computer-illiterate. And Ding was such a tech novice he needed help posting selfies when he went on hiking trips, according to a former business partner. But if they were in league with the hackers, this wouldn't necessarily have mattered. The hackers had the tech side covered. What they needed Gao and Ding for was the physical side of the operation, according to Katz.

The more he found out about the pair, the more Katz realized that their respective life stories made them ideal choices for the job. 'Gao was the "hard man",' says Katz. 'He was big in the Chinese illegal gambling world. China does not allow casinos, but he ran illegal casinos in China, and he was known as a wealthy man.'

One summer in 2004, according to court documents uncovered by Katz, thugs working for Gao beat up a group of men whom they mistook for another gang that had robbed them. Unfortunately for Gao, the victims turned out to include police officers, and he found himself serving an eighteen-month prison sentence.

It wasn't to be his last brush with the law. He was arrested by the Chinese authorities again in 2012, at which point they discovered he ran one of the biggest gambling networks in the country, spanning twenty-nine provinces and making him more than $8m, according to Katz.

Like Gao, Ding was also a big wheel in the casino world. 'Ding definitely made good money from this,' says Katz. 'He and his wife ended up buying a big mansion. They were robbed at one point, and they had more than $600,000 worth of items stolen from their house. That included two Swiss watches, and a kilo of gold. They also had about $25,000 in cash at the house.'

Running illegal gambling operations was Gao's and Ding's main business, according to Katz's research, and that gave them a very useful set of skills for anyone interested in money laundering. '[They were] used to moving large sums of money on behalf of other people, whether it's legal or not.'

Importantly for our tale, Gao's and Ding's stories converge on one place in particular: Macau. On his release from his second prison stint, Gao travelled to Macau and went on to set up a company there in 2014. He invested in businesses running casino VIP rooms, including Eastern Hawaii Leisure, the company run by Kim Wong.

Ding also set up an investment company in Macau, in 2007. And with his wife he went on to put down some considerable roots there. 'They bought a Macau high-rise now valued at $1m. About a half-hour's drive from there, the couple owns a four-storey mansion surrounded by a koi pond, bonsai trees and at least seven security cameras. The lot alone is worth $5m, local real-estate agents estimate,' Katz and his colleague wrote in their Bloomberg News article.

By the time the Bangladesh Bank heist happened, Ding was a card-carrying member of Macau society – of the twenty Chinese gamblers the Philippines Senate tried to trace, Ding alone held a Macau passport.[4]

Gao and Ding aren't the only connections between the bank heist and Macau. The two main junket operators to which Ding sent the stolen money, Sun City and Gold Moon, are both based in Macau (the two companies' representatives appeared at the Senate hearings and agreed to co-operate in providing information as to what happened).[5] And of course various contacts of Tadashi Sasaki, the man involved in moving funds through Sri Lanka, also track back to Macau.

Macau is a patch of land less than 50 square miles in size, and yet, from what we've uncovered, it is a sinkhole for multiple links to the Bangladesh Bank heist and the network of middlemen and fixers caught up in it. Those who've lived there aren't surprised to hear this. As they'll tell you, Macau has a dark and seedy history.

'Macau's heyday came around the sixteenth century,' says casino expert Muhammad Cohen, who's a former long-time Macau resident. It was a booming commercial outpost for the Portuguese: 'the sole outlet for trading between the West and Canton, which is now Guangzhou'. But then its fortunes changed, says Cohen: 'The harbour silted up due to the flow from the Pearl River. Hong Kong emerged as a better deep-water port. China opened up more ports to more Westerners. Macau saw all its business taken away from it. And Portugal, which ran it, became a second- or third-rate power in Europe. So what was Macau to do?'

The answer, says Cohen, was to turn to the 'dark arts'. 'Gold-bullion trading was illegal in the rest of the world, but was done in Macau. Prostitution was legal in Macau. Smuggling was huge. All these things were specialties in Macau. That became its raison d'être. And of course, the biggest of the dark arts that they capitalized on was gambling.'

For many people, Las Vegas is the spiritual home of the casino, but its industry is dwarfed by the scale of Macau, which is the biggest market in the world, almost four times the size of its Nevada counterpart. In 2019 the Las Vegas strip generated under $9bn, compared with Macau's $35bn.[6] Like Hong Kong, Macau is a Special Administrative Region of China, and they're the only places in China where casinos are allowed. What this created was a similar situation to the one we saw in Japan – as people moved in to take advantage of the legal loophole and enjoy some gambling, organized crime started to become a problem.

As Cohen explains: 'In China, there is no legal recourse for collecting a gambling debt. So if you want to collect a gambling debt, you have to do it through extra-legal means, which may mean dealing with organized crime to have somebody come threaten the debtor, and things like that.' This was the milieu in which Gao and Ding were moving, according to Katz's research.

But it wasn't just organized crime making use of Macau's status as a seedy fringe location. Several remarkable stories reveal that this Chinese region has played a key role for North Korea as well.

Beneath the lights of a crowded TV studio, a woman sits before the cameras and assembled audience members. She's strikingly beautiful, in her late twenties, dressed in a dark skirt suit and white shirt. She seems painfully shy. Her voice is almost a whisper at times, and in between her answers she stares down at her lap. The interviewer gradually coaxes her story from her – a story that seems almost unbelievable, given her meek demeanour. The woman's name is Kim Hyun Hee, and just a few years earlier she had killed 115 people.[7]

It was 1987 and South Korea was on the brink of hosting the Olympics the following year. As we saw in Chapter 2, this had been a great source of anger and wounded pride for the North's leadership. According to Kim Hyun Hee, they set out with a horrific plan to teach their enemy a lesson, and she was to play a key role.[8]

She says she was trained as a spy in North Korea, then teamed up with another North Korean agent and given further training in Europe. In 1987 she received an order that had been 'ratified' – meaning it came directly from either Kim Il Sung or Kim Jong Il. She and her fellow agent were to board a Korean Air flight from Baghdad in Iraq to Seoul in South Korea. They were to leave a bomb hidden inside a radio in the luggage rack, then disembark when the plane transited through Abu Dhabi. The bomb would explode, killing all on board. If Kim and her accomplice were discovered, they were to take the cyanide pills hidden inside cigarettes that they'd been issued with. On 29 November 1987 they put the plan into action. It worked flawlessly except for one detail – when they were caught after fleeing to

Bahrain, Kim wasn't able to take her suicide pill. She survived. Meanwhile, all 115 passengers and crew on board the flight were killed.

She was travelling on a false Japanese passport, but the Bahraini authorities were suspicious and eventually handed her over to the South Koreans. She was flown back to Seoul, where she confessed. She said her commanders had told her that bringing down the airliner would weaken the South and hasten the reunification of the Korean peninsula.[9] She was tried, pleaded guilty and was sentenced to death. But there was to be a second escape from death for Kim Hyun Hee. South Korea's President pardoned her, on the grounds that she had been brainwashed by the North Korean regime and did not realize the full impact of her actions. She now lives under protection in South Korea.

What's all this got to do with Macau? Well, during her interrogation, Kim Hyun Hee revealed that she and her accomplice had spent time in the territory preparing for their attack. In order to fit in with their Japanese cover identities, they had to learn skills alien to most North Koreans, like shopping in supermarkets, using credit cards and visiting nightclubs.[10]

It's no surprise that Macau might be the place North Korea chose to train its spies in how to blend in with decadent Western ways. The regime already had a convenient base in the region: Zokwang Trading. As we discovered in Chapter 3, this tiny firm based on the fifth floor of a generic office block was actually a front company for the North Korean regime, complete with pictures of Kim Il Sung and Kim Jong Il on the walls. Zokwang Trading employees had been caught trying to pass off superdollars, the fake high-quality $100 bills. And those same superdollars had been laundered, according to US authorities, through the Macau-based Banco Delta Asia.[11]

Over the decades North Korea had shaped itself into a secretive state intent on sealing itself off from the outside world, and providing for its population with its policy of *Juche*, or self-reliance. In reality, the country desperately needed some kind of conduit: a nearby portal to the outside world through which resources and people could move, whether legally or illicitly. That's what Macau was for North Korea. It helped that it was awash with gambling money and underworld dealings. Also helpful was Macau's political position – it was technically under the umbrella of North Korea's ally China, but, thanks to its Special Administrative Region status, Beijing held less sway there.

It wasn't just secret agents and dodgy money North Korea was moving in and out of Macau. One veteran reporter recalled sitting with his TV camera crew on a hill outside Macau's airport and filming the cargo being loaded on to the territory's regular flight to Pyongyang (which no longer operates). The payload included luxury goods like wide-screen TV sets, all no doubt bound for the homes of North Korea's elite class.[12]

There's one story that ties together all these strands: Macau, North Korea, gambling and crime. It's the remarkable tale of Kim Jong Nam.

As you might guess from his surname, Kim Jong Nam was born into North Korea's ruling family. Remember how Kim Jong Il was so obsessed with movies that he'd sometimes turn up to oversee film shoots? It seems he had another incentive to hang around on set: glamorous actresses. He'd been married in 1966 to a woman chosen for him by his father, but they'd divorced a few years later. Shortly after that he fell for a film star called Song Hye Rim. She was married, but Kim reportedly forced her to divorce her husband. He kept the relationship a secret from his father (and of course the general population), even when they had a son together. That son was Kim Jong Nam.[13]

Despite his hidden status, Kim Jong Nam was raised with all the trappings of the ruling family. Diplomats were ordered to buy diamond watches, gold-plated guns and a miniature Cadillac for the boy. At age twenty-four he was dressed up in the uniform of a high-ranking marshal, and generals were ordered to salute him.[14]

But, instead of keeping him in Pyongyang, Kim Jong Il sent his son off to Moscow and Geneva to be educated, giving him a taste of the outside world. When he returned, the name 'Kim Jong Nam' began to appear in the state media: a sure sign he was being prepared for leadership.

But it seems Kim Jong Nam wasn't quite ready for the sober and stressful life of running a country.

In April 2001, by then married and a father, Kim Jong Nam fancied taking his son to Tokyo Disneyland. He attempted to avoid detection by using a fake ID: a Dominican Republic passport bearing a Chinese name that translates into 'Fat Bear'. Japanese authorities reportedly got word from a 'friendly foreign intelligence service' as to what was about to go down,[15] and they arrested Kim Jong Nam as soon as he arrived in the country. The incident went public and was hugely embarrassing for the North Koreans – after all, here was the presumed future leader of the avowedly socialist country chasing a big dose of capitalist fun in Disneyland, of all places.[16]

Perhaps keen to avoid a huge diplomatic spat, the Japanese government deported Kim Jong Nam and his entourage without charging them. But life would never be the same for him. Even for one of the most privileged people in North Korea, his attempted journey from Hermit Kingdom to Magic Kingdom had been a step too far. Kim Jong Nam went into self-exile. He's believed to have set up his wife and son in Beijing, but he ended up moving with his mistress and their children to . . . Macau, of course. And it seems that once there he took advantage of all the city's usual distractions. 'Living Las Vegas in Asia,' he wrote under a pseudonym in a 2010 Facebook post.[17] He was enjoying his freewheeling life in Macau: eating out, drinking and dabbling in a little gambling. His love of the nightlife was also useful for journalists looking for an insight into North Korea and the reclusive Kim family, because they could lie in wait at the city's casinos to score an interview.

From the safety of Macau, Kim Jong Nam also became increasingly critical of the North Korean regime. Some of the reporters who circled him occasionally got quotes expressing negative opinions about the North's leaders. These views had been tolerated by Pyongyang, and, perhaps more importantly, by his father, Kim Jong

Il. But that changed in December 2011. Kim Jong Il died of a heart attack, and Kim Jong Nam's half-brother, Kim Jong Un, was now in charge. The two had been raised separately. Kim Jong Nam once said he had never even met his younger sibling. So there was no close bond to protect Kim Jong Nam. Added to which, his half-brother was newly installed as leader, insecure and, as we've seen from previous chapters, desperate to cement his position at any cost – even if it meant killing off family members. None of which was good news for Kim Jong Nam.

As he partied in Macau, an audacious plot was being hatched to shut him up for good.

Kuala Lumpur Airport in Malaysia, 13 February 2017. It's 9 a.m., and an unremarkable-looking man is using the self-check-in kiosk for a flight to Macau. A woman bumps into him and quickly smears something across his face. As the man reels back in confusion, another woman darts in and rubs a cloth over his mouth. Then both women walk away calmly. No one else seems to notice. The whole incident has taken less than five seconds.

The man feels something is wrong, and goes to the airport security staff, who in turn lead him to the health clinic. By the time he gets there he's dragging his feet and sweating. CCTV footage shows him slumped in a seat, barely conscious. Within two hours, he's dead. It would later emerge that he was travelling on a North Korean diplomatic passport with the name Kim Chol – a very common North Korean name. The Malaysian authorities go to inform North Korea's Embassy of the death of one of their citizens, but somehow the news leaks. Photos of the dying man slumped in a chair in an airport clinic shoot around the world. It soon becomes clear who he really was: Kim Jong Nam.

The man who was once set to take over North Korea and who then became one of its critics had been murdered in a slick operation. All eyes were on Malaysia – could it track down the culprits and unravel the case?

Within days of the attack, the Malaysian police captured the two women who'd been caught on CCTV smearing Kim Jong Nam's face with the substances that killed him. One was Vietnamese, one Indonesian. They told an incredible story. Both were from relatively poor backgrounds and were seeking to improve their lot by breaking into showbiz. They said they were approached by a Japanese man with a very tempting offer to work on a YouTube prank show. Over the course of several months they carried out a few stunts for their new boss, spraying liquid at unsuspecting victims. When they asked when the footage would be aired, they were given vague replies. And then the Japanese man gave them a new assignment: go to Kuala Lumpur Airport and wipe some liquid on a guy's face. It would all be captured on camera, just a bit of fun like the other stunts, the two women thought. In fact, it was an assassination. Separately, the two liquids they were given are harmless. But combined they create VX, the most toxic nerve agent ever produced. It's a chemical weapon that can disable the nervous system in minutes. And toxicology reports revealed VX killed Kim Jong Nam.

The two women were eventually released – one had her murder charge dismissed, the other pleaded guilty to a lesser charge.[18] But in the course of their investigation, Malaysian authorities discovered the women weren't acting alone at the airport. Studying the CCTV, police reportedly spotted four North Korean agents on the ground at the time of the attack. They flew out of the country shortly after, taking a circuitous route apparently designed to avoid any airspace where the planes could be forced down so the men could be apprehended.[19] Within days the Malaysian police were pointing fingers at North Korea. It brought an angry response from the regime, which firmly denied any involvement. The incident sparked a massive diplomatic row. At one point North Korea banned Malaysian citizens from leaving its territory, and Malaysia reacted by banning North Koreans from leaving Malaysia. Up until this point the two countries had been on pretty good terms (which is probably why Kim Jong Nam felt he could travel there on a North Korean passport rather than a falsified one of the kind he used to try to access Japan). So there's an intriguing question: if Kim Jong Nam was assassinated by North Korean agents, why didn't they do it in Macau, where he lived, and where North Korea has long-established links? Why do it in Malaysia and risk alienating one of its few international friends? Some believe it's because North Korea didn't want to upset its main ally, China, by carrying out the assassination on their soil.

Others have different questions about the murder in the airport. If VX nerve agent is so deadly, they ask, how come no one else was affected? In particular, how come the two unwitting assassins themselves didn't get sick? There is much Internet discussion, and many an armchair toxicologist has weighed in on the debate. There was yet more speculation when it was reported that Kim Jong Nam had become an informant for the CIA, and may have travelled to Malaysia to receive a pay-off.[20]

Of course, none of it ultimately mattered to Kim Jong Nam and his family. The man who might once have ruled North Korea was never to return to his adoptive home of Macau alive.

Kim Jong Nam, the Korean Air bomber, the superdollars, the Sri Lankan fixer, the casino junkets – Macau is the central link between them all. And of course Gao and Ding, the men accused of organizing the money-laundering gambling jaunts in Manila. What happened to them? Did journalist Alan Katz and his colleague ever finally track them down? 'No, we did not,' says Katz. 'And the reason is it didn't actually end very well for them. They got away scot-free from the Philippines, disappeared, but they reappeared in China. And, by early 2017, both had been arrested.'

As Katz and his colleague explored the circumstances surrounding the arrests, they came across some worrying signs that the men were in serious trouble. 'When they were taking Gao away, his wife asked one of the policemen, "Where should I tell the lawyer to call to try to either get him out on bail or to follow up on this?" And the policeman said to her, "Oh, don't bother calling a lawyer." And that's a very odd response, because China is actually quite a big believer in lawyers.'

Katz himself never got to the bottom of what happened. 'We still don't know really why they were arrested. Someone appears to have decided that what they were doing in the Philippines was not to their liking. It's possible they could have been involved in other projects that were also not to someone's liking, but that would be quite a coincidence.'

Gao and Ding performed a function, says Katz, after which they dropped out of the picture: 'They had a specific job to do, which was to launder the money through the casinos in the Philippines and get the money out of the Philippines, likely back to Macau. They were good enough at their job that they laundered the money and it became untraceable. But that was where their job ended. The people who would then be getting the money from Macau to North Korea would have been a different set of people.'

Katz is assuming here that if North Korea was behind the heist, the money must eventually have been physically moved back to Pyongyang after Macau. But it's quite possible that wasn't the end-game at all. Experts we spoke to for *The Lazarus Heist* podcast explained a situation whereby money received in somewhere like Macau can simply remain in the region and be used to buy goods that can then be sent back to the regime, like the massive TVs the journalist watched being loaded on to planes bound for Pyongyang. Or it can be used to pay off middlemen. The money effectively becomes an overseas 'credit' that can be utilized at will by the regime.

So this is the ultimate – and somewhat dissatisfying – conclusion of the Bangladesh Bank heist story. It's where the parallels to Holly-wood heist movies must end, because this story does not conclude as it would do in the films. There's no big champagne party where Kim Jong Un rolls around among the banknotes while his gang discuss the lavish retirement villas they'll buy with their share of the loot. Neither is there a scene in which the police finally round up the crooks and hand back the stolen cash to a grateful victim, leading the culprits away in handcuffs as the credits roll.

No, this is the real world, and it hasn't been carefully scripted to satisfy a cinema audience. The global cast of characters in this story will not be brought back for a sequel. Like Tadash Sasaki and Kim

Wong, they simply shrug off responsibility; or, like Weikang Xu and Shalika Perera, they disappear in mysterious circumstances; or, like Gao Shuhua and Ding Xixhe, they meet a worrying fate; or, like Maia Santos Deguito, they end up with a prison sentence while insisting they were only pawns in the game. And it's not just the cast who sink into the cracks. So does the money. It doesn't end up in neat bundles stacked inside a leather briefcase to be handed over at some discreet rendezvous on a park bench like in the movies. It simply melts away somewhere in an East Asian country, becoming almost impossible to trace.

If you're feeling deflated by this conclusion, spare a thought for Kim Jong Un. If his regime was behind the entire heist, as the FBI allege, you have to wonder how satisfied he was with the outcome. Think about it: this heist started with an audacious plan to steal a billion dollars from right under the noses of Bangladesh Bank, then race it across the world before laundering it over the card tables of Manila and pulling it into the safe haven of Macau. Yet, at the end of the day, what his operatives actually handed over was probably a few tens of millions of dollars rather than the billion they'd promised.

Of course, a large part of that shortfall came as a result of bad luck ('Jupiter') and poor spelling ('Fundation'). But at a deeper level what ate away the hackers' profits was the fact that, no matter how cunning and technically skilled they were, they were still reliant on the traditional money system. They were raiding a national bank with a dollar account; the money had to be transferred through the international banking network via SWIFT; then it had to be converted into cash, into casino chips, then back into cash again. At every step of the way this required a network of middlemen and fixers, all of whom needed to be paid off (whether they were aware of the full scale of the heist or not), and any one of whom might become a leak in the operation, allowing law enforcement to disrupt the heist.

If only there were a way of avoiding all these hurdles – a way of accessing wealth without bothering with what hackers call 'meatspace': the messy, unreliable world of human beings and their greed and fallibilities.

Luckily for the Lazarus Group's operatives, this dream was about to become a reality. The explosive growth of the Internet had created a parallel money system. Not only was it awash with cash, it was considerably less well protected than the traditional financial world. If the hackers could crack it, they could make sums that would dwarf the tens of millions they'd finally netted from Bangladesh Bank. But, first, they had to master how this new world functioned.

The Lazarus Group was about to make another huge technological leap forward.

And it would also bring the FBI's investigators back into the game. They would unlock another piece of the Lazarus Heist jigsaw and reveal something deeply concerning for all of us. The group's hacking had become, quite literally, a matter of life and death.

13

WannaCry

It's 10 a.m., on a sunny Friday in May 2017, and Patrick Ward is finding it hard to concentrate on the trashy crime novel he's been reading. He's sitting in a hospital bed at St Bartholomew's in Central London, hours away from the surgery he hopes will change his life. It took a while to get to this point. It all started a few years before.

'I was playing football and noticed the shortness of breath and I just thought it was some sort of pain in my throat. I went to the doctor and he told me to stop everything,' says Ward.

It turned out he had an enlarged heart, a hereditary condition which meant it struggled to pump enough blood through his body. He'd been an active person, but now at forty-seven he had to take breaks just to walk up a flight of stairs. The condition was having a serious effect on his life. The doctors eventually offered a solution, but a highly risky one: open-heart surgery.

'It was a major, major decision,' says Ward.

It's also a very specialized operation and not many surgeons in the UK carry it out. So Patrick has to wait for two years. But, eventually, on 12 May 2017, it's his turn.

'I was mentally prepared to have many, many weeks off work, to have my chest cut open. And I wanted it at that point. I was going to get my life back again,' he says.

Everything seems to be proceeding to plan. The surgeon drops by to check on him mid-morning. But, just after 1 p.m., minutes before his surgery is due to begin, Ward starts to notice some commotion outside his room.

'I got up out of the bed and walked out to the nurses' station to see blank monitors everywhere and people looking very worried.

Nurses and orderlies and various other people just wandering around the place, not quite knowing what to do.'

Across London, in another hospital run by the UK's National Health Service, the NHS, a similar scene is taking place. Tony Bleetman is a consultant in emergency medicine and he's just arrived for his shift at the Accident and Emergency Department. 'As I walked into the office, it became clear that something had gone drastically wrong with all the computers. There was a message on the screen, on everybody's computer screen,' he recalls. Against a red background, the text reads (*sic*):

> Oops your files have been encrypted. Maybe you're busy looking for way to recover your files. But do not waste your time. Nobody can recover your files without our decryption service.

Hackers have broken into the hospital's computer system and scrambled all the data. They're offering to unscramble it, but for the price of several hundred dollars, paid in the virtual currency Bitcoin. And there's an extra twist. After three days the ransom money doubles. And if nothing is paid within a week, the hackers' message says they'll destroy all the data forever.

The dropdown menu offers instructions for payment in twenty-eight different languages – it seems whoever's behind the attack is setting themselves up for international success. As a public-sector organization, the hospital is in no position to pay the ransom. And so, in an attempt to control the outbreak, it switches off the computer network.

'We couldn't register new patients on a computer,' says Bleetman. 'We couldn't access their medical records. We couldn't track their location, what's happening to them and who's looking after them and what their blood results are. We couldn't access X-ray or CT images on the computer.'

Today's doctors need access to state of the art technology. When time is tight, it can help make quick, life-saving decisions. For example, if a patient turns up with symptoms of a stroke, one possibility is that part of the brain is blocked by a clot; another possibility is that a brain vessel might be bleeding. If you give clot-busting treatment in the first case, you're saving a life. But, if it's the second, the same treatment could lead to death. The only way to know for sure is to carry out a brain scan. The same is true for the whole of emergency medicine, from car accidents to cancer. Scanning is an essential frontline asset. But that technology, along with basic admin IT, is now unavailable to Bleetman and his colleagues thanks to the cyber-attack. So they adapt. Non-critical patients are turned away. Some critical patients are diverted elsewhere. But that becomes increasingly difficult as other hospitals succumb to the virus.

'At least one of the London trauma centres was not accepting patients because the trauma surgeons were unable to access the images which they often rely upon when embarking on emergency surgery. And there was restricted access for a time for heart-attack centres,' says Bleetman.

Meanwhile, back at St Bartholomew's Hospital, Ward is still waiting to be taken to the operating theatre. Unsure what's happening, he turns to his smartphone. That's when he starts to see the news headlines and realizes it's not just his hospital affected. And then his surgeon finally reappears with bad news. 'The hospital's computer system had been hacked, their systems were all down,' recalls Ward. 'I said, "Well, we don't need that. You're operating on my heart. What on earth do you need a computer for? Come on, I've waited two years for this operation." This cannot be happening to me now. I thought he was having a laugh to begin with.'

But the surgeon is deadly serious. He tells Ward: 'I'm really sorry, but we need the computers for your blood results. We need that for your tests. It's an integral part of the operation. There's nothing we can do. The operation is cancelled. You can leave.'

Ward stumbles out into the daylight, still with the bandages on his hand from the cannula that had just been removed. He's reunited with his family, who had travelled to London to support him. He immediately bumps into a BBC News film crew who've been hovering around the exits scouting for interviewees. Ward recounts his own experience and then asks the question on everyone's minds: 'Why would anyone want to hack a hospital that's trying to do good?'[1]

What Ward doesn't realize is that it's not just hospitals. The virus is spreading around the world, hitting everything from the German railway company Deutsche Bahn to Russian financial firm Sberbank.[2]

In the space of an afternoon, it scrambles the data on some 230,000 computers in 150 countries around the world. Estimates of the damage range from $4bn to $8bn.[3]

It's the event people in cyber-security have dreaded for years: a worldwide computer pandemic that spreads automatically. It seems unstoppable. But it wasn't. Someone brought the virus outbreak to a screeching halt. And the story of who and how is one of the craziest tales in cybercrime history.

Friday, 12 May, the day the virus struck, was supposed to be a day off for Marcus Hutchins. Wholesome, with a winning smile and a mass of curly hair, the 22-year-old was already earning a six-figure salary as a researcher for an American cyber-intelligence company. He was working on viruses, or 'malware', as they call it in the trade.

Like many techies, he'd started young. After he dismantled the family PC aged just thirteen, his parents had bought him his own computer to experiment on, and he'd never looked back. At seventeen he'd started a blog called Malware Tech. His posts became famous for their detailed breakdowns of computer viruses. He'd accumulated many followers online, but they had no idea of his real name or what his life was like, because the profile photo on his blog was a pouty-faced cat wearing enormous sunglasses. Hutchins is shy, and blogging from behind a pseudonym suited him just fine.

There's a cliché about hackers being young men working from their bedrooms. Except, in Hutchins's case, it wasn't a cliché. 'I was still living with my parents. I had a bedroom where I had this computer set-up and a server rack,' he tells me.

All of this high-tech work was taking place in a sleepy seaside town in the south-west of England called Ilfracombe, a few minutes from the beach where Marcus surfs. It's a quaint little place in Devon, with twisty roads and ice-cream shops: not the kind of location where you expect to find world-leading tech experts. Hutchins's own family had no idea what he was up to in his bedroom, except that it was vaguely connected to computers. 'I've always been quite a reserved, private person,' he says. 'So I kept the job side of my life very separate from my personal life. I didn't really share a lot of what I do with my parents or my friends or my family.'

That Friday, Hutchins starts the day by taking it easy. He gets lunch at the local fish-and-chip shop. But when he comes back and sits down in front of his computer, he discovers a virus outbreak is in full swing.

'There're NHS hospitals all across the UK reporting they've been hit by the same malware,' he recalls. 'So that was the point where I'm like, "This is something serious."' He immediately contacts a cyber-security friend and gets hold of a sample of the virus (such collaboration is relatively commonplace in the world of tech security).

What Hutchins is now looking at is a specimen of ransomware. You've probably heard of it – at the time of writing it's the most lucrative hacking phenomenon in the world. Just one strain of ransomware made one gang more than \$325m in a single month.[4] Over the years this part of the cybercrime industry has been gradually honed into a highly effective form of digital extortion.

It's also refreshingly simple to explain compared with many other, more intricate cybercrime tactics. In a ransomware attack, hackers infect your computer with a virus that scrambles, or 'encrypts', your files. Then they charge you a ransom to unscramble them, most often paid in the virtual currency Bitcoin, which, if used correctly, makes the transaction impossible to trace back to the culprit.

Sounds easy enough for a techie, but how do you go about obtaining a program capable of encrypting files? Well, handily for the hackers, Microsoft makes this very thing. If a PC user wants to encrypt their own files (perhaps for security or privacy reasons), they can use a tool called Windows Crypto. Once it's done scrambling the files it puts WINCRY at the end of the file name. Of course, if you're scrambling your own files, you hold the decryption key, so you can unscramble your files whenever you want.

The people behind the May 2017 virus used the same software to help encrypt victims' files but with a twist: *they* kept the decryption key and charged victims a fee to get it back. They also had a sense of humour: they renamed WINCRY to WannaCry – because that's what you wanna do when you find out your precious photos, emails and music collection are being held to ransom.[5]

The business model of ransomware may be straightforward, but it still faces the challenge of many cybercrime campaigns: scale. In order to make a profit, you need wide distribution. How are you going to get your ransomware on enough machines to earn the big bucks? Traditionally the answer has been spam email. But Wanna-Cry used a frightening new tactic, as Marcus Hutchins discovered as he peered into the virus code. 'WannaCry spread from computer to computer, which meant you didn't have to open a malicious email or click a strange link. It was just able to hack your computer remotely,' he says.

In our modern world of interconnected tech, this meant that the virus was out of control, spreading indiscriminately.

'People had assumed that they were going after the NHS,' says Hutchins. 'But, seeing all this data, it was clear that this was not targeted to the NHS. It was not even targeted to the UK. This was just hitting anything, everywhere in the world. It was at a phenomenal scale, like nothing I'd ever seen before. It was just infections coming in the thousands every few seconds. It was overwhelming.'

Marcus isn't the only one becoming deeply unsettled by the virus's spread. Three miles from the hospital from which Patrick Ward has just been discharged, in a backstreet behind Vauxhall Underground Station, is a nondescript office block bristling with CCTV. It's the headquarters of the UK's National Crime Agency, the NCA. That Friday morning members of staff are turning up the volume on the office TV. Sky News is reporting a cyber-attack on a hospital in the north-west of England. Other reports soon start to flood in to the NCA, most of which end up on the desk of Mike Hulett, who is Director of Operations for the Agency's National Cybercrime Unit.

'It becomes pretty rapidly apparent around lunchtime on that day that this is not just an isolated incident affecting one hospital or one organization,' he says. Working with the UK's newly formed National Cyber Security Centre, the NCA officers have to figure out how the virus is spreading so quickly. It first hit in Argentina around midnight, and within half a day it was raging across Europe. Hulett and his team discern that the malware is exploiting a particular 'port' – a digital doorway built into computers that allows different machines on the same network to communicate with each other: Port 445, to be specific. On some machines, Port 445 doesn't just allow communication from other computers on the same network, but is also set up to be 'public facing', meaning that anyone, anywhere in the world, can send the computer messages using the port – including computer viruses. This is how WannaCry is spreading around the world. It hops from computer to computer within a network, infecting each one it lands on and scrambling its files. Then it calls out to random computer addresses around the world, hunting for a machine with a public-facing Port 445. Once it finds one, it hops over, infects it and begins to spread within that computer's network too.

The more connected the organization is, the easier it is for WannaCry to spread. And this means that, while it may not have been the intended target, the NHS, as one of the world's largest employers, becomes one of the hardest hit.[6]

As Hulett notes: 'The ability to connect across the country so that your results and tests and so on can be sent quickly from institution to institution means that you've got quite a widely interconnected system particularly susceptible to infection.'

Meanwhile, in his bedroom in Devon, Marcus Hutchins is still dissecting the WannaCry code and spots something unusual. Before infecting a victim, the virus would try to visit a particular website that had a long, seemingly random address. If it found the website was offline, the virus would kick in, scrambling the files, demanding a ransom and attempting to infect other machines. But if the virus found the website was up and running, it would stop, leaving the victim's files untouched. So Hutchins has the idea of checking who actually owns the website that the virus is trying to visit.

'And nobody owned it, so I immediately registered it,' he says. It costs him less than £10 – a cheap investment that would have, as accountants say, 'considerable upside'. By taking control of the website, Marcus has, in fact, brought the outbreak to a halt. The virus code sees that the site is up and running, and so it stops, no longer infecting any computers or trying to spread itself. 'Within seconds of registering the domain, the infection rate just started declining,' he says. 'Usually stopping malware is this huge feat where you're fighting for weeks or months battling the guys on the other end. You're coming up with clever ways to dismantle their infrastructure. I had never come across something so easy.'

Marcus has just stopped one of the world's most dangerous virus outbreaks for the price of a large fish and chips.

Which raises an intriguing question: why would the virus writers build in such an easily discoverable off-switch? The most compelling explanation is that WannaCry was released before it was ready. Virus writers often build in this kind of off-switch as a safety brake when they're developing a piece of malware in the lab. That way, if the virus accidentally escapes, they have a handy way of stopping it quickly. Usually the off-switch would be removed or obscured before the virus is unleashed, but in this case it wasn't. And there were other indications that WannaCry wasn't quite finished. Normally, ransomware wranglers would create a new Bitcoin wallet address for each victim (such addresses can be created at the click of a mouse thanks to Bitcoin's virtual nature), which makes the transactions harder to trace. But, in the case of WannaCry, there were only three Bitcoin addresses written into the code, holding out the prospect that the payments could eventually be traced back to a culprit.

For Hutchins, finding the off-switch was an unexpected windfall. He may have felt it was almost too easy, but that didn't stop him from becoming famous overnight. Soon the British tabloids found out his identity and ran headlines about the 'accidental hero' who had saved the world without even leaving his bedroom. 'They had my name,' says Hutchins. 'They had a photo of me that they found on someone's Twitter feed. And, at that point, they were camping out on my lawn, outside the front gate of my house. It was horrifying. I was never really a fan of the idea of fame. I never wanted it. And suddenly now everyone who's been following my blog and anyone reading the world's media knows who I am, which was just terrifying.'

It was also a big worry for Hulett and his colleagues at the National Crime Agency. They feared that whoever was behind WannaCry might now go after Hutchins. 'From a physical, real-world-risk perspective, we're looking at it thinking, "You've spoiled someone's party, and I don't know whose party you spoiled,"' he says. 'It could be some other kid in their bedroom somewhere, or it could be some nasty organized-crime gang, or a state.'

Hutchins may have dreaded the spotlight, but his new-found fame did come with some rewards: he gained thousands more social media followers. A local restaurant offered him free pizza for a year. And his family – including his mother, who's an NHS nurse – finally understood what he does for a living. But, as we shall see, his celebrity came with an awful cost that would throw his life into turmoil. Because Hutchins had been hiding a secret all the way along, something that would go on to cast a long shadow over his heroic acts.

Meantime, thanks to his work, the WannaCry attack was over. The damage was far from fixed, however. The victims whose data had been scrambled didn't get that data back. The impact was particularly severe within the NHS. In England, for example, a third of the groups that run NHS hospitals were either infected or had to disconnect computers to protect themselves. Almost 7,000 appointments had to be cancelled, including more than a hundred urgent cancer cases.[7] NHS staff I spoke to told me they worked extra hours to rebuild their systems and get patients' appointments back on track – including Patrick Ward's: a couple of months later he got his operation, which, as he had hoped, gave him back his health.

For Mike Hulett and his colleagues at the National Crime Agency's Cybercrime Unit, however, the real work had only just started. 'Very often what we find with cyber-cases is the incident itself is over quite quickly,' he says. 'What always takes longer, though, is the investigation that goes into it. We've got one of the most destructive and impactive cyber-attacks that we've seen for many years in the UK, and it's our job to try and identify and bring whoever's responsible to justice.'

At first, WannaCry looked like a typical piece of ransomware. When police investigate these attacks, they can sometimes use the same tactic applied in kidnapping cases: get into direct negotiation with the extortionists and try to track them down. In some past ransomware instances, the police were able to contact the crooks, and even on occasion managed to pinpoint their exact location and make an arrest. But Hulett and his team had no such luck with WannaCry – because whoever had unleashed it appears to have had no interest in helping their victims to pay the ransom and recover their data. 'To my knowledge, there weren't any cases around the world where someone had successfully paid the amounts and received a decryption key in return,' he says.

So the NCA was now dealing with a ransomware campaign in which the people behind it didn't seem interested in getting the ransom. That rang alarm bells. 'In this case, you've got something which appears to be, on the face of it, a financially motivated crime but there's no real way of actually making money out of it,' says Hulett. There's one obvious theory: that it's not a cybercrime gang but a nation-state. Realizing that the investigation would have international scope, the Brits began to share their findings with their American counterparts, and that's when things started to get really uncomfortable. Because, as they dug deeper into the malware, the investigators found worrying evidence that, incredibly, some of the code had originated within the US intelligence community itself.

*

The version of WannaCry that hit in May 2017 was just the latest iteration: there had been at least two previous versions with very similar code, suggesting the same author or team was behind all three campaigns. But the earlier versions weren't particularly successful. What made the May 2017 iteration so much more destructive was the inclusion of two new pieces of code. They had typically esoteric names – Eternal Blue and Double Pulsar – but it was these two components that had turned WannaCry into a digital pandemic.

Previously hackers would have to send their viruses to victims by email and try to trick them into activating them, which is what happened at Sony and Bangladesh Bank. Eternal Blue and Double Pulsar do away with all that. Between them they automatically spread the virus from computer to computer using the Port 445 technique, and then automatically detonate it when it arrives on a new computer.[8] No more would the hackers have to send dodgy emails and wait for their victims to click. This virus spreads itself. That's new, and for the tech-security community it's a frightening development.

What's even more terrifying perhaps is that these dangerous new hacking tools were not the work of a shadowy cybercrime gang, but were actually developed by the US National Security Agency. In order to understand how they ended up infecting computers around the globe, you need to take a trip into the murky world of the exploit traders, or, as some call it, the cyberweapons market.

It works like this. Imagine you're a talented hacker and you come across a flaw in a major piece of software (like the Port 445 trick described above). You then come up with some code that capitalizes on that flaw, called an 'exploit'. You've got a few options: you can be honest and tell the company whose software you've hacked in the hope they fix the flaw; you can be dishonest and try to use your new-found hack to make illegal money for yourself; or you can take the middle way – sell your knowledge to someone else and let them make the tricky ethical decisions about how to use it.[9]

This third path leads to the cyberweapons marketplace, where brokers buy exploits from hackers and sell them on to organizations which want to use them. It's a world as secretive as it is lucrative. There are occasional insights into just how lucrative. One broker, for example, offered $1m to anyone who could find a flaw in TOR, the software behind the so-called 'dark web' of hidden sites. The broker's company claimed it would sell on the exploit only to governments and law-enforcement agencies.[10] Many cyberweapons brokers make the same claim, but, let's face it: selling these tools to a government is no guarantee that they'll be used ethically.

It's not just freelance hackers who are constantly trying to find these flaws in the software we all use so they can exploit them. Governments do it in-house, according to former National Security Agency analyst Priscilla Moriuchi: 'Governments are going to devote time to discover vulnerabilities in software and are going to develop exploits for them. We might not like it. And we don't like it when our adversaries do that.'

If the world were a kinder place, as soon as any government found out about a tech vulnerability, it would share that information with everyone else so we could all be protected. But the world isn't like that. Governments' hackers actively hunt for these vulnerabilities, and when they create an exploit for them they regard those as weapons – tools to break into other governments' systems. Making your opponents aware of your exploits blunts their effectiveness. Who ever heard of a government giving away its weapons?[11]

In the case of the Eternal Blue exploit, it appears that the NSA knew about the Microsoft Port 445 vulnerability as early as 2012, but kept it secret for more than five years. Then something remarkable happened. A group of hackers called the Shadow Brokers – which, some say, is connected to the Russian state – managed to steal this deadly piece of software, along with its Double Pulsar buddy, and put them up for auction. 'Ultimately the auction didn't work,' says Mike Hulett. 'So early in April 2017, the exploit was released into the wild. They gave away this cyber-tool so it was there to be used by anybody.'

Suddenly the Americans watched as their advanced cyber-weapons leaked out into the online underworld. It was as though someone had turned up to a backstreet arms bazaar where they're selling handguns and petrol bombs and started handing out free Stealth Bombers.

By early 2017 Microsoft had been warned about the Port 445 vulnerability and had issued an update to fix it. But the update wasn't automatic or compulsory, so millions of computers remained vulnerable. They were therefore sitting ducks when the hackers unleashed their new strain of ransomware, now with upgraded capability courtesy of the NSA.

As Mike Hulett explains: 'You've got a reasonably crude bit of ransomware attached to, effectively, a weapons-grade exploit, something that was originally designed by the NSA for whatever purpose the NSA needed it for. But this is now something which is being weaponized and used against countries all over the world [including the US]. So a certain irony there, one would say. Part of the reason why the FBI and other US agencies were so keen to put a lot of resource into finding out who was responsible.'

And, on that front, the NCA and the FBI were about to get a break.

At this point, the FBI in Los Angeles was still working on the attacks on Sony Pictures Entertainment and Bangladesh Bank. 'We've got the FBI looking at Sony back in 2014 and we've got the UK looking at WannaCry in 2017,' says Hulett. 'We're working back in time and they're working slightly forward in time. And, ultimately, what we're trying to do is to build a chain that goes from one to the other.'

The British investigators found a vital link in that chain. As they analysed some of the earlier versions of WannaCry, they found a clue. Hidden within the code was a chart full of data that helped the hackers to remotely control the computers they'd taken over.

That caught the interest of the FBI team in Los Angeles and Tony Lewis, the Assistant US Attorney in California. 'Once that data table was discovered, it was searched for in other malware,'

says Lewis. 'Lo and behold, we found the same data table in malware found at Sony Pictures, and malware found at other financial
institutions that were victims of the same actors.'

The 'actors' he's talking about are the members of the Lazarus
Group. According to both the FBI and the NCA, WannaCry was
the work of North Korea's elite hackers.

North Korea denied all this, and through a spokesperson
described the accusation as 'a grave political provocation by the US
aimed at inducing the international society into a confrontation
against the DPRK by tarnishing the image of the dignified country
and demonizing it'.

But if the law-enforcement agencies are right, it presents a worrying picture: the Lazarus Group's hackers have evolved from breaking
into a Hollywood studio, to tackling a national bank in Bangladesh,
to now unleashing a global, digital pandemic that's taken hospitals
out of action. But, as the summer of 2017 rolled on, it wasn't just in
cyberspace that North Korea appeared to be ramping up its
activity.

On 4 July 2017 North Korea launched its first Intercontinental Ballistic Missile (ICBM). It had been fired on a 'lofted' trajectory,
meaning it travelled almost vertically up and down and therefore
landed fairly close by, in the Sea of Japan (to the consternation of
the Japanese government). But if fired on a longer trajectory, it is
estimated that it could have reached Alaska.[12] If the launch date had
been calculated to enrage North Korea's old enemy the US, it
worked. Not that then-President Donald J. Trump needed much
encouragement to fly off the handle. He went on to deride Kim Jong
Un as a 'madman', nicknaming him 'little rocket man' and describing
him as on a 'suicide mission'.[13]

Trump's rhetoric made little difference. Within a month there
was a second ICBM launch. This time, estimates reckoned it might
be able to reach as far as Los Angeles.[14] The North Korean issue was
heating up on all fronts – military, diplomatic and cyber. You might
have thought all of this would worry Marcus Hutchins, the young
man who successfully brought WannaCry to a halt. As Mike Hulett

put it, he'd brought someone's party to a stop. Now it was being alleged that the party host was none other than Kim Jong Un, fast emerging as one of the most dangerous men on the planet. But Hutchins had other things on his mind: 'I had just been arrested by the US government. So I had bigger problems at the time.'

Hutchins's story had just taken another wild twist . . .

In August 2017, after probably the most intense few months of his life, Hutchins flew to Las Vegas to attend DEF CON, the world's largest annual hacking conference. Thanks to his work on Wanna-Cry, he was treated like a celebrity. 'I had a lot of people approaching me for photos and even some people asking for autographs,' he remembers. 'It was more attention than I had ever got in my entire life. And I was somewhat uncomfortable with it. We had booked this mansion quite far from the Vegas Strip. So I kind of ended up just hiding in the mansion and partying for most of the holiday.

'We got to do some crazy things. We went to shooting ranges, drove Lamborghinis, and we obviously had this nice house to party in. So it felt like the holiday of a lifetime until I got to the airport. And then that's when things went south.'

Having hardly slept and with the beginnings of a considerable hangover, Hutchins managed to make it through check-in for his trip back to the UK. 'When I got to the lounge to wait to board my flight, there was a tap on the shoulder. "Are you Marcus Hutchins?" To which I obviously answered "yes".'

It was US customs officials. At first Hutchins assumed they wanted to ask him about his role in stopping the WannaCry attack. But, as they interrogated him for an hour and a half and other law-enforcement bodies got involved, he realized this was about something else. His past was catching up with him.

'When I was a lot younger, I used my skills for some less-than-good things. I got involved in some criminal hacking.'

When Hutchins first discovered the world of malware as a teen-ager, he actually started to write some of it himself. He became good at it and someone eventually approached him for help. 'I was basically a contract programmer for a guy who sells malware on the Internet. I wrote some malware and another person wrote some code to steal money from banks, and that got combined with my malware. I got paid for the bit of code I wrote. It was never really my intention to have anything to do with bank fraud or stealing money. I really screwed up. I partnered with someone I shouldn't have, I got in way too deep.'

From that moment on, Marcus knew his fate was sealed. 'That was the minute when I just knew that at some point in my life I was going to prison. I knew that this was coming.' What he didn't know was that the moment would arrive at the very point he'd become world-famous for using his tech skills for good. Within twenty-four hours Hutchins went from partying in a Vegas mansion to staring at the walls of a prison cell. 'Life comes at you fast,' he says. 'I basically just found myself in a concrete box lying on this hard floor.'

After a couple of weeks Hutchins was released. The cyber-security community reportedly came to his rescue by putting up the bail. The judge allowed him to live in Los Angeles under house arrest while awaiting trial. In July 2019 Hutchins flew to Wisconsin for his hearing in a Milwaukee Federal Court. And, after weighing the importance of his role in stopping WannaCry, the judge showed some leniency. Instead of ten years in prison, he sentenced Hutchins to 'time served', meaning he could go free.[15] He's now settled in the US and has made a new life for himself in California, still working in tech security. And, as an added bonus, the surfing is a heck of a lot warmer than on his native beaches in Devon.

Meanwhile, some in the tech-security community had been totting up the profits made by the WannaCry attack and come to a surprising conclusion. It appeared to be a disaster for the hackers. The ransoms paid added up to just a few hundred thousand dollars: peanuts compared with the hundreds of millions raked in by other ransomware campaigns. The WannaCry hackers had created the world's most effective virus outbreak in recent history and made barely enough to buy a Lamborghini.

But perhaps looking at the profit margin was missing the bigger picture. If WannaCry was the work of the Lazarus Group, the key point wasn't necessarily how much money they made. It was about what they did with it. They managed to make the cash disappear. And, this time, it didn't take months of work and teams of middlemen and fixers scattered across the world. It was all done digitally and took just a couple of days. I got a deeper insight into this process than most, because I spent months on a wild goose chase trying to track down the WannaCry money.

Bitcoin is often billed as an 'anonymous' digital currency. That's not always true. Bitcoin transactions take place by sending funds between digital wallets, each of which has a unique ID – a long string of letters and numbers. Every transaction between every wallet is published online for all to see (this is called the 'blockchain'). This might seem counterintuitive for a currency aiming for anonymity, but it's an essential part of the Bitcoin system. There's no bank or government to oversee it, so it's only by making all the transactions public that you can ensure no one pulls a fast one by, for example, trying to send the same funds to two different wallets simultaneously. Besides, Bitcoiners argue, even if all the wallet IDs and transactions are public, that doesn't mean the users' real-world identities are revealed.

But that logic only goes so far. For example, if I ask you to pay me via my Bitcoin wallet and I give you the wallet ID, you can now link that ID to my real-world identity. Sure, I can set up a new wallet at the click of a mouse, but as soon as I transfer money from that new wallet to my old one or vice versa it will show up in the blockchain record, and you can tie the new wallet ID to me.

So it's sometimes possible to trace transactions through this public blockchain record and track them back to a real person. Which is exactly what I tried to do with the WannaCry ransom payments.

You may recall that the virus code contained only three Bitcoin wallet IDs, meaning all the ransoms ended up being paid into one of those three wallets. On 3 August 2017, weeks after the WannaCry outbreak, at 3 a.m. UK time, all three wallets were cleaned out within a matter of minutes. Using the blockchain, I was able to trace where the payments went. It led me on a merry dance. Whoever was withdrawing the money had set up dozens of wallet IDs and was moving the Bitcoins through them fast (this is a digital version of the 'layering' process in money laundering. In cryptocurrency circles it's called 'tumbling'). But, thanks to the blockchain record, I was able to keep up – just. The majority of the money ended up in only one wallet, and after a great deal of work I finally managed to link it to an individual. Incredibly it seemed to belong to a guy living in Croydon, South London. Could the man behind one of the world's most disruptive cyber-attacks really be living just a bus ride away from me? Even for the wild story of WannaCry this seemed too good a twist to be true. And it was. The man had nothing to do with the hack – his details had been hijacked by whoever was laundering the WannaCry money.

In fact, the Bitcoin wallet that received the funds belonged to a company called HitBTC. It's a money-exchanging firm that specializes in swapping cryptocurrencies like Bitcoin for 'fiat' currencies like the pound and dollar, and vice versa. Such firms have Bitcoin wallets that send and receive thousands of transactions per day – a good place to hide some stolen money. When I contacted HitBTC to ask what had happened to the WannaCry money, it didn't answer my questions, and instead referred me to their Anti-Illegal Activity Policy. It seems in this case the policy didn't succeed in stopping the illegal activity. The WannaCry money had vanished into the sea of digital cash sloshing around HitBTC, and was almost certainly withdrawn in a way that was now impossible to trace. The hackers had got clean away with the loot. And compared with the months taken to harvest the Bangladesh Bank cash, all this had taken less than forty-eight hours.

So it seems the idea of WannaCry wasn't necessarily to make a profit – it was a dry run in cutting-edge money laundering. The Lazarus Group's hackers had learnt a new skill. Now they would apply that skill to making sums that would put the Bangladesh Bank heist into the shade.

14

Old Tricks, New Money

As historic moments go, it's somewhat underwhelming: there's no red carpet, no glitzy venue, no flags or fanfare. Just a patch of sandy earth and some shabby blue prefabricated buildings. But it's here, for the first time in sixty-five years, that a North Korean leader would visit the South, the land of its mortal enemy. The venue is Panmunjom, a 'truce village' inside the Demilitarized Zone separating the two countries. The South's President, Moon Jae-in, is waiting patiently, careful to stay behind the two-inch-high strip of concrete that marks the border between the two nations. As you watch him, it's hard not to feel the ridiculousness of such boundaries – it's like a kid pretending there's an impenetrable force field in front of them.

Then Kim Jong Un approaches from the Northern side. Gradually his phalanx of security guards and dignitaries falls away, and it's just him, striding along in the sun with his trademark black baggy suit. As he steps on to the pathway leading to the border, he smiles: a broad, natural grin. Moon holds out a hand, also smiling. Kim takes it. And then Moon invites him over the dividing line. The force field is broken. Kim Jong Un is in South Korea, the territory that's been his country's arch-enemy for decades (if only by a yard or two). There are moments of unexpected comedy: camera crews on both sides want to get a shot of the handshake with a clear background, but they keep getting in each other's way. Moon and Kim are caught in the crossfire as the media crews yell at each other and sprint out of the way. Then another bizarre moment as Kim seemingly spontaneously takes Moon by the hand and leads him back across the concrete strip. The photographers are laughing now and applause breaks out. The *Washington Post* is live-streaming the event on YouTube, and, as the two make their way back on to the Southern side of the border, one of the viewers leaves a note in the comments section: #PEACEFORKOREA.[1]

At that moment it was an aspiration that probably seemed as close as it had at any time in the last six decades. The April 2018 meeting was part of an unprecedented thaw in relations. In February of that year North Korean athletes had attended the Winter Olympics in Pyeongchang in the South. They had marched into the opening ceremony alongside their Southern counterparts under a unification flag, and even competed alongside them in the women's ice hockey.[2] Compared with the bitter dispute over the 1988 Summer Olympics in Seoul, which some linked to the bombing of the Korean Air flight, it looked like a remarkable breakthrough.

In May 2018 North Korea agreed to blow up some of the tunnels it had used for nuclear testing, interpreted by some in the West as a further sign the country was finally moving towards a compromise. Video of the explosion was released and aired on TV news channels around the world.[3]

But, away from the cameras, North Korea's hackers were not turning their digital swords into ploughshares. Far from it, in fact. According to the FBI, they had taken the cryptocurrency skills they learnt in the WannaCry attack and were now using them to pull in vast amounts of money in a global crime spree.

Ljubljana, the capital of Slovenia, might not be the first place that comes to mind when you think of high-tech financial services. But that's one of the things about the new world of cryptocurrency: the action isn't necessarily happening in New York, Hong Kong or London. It's equally likely to be taking place in a little office somewhere off the beaten track, staffed by a small team of techies and dreamers. Such was the case with the Slovenian firm NiceHash. The company's business model is quite tricky to explain to those unfamiliar with the inner workings of cryptocurrency. Suffice to say, its main aim is to provide a marketplace where people interested in this new type of money can buy or rent services from those with the technological know-how and computing power to make it happen. NiceHash then takes a commission for linking them up with each other.

It may be niche, but NiceHash was making serious money back in 2017, partly thanks to the meteoric growth that Bitcoin and other currencies were experiencing throughout that year. In January you could have bought one Bitcoin for around $1,000. Twelve months later you could have sold it for just over $19,000 (if you're comparing that to the returns you got from your bank account during the same period with dismay, keep reading: investing in digital currencies may be lucrative but it's also fraught with risk).

Like many cryptocurrency businesses, NiceHash allowed customers to keep their funds in Bitcoin wallets administered by the company.[4] They could log in, check their balance, and then send and receive money to and from other NiceHash users. But, on 6 December 2017, as Bitcoin's price surged above $11,000, NiceHash's customers logged in to find an unpleasant surprise. The money had gone. Hackers had broken into the company's systems and stolen thousands of Bitcoins. The firm scrambled to get on top of the situation, remembers Marko Gašparič, who was their Product Manager at the time. 'At first I didn't think it was real,' he says. 'It's an emergency situation, everyone was called back to work. We were under attack. We tried to do everything we could to save our business and protect our customers.'

What really worried those at the company was that NiceHash was no easy target for the hackers. Gašparič says they took security very seriously. Whoever had broken in had managed to get round all their protections and controls. 'It was very well planned,' he says. 'I do not believe that an amateur or an individual person could execute such an attack.'

Soon enough, the case came to the attention of the FBI, and, after analysing the theft, they reached the same conclusion. NiceHash had been attacked by one of the world's most professional hacking crews, the Lazarus Group. The tactics were depressingly familiar. It sent a phishing email to NiceHash on 4 December, tricking an employee into downloading a virus which gave them access to NiceHash's network. By 6 December, the Lazarus Group's members had enough understanding and control of the company's systems to transfer out Bitcoins worth $75m.[5]

'This is the largest theft in the history of Slovenia,' says Gašparič. NiceHash eventually reimbursed all its customers in full, setting aside a proportion of its profits each month to do so.

Compared with previous thefts attributed to the Lazarus Group, the NiceHash raid was a quantum leap. In just two days it had made almost as much money as it had during the year it'd spent on the Bangladesh Bank job. And this time there was no network of Chinese gamblers or Japanese fixers to pay off. Instead, the entire haul would potentially go direct to the hackers' own Bitcoin wallets, the anonymous stores of money sitting in cyberspace.

The benefits of this new type of criminal enterprise were apparently not lost on the Lazarus Group's hackers. They hopped on the crypto bandwagon with gusto. NiceHash was just one example: throughout 2017 and 2018 the gang hit a slew of cryptocurrency businesses, according to the FBI's investigators as they raced to keep up. The hackers got their modus operandi down to a fine art. A phishing email would arrive in the inbox of an employee, who would inadvertently download a virus, and within a short time tens of millions of dollars would be transferred out from the digital wallets of the victim's company, never to be seen again. The rapidity of the money movements was bewildering, and frequently foxed any efforts to recover the stolen money.

For example, one cryptocurrency firm tried a clever tactic to fight back after it was robbed: it created a system whereby the wallets into which the stolen funds were transferred were marked with a tag reading 'do_not_accept_trades: owner_of_this_account_is_hacker'.[6] This would make the stolen money 'effectively unusable', said the firm. But the hackers responded by simply setting up hundreds of wallets and moving the money so fast that the tagging system couldn't keep up. The funds were never recovered.

The Lazarus Group's operatives were also getting smarter at tricking people into downloading its viruses, according to security researchers. It had started using social media sites such as LinkedIn to lure its victims. In one case, a techie from a cryptocurrency firm received a recruitment message about a juicy new role at a rival company which seemed tailor-made for their skill set. That's because it was – the hackers had researched their target on LinkedIn and drawn up a job spec that was guaranteed to appeal. But, before the victim could open the Word file containing the application form, they were presented with a pop-up screen telling them that the document was protected by European data protection regulations. To access the job application, the recipient was told they would have to click to 'enable content'. That was all it took. By clicking, they unwittingly activated a digital backdoor hidden inside the Word file and allowed the hackers access to their computer, and thence to the company's network. Perhaps there's some consolation for the victim in the fact that, according to the security researchers, the hackers were using exactly the same trick in around twenty other countries at the same time.[7]

But, as we learnt from the Bangladesh Bank heist, getting in is just the start for the hackers. Escaping with the money is a whole different ballgame. Although cryptocurrency exchanges seemed to be a softer target, and although stealing from them allowed the hackers to digitally zip the stolen money around the world extremely quickly, they still faced challenges. At some stage those ill-gotten digital gains would need to be converted into pounds, dollars and so on. After all, if you want to buy a top-of-the-line Mercedes or a crate of high-end cognac – the kind of luxury goods North Korea's elite craves – you can't easily use Bitcoin (at least, not at the current time). The hackers faced a second obstacle too: because of the surge in crypto-crime, the exchanges were getting more careful about the transactions they handled, and putting in more security checks to prevent money laundering.

But, according to the FBI, by the end of 2018 the Lazarus Group was becoming increasingly adept, not only at getting round these new impediments but also at turning its stolen virtual currency into cash. And, to do so, the group was forging new links with networks of skilled, high-tech criminals who were only too willing to lend a hand, as one intriguing case illustrates.

The FBI had been investigating the theft in late 2018 of around $230m from an unnamed cryptocurrency exchange.[8] Tracing the money had led the investigators on the same kind of perplexing journey I'd endured trying to track the ransom payments from the WannaCry attack covered in the previous chapter. The money disappeared into a tangle of digital wallets. Of course, the FBI has far more resources than I do, so you'd expect it to have a lot more luck. Sadly not: as they delved down and down into the transactions, the investigators realized the hackers had come up with a clever strategy to throw them off the scent, and also circumvent the anti-money-laundering tactics that the cryptocurrency exchanges were now implementing.

The hackers had realized that trying to swap thousands of Bitcoins for millions of dollars in one go would ring alarm bells at the exchanges. So they began to use a tactic called a 'peel chain'. They would carve off a fraction of the total amount of Bitcoin they wanted to launder and send it to a cryptocurrency exchange for conversion into fiat currency like dollars. Then they'd send the rest of the Bitcoin hoard to another wallet, peel off another small fraction, send it to an exchange for conversion to dollars, and send the remaining Bitcoin to yet another wallet. And so it went on, sometimes hundreds of times. They automated the transfers using a computer, meaning that dozens of transactions could be done in a minute. Tracing it all quickly became a nightmare for the investigators.[9]

But, despite the hackers' best efforts, the FBI and its partners were able to trace some of the money to several cryptocurrency exchanges. And that led to more good news for the investigators. Some of the exchanges had implemented a new security check: in order to set up an account, customers now had to identify themselves by emailing across a selfie holding up some kind of official

ID, such as a driving licence or a passport. The FBI knew which accounts had been used to launder the money. If it could get the photos of the account holders from the exchanges, it should be able to get the real-world identities of those involved. The next step could be a knock at the door – and potentially a criminal conviction.

The investigators received the first of the account holders' photos from one of the exchanges. The picture showed a young Asian man with neatly coiffed hair sitting in a big computer chair and holding up a South Korean government ID. It looked like the investigators had lucked out – this man was a key connection in the plot to steal $230m from an unnamed currency exchange, and now they had all his personal details. But there was a snag. A second account holder's photo arrived. This time the man was Caucasian and he was holding up a German government ID card. But there was something familiar about the shot. The investigators looked closer and realized this man was wearing exactly the same T-shirt as the man in the first photo. Not only that, their fingers were in exactly the same positions. The photos looked incredibly realistic, but they were both fakes – digitally altered versions of a legitimate picture that had been ripped off the Internet.

The accounts at the cryptocurrency exchanges had been set up by the Lazarus Group, whose hackers had swapped the heads on the two photos and changed the ID documents to match, just to fool the currency exchanges into allowing them to create the accounts.[10]

Hackers 1, FBI 0.

But the Lazarus Group's hackers weren't out of the woods yet. Having finagled the money into the cryptocurrency exchanges, they would now need to extricate it and turn it into cash. For that, according to the FBI, they used two Chinese accomplices who'd advertised themselves for exactly this kind of service (for a fee, naturally). They were experts in moving money seamlessly from the digital realm to the 'real' world and used a bewildering network of resources to do so. One of them was described as having accounts at nine different Chinese banks. The other managed to launder some of the stolen Bitcoin by selling it in exchange for iTunes gift cards, which could in turn be sold on for cash.[11]

Throughout 2017 and 2018 investigators watched as North Korea's hackers became ever-more adept, not only at successfully robbing cryptocurrency exchanges but at vanishing the money too. It didn't stop there. The Lazarus Group was already cooking up its next cryptocurrency plot – one which showed just how much it understood about this new financial technology.

In October 2017 Jonathan Foong Kah Keong was approached with an interesting offer. He'd been active in the maritime industry in Singapore for decades via his company Singclass, and was contacted by a man who 'needed my expertise on shipping issues', according to Foong.[12]

The man said his name was Tony Walker, and he had an idea he wanted Foong to help with. It was a bit complex, but, if it worked, the returns could be massive.

Essentially, the scheme was all about investment in shipping. Walker's idea was that people would be able to invest money to take a share in a particular vessel. For example, they could pay $100 for a chunk of *The Empress*, or whatever the boat was called. But, instead of getting a piece of paper denoting their share, the investor would be given it in the form of digital currency, sort of like Bitcoin but for ships ('Boatcoin', if you like). Investors could then buy and sell these Boatcoins. It was a traditional infrastructure investment scheme, but with a cryptocurrency twist.

Walker had put together a slick business presentation for potential investors. The scheme was a win-win, he said: shipping companies would get much-needed money, and ordinary investors would get a chance to break into the esoteric world of maritime finance via the hot new trend of cryptocurrency. The firm was called Marine Chain. It was registered in Hong Kong on 12 April 2018, a swish website was launched, and Walker set the initial target for investment at $20m.[13]

He then went about recruiting an international team to run the company: a French Chief Technology Officer living in Hong Kong, a Chief Security Officer in the US, a Sustainability Officer in Finland and more. He also hired legal teams in four separate Hong Kong firms to advise on the business.[14] Walker was throwing money around as he readied his multimillion-dollar scheme for launch.

But, despite the flurry of activity, Walker himself was strangely absent from the fledgling company's meetings. He issued directions over email and text and joined meetings via online chat, claiming to be in various countries where he was meeting 'potential investors', including Italy, China and the US.

There was also confusion about the precise role of Walker. It seems some of Marine Chain's consultants were given the impression he was only supposed to be an adviser to Foong, and were perplexed to find themselves receiving orders directly from him.

Behind the scenes there were more warning signs. He may have used the name 'Tony Walker' when approaching Foong and talking to investors, but the mysterious man behind Marine Chain then told Foong it was only a pseudonym; his real name was Julien Kim, which was the name he used when signing contracts. Furthermore, Kim started to make strange demands about the business: he wanted Foong to own all the shares in the company. Foong pushed back, telling Kim in a text message (*sic*): 'Bro too much responsibility not much time to look after the operational aspect.'[15] Nonetheless, Foong began to work for Marine Chain, talking about the company at events, sometimes being described as its CEO.[16] He also paid the company's suppliers, as he was directed to by Kim. Then one day the messages from Marine Chain's founder suddenly stopped, and so did the money. Kim disappeared in July 2018, leaving Foong with a stack of bills to pay. He tried to get in touch with Kim, as did others working for Marine Chain, but to no avail. The company was wound up in September 2018. Meantime Kim had vanished as mysteriously as he'd arrived. Perhaps he got spooked by what was emerging about Marine Chain on Internet forums. Online sleuths had been sniffing around the company, and were making some worrying claims about the truth behind the firm – and the mysterious man who'd created it.

On 5 April 2018, just as Marine Chain was gearing up for company registration, a user named Arsenalfan5000 on the Reddit online forum posted a comment entitled 'Marine Chain.io: North Korea scam currency'. Arsenalfan5000 pointed out that the company's website appeared to be a straight-up copy of a similar firm's. Then they added something even more damning: 'It looks like at least one of the founders is North Korea national hiding behind a fake LinkedIn profile.' Quite how a Reddit user could claim to have discovered a North Korean connection is unclear, especially given the amount of secrecy Tony Walker aka Julien Kim placed around his identity. And Arsenalfan5000 didn't seem like an expert: the account on Reddit had posted only once, leaving this single comment about Marine Chain, and hasn't uttered a peep since. Some suspect that Arsenalfan5000 is actually a cover identity for someone connected to an intelligence service, leaving a breadcrumb of information online for others to find. Because it turned out he or she was bang on the money when it came to the Pyongyang connection.

Soon after Marine Chain went out of business, others started to publish links tracing the company back to North Korea.[17] Foong had a long history with the country: his company was connected to at least two North Korean cargo ships.[18]

It makes perfect sense that a dodgy shipping scheme like Marine Chain would link back to North Korea. As sanctions have bitten ever-deeper into the regime's connection to the outside world, marine cargo has become an increasingly vital way to smuggle banned goods into the country. As a result, shipping has also become a key focus for those tasked with monitoring the enforcement of sanctions against North Korea. Twice a year the United Nations Security Council publishes a report from its Panel of Experts, which tries to detect any attempts made by the Pyongyang regime to evade the sanctions. The reports are several hundred pages long, and usually around half is devoted to allegations that shipping routes have been used to flout the restrictions. The detail is incredible: there are grainy undercover photos of rusting container vessels out at sea; copies of passports of those accused of running smuggling operations; photocopies of page after page of cargo manifests. Shipping is an obsession for those keeping watch on North Korea.

All of which explains why a North Korean might set up a shipping-investment company from behind a pseudonym. But it doesn't explain how Julien Kim intended to use Marine Chain for the regime. After all, from the looks of it all he did was spend money on it, hiring expensive advisers and shelling out for other services via Jonathan Foong Kah Keong. Perhaps Marine Chain was an experiment that didn't pan out? Maybe Kim realized that a cryptocurrency-based shipping investment scheme just wasn't going to work? Or maybe he got spooked by the Internet chatter linking him and his company to North Korea? Whatever the explanation, it wasn't the end of the story of Julien Kim – he'd go on to play a pivotal role in another North Korean scheme – this time, one which would be far more successful than Marine Chain.

And it turns out Marine Chain wasn't a total failure, because, according to the FBI, it taught North Korea's hackers something: there's a world of people out there who are very interested in all things cryptocurrency, and they're prepared (like those who joined the Marine Chain team) to sign up to a murky enterprise in the hope of getting rich. The Lazarus Group would now use this fact in the next wave of its high-tech crime spree.

Celas Trade Pro appeared on the cryptocurrency scene in May 2018, the month after Marine Chain was registered. Celas's website was in tones of cool blue: a colour that oozes financial probity. Its offering was simple: users could download a piece of software which would allow them to trade in cryptocurrencies; to ride the whirlwind of price spikes that was making millionaires out of a lucky few. Sure enough, once downloaded, the software opened up with an impressive-looking interface through which the budding financier could trade Bitcoin for dollars. Of course, in order to do so the user would have to grant the software access to his or her Bitcoin wallet, and that's where Celas's evil side kicked in. The software came with a hidden addition: a computer virus that aimed to prise open the victim's Bitcoin wallet and steal whatever was inside.[19]

In fact, Celas was a scam set up by North Korea's hackers to steal even more cryptocurrency. The Russian cyber-security company Kaspersky analysed the virus that victims unknowingly downloaded from Celas's website and found a piece of malware previously attributed to the Lazarus Group.[20] (This was somewhat ironic, given that Celas Trade Pro's website proudly featured the Kaspersky logo, alongside those of McAfee, F-Secure and ESET – all of them cyber-security companies that have investigated the Lazarus Group's activities over the years, and whose logos were used without their knowledge or permission to make the Celas site look more legitimate.)

For their Celas project, the Lazarus Group's operatives had ripped off a legitimate piece of software to create a convincing-looking trading platform, and hidden their viruses behind it. They had then sent emails to cryptocurrency-exchange employees plugging the new Celas Trade Pro service and urging them to try it, in the hope they would download the virus, giving Lazarus's hackers access to the exchange's inner workings and allowing the group to steal its funds.

Kaspersky blew the whistle on Celas in August 2018. The hackers didn't seem to care. They just rebranded and moved on, again and again.

WorldBit-Bot was launched in October 2018, according to the FBI, to be followed over the next two years by iCryptoFx, Union Crypto Trader, Kupay Wallet, CoinGo Trade, JMT Trader, Dorusio, CryptoNeuro Trader and Ants2Whale (a reference to crypto-currency slang for going from a small, poor investor to a big, rich one). They all had different websites but offered the same trading platform, with the same malicious software hidden inside, nicknamed 'AppleJeus' by security researchers. Every time one iteration was exposed as a scam, the Lazarus Group's hackers simply launched the next one. And it worked: in August 2020 someone inside an unnamed financial-services company in New York downloaded

CryptoNeuro Trader. The viruses kicked in. The Lazarus Group walked away with $11.8m.[21]

At the time of writing the most recent hack to be attributed to North Korea's cyber-attackers is not only one of the largest in cryptocurrency history, but it also shows the speed with which the group evolves its tactics.

In September 2020 the cryptocurrency-exchange KuCoin announced it had been hacked – security researchers reported that $275m had gone missing.[22] Instantly, suspicion started to fall on the Lazarus Group. But this time attribution would be even harder. The hackers had learnt from their past jobs, and made some tweaks to their tactics.

As we discovered earlier, cryptocurrency exchanges had begun to demand photo ID from users in a bid to tackle fraud and money laundering. In the KuCoin attack, the hackers would get round this by taking the money to 'swap services'. In a traditional exchange a user would, for example, pay Bitcoin into the exchange's wallet, and then the exchange would pay out in dollars. This meant the exchanges were responsible for handling their customers' money, and, as a result, had introduced stricter money-laundering controls to stay on the right side of the regulations. The new breed of 'swap services' worked differently. They simply linked up those who wanted to sell with those who wanted to buy, and let them transact directly (with the swap service taking an introduction fee). The swap services never actually possessed the money themselves, therefore they felt no need to do money-laundering checks.

However, investigators were still able to spot the Lazarus Group's fingerprints on the KuCoin job. Even though they were using a different kind of exchange, the hackers were still sending the money using the same peel-chain amounts they had previously, and sometimes using the same Bitcoin-wallet addresses too.[23]

And so the KuCoin hack joined the growing list of cryptocurrency raids attributed to the Lazarus Group. It's hit dozens of targets since 2017. Coming up with a total for just how much the group has earned from all of this is tricky for a number of reasons. First, as we've seen, the value of these currencies is far from stable (for example, the money stolen from NiceHash was worth $75m at the time of the theft, close to $130m a fortnight later, and then around $20m a month after that). Second, despite the hackers' best efforts, exchanges can occasionally claw back some of the stolen money (for example, KuCoin claims to have recovered $204m).[24] And third, attribution of such hacks is of course always open to interrogation. One of the biggest cryptocurrency heists of all time, the theft of $530m from Japanese firm Coincheck in January 2018, was blamed on North Korea by the South's intelligence services, but the United Nations Security Council doesn't seem to include it in its round-up of Lazarus's jobs.[25]

Nonetheless, if you tot up all the cryptocurrency hacks attributed to North Korea using the value of the currency stolen at the time of the theft, the total is an eye-watering $1.3bn. If that's accurate, perhaps it made up for any sense of disappointment the Lazarus Group's members might have felt about the Bangladesh Bank job. The gang got their billion-dollar heist after all.

But the total amount isn't necessarily the most important point here. What these cryptocurrency attacks show is the staggering speed with which North Korea's hackers can not only embrace new technology, but exploit it while continually staying on its cutting edge. There is a vanishingly small number of people on the planet right now who have a really deep understanding of the things I've touched on in this chapter: blockchain, peel chains, swap services and so on. The idea that some of those people live in a country like North Korea is simultaneously fascinating and deeply concerning.

As former US National Security Agency North Korea analyst Priscilla Moriuchi puts it: 'We see this time and again when we look at our cyber-operations, how they're utilizing contemporary Internet technologies. The North Koreans are really on the leading edge and they're quite adaptable. They have a better understanding of our technology and our culture and our society than we really ever give them credit for.'

But, for all its cutting-edge cryptocurrency work, the Lazarus

Group wasn't done with the traditional banking sector quite yet. Just like all good heist movies, there was time for one more big job. And, just like in the movies, it would not go to plan. This time, North Korea's middlemen would not slip through the cracks. And what emerged would shed light on just how far North Korea's international network now stretches.

15

Going Back for More

It's Tuesday, 12 June 2018 – time for another moment in the lime-light for Kim Jong Un. Unlike his border meeting with Moon Jae-in two months before, this time there's a red carpet, a plethora of flags and a glitzy venue: the Capella Hotel on Sentosa, an island off Singapore. Kim's diplomacy drive has had an upgrade: he's about to meet the US President.

And this time there's also no disorganized scrum of photo-graphers getting in each other's way. Every element of this meeting has been stage-managed down to the last detail. Donald J. Trump appears from the right, wearing his 'doing-something-important-on-the-world-stage' face. Kim strides in from the left, smiling but looking slightly nervy. The two men shake hands. The sound of photographers' shutters is cacophonous, and Kim seems a little taken aback. 'They never stop,' Trump can be heard telling him – sounding surprisingly huffy for a man so used to celebrity.[1]

The meeting is remarkable given the fractious relationship between the two leaders, who'd spent the best part of the previous year trading insults. After North Korea's 2017 missile tests, Trump warned the country would 'be met with fire and fury like the world has never seen' if it continued with its 'threats' to the US.[2] He called Kim 'little rocket man' in a speech at the UN. Kim called Trump a 'dotard'.[3] To those monitoring North Korean affairs, such rhetoric must have been deeply worrying, escalating tensions in a game with the highest of stakes. And yet, thanks to Trump's bewil-dering approach to foreign policy, here the two leaders were, shaking hands and exchanging pleasantries under the bright Singa-porean sun.

It was the beginning of the 'bromance' between the pair, who exchanged what Trump described as 'beautiful letters' in the months following the meeting. 'We fell in love,' he said.[4] A year after the Singapore summit Trump would be at the Korean border in Panmunjom. Like Moon Jae-in, he would step over the two-inch-high borderline into North Korea – the first sitting US President to do so.[5]

There was considerable doubt about Trump's approach and whether it would yield results from the savvy Kim (scepticism which turned out to be well founded as time went on, with few tangible concessions from his regime), but at least there was dialogue. In front of the cameras the diplomatic mood music around North Korea appeared to be good.

Away from the public gaze, however, it was once again a different story. North Korea's hackers were already circling their next target, and further developing their global criminal network. This time their search for accomplices would lead them to forge some truly remarkable alliances.

As we learnt in Chapter 1, by June 2018 the Lazarus Group had already hacked into Cosmos Co-Operative Bank in India. As Trump and Kim were sitting down to talks in Singapore, Kim's hackers were worming their way through to the software that ran the bank's ATM approvals process, and taking control of it. They were also stealing customers' account details. The next stage of the plot was to encode those stolen details on to blank cards, and then distribute the cards to accomplices, who would use them to withdraw millions of dollars from cashpoints around the world. But, to accomplish that, the hackers needed help. Specifically they needed someone who could assist them in creating the counterfeit cards, and who had access to a network of people who could do the legwork of visiting the ATMs. According to the FBI, this is where Julien Kim, aka Tony Walker, comes back into the picture.

We met Julien Kim in the previous chapter: he was the shadowy character who set up Marine Chain, the high-tech shipping-investment scheme in Hong Kong. He'd then disappeared and left his co-workers high and dry. The FBI had been investigating his activity; it now believed his real name was Kim Il and that he was another member of the Lazarus Group.[6] As the Marine Chain episode showed, Kim Il was skilled at making connections, and for the Cosmos Bank hack that would come in very handy indeed.

Kim Il was in touch with a contact in Canada who went by the pseudonym 'Big Boss'.[7] He was offering exactly the kind of service the North Korean hackers needed: to take the stolen customer information and create counterfeit cards. And, as an added bonus, Big Boss also had access to a crew of more than twenty 'runners' both in Canada and in the US – people who could take the cards to cashpoints and make the withdrawals.[8] It's unclear how much Big Boss knew about Kim Il, the person with whom he was now dealing. The interaction was almost certainly all done online. And, given Kim's previous history of disguising his identity, it's very likely Big Boss didn't know his new paymaster was suspected by the FBI of being a North Korean government employee. It's possible that he didn't care whom he dealt with, so long as he got paid. Whatever the truth, Big Boss was ready to help, and the stage was set for the Cosmos Bank heist. It was all lined up for a weekend in August. In just a few hours the bank was taken for more than $11m. The money was withdrawn from ATMs, much of it by Big Boss's teams of runners.[9]

The total take was far less than the amounts the Lazarus Group made from the cryptocurrency raids described in the previous chapter. But the Cosmos job was clearly deemed a success by the hackers, because within a couple of months they would run the same scam using the same techniques and accomplices. This time the target was BankIslami in Pakistan. Once again, Big Boss helped the hackers to harvest the ATM money using his crew of runners. The haul was $6.1m.[10] North Korea's hackers were beginning to master a new way of turning digital crime into cash thanks to international collaborators like Big Boss. But the investigators who'd been pursuing the Lazarus Group were readying a surprise. The years of work that the FBI and its colleagues in the Attorney General's Office (as well as its partners in private industry and other domestic and overseas agencies) had put into tracking the group were about to bear fruit.

Just as North Korea was preparing to celebrate the 70th anniversary of its founding, on 9 September 2018, the US Department of Justice unveiled an early birthday present guaranteed to enrage Kim Jong Un.

It's 6 September 2018: a conference room in Los Angeles. Eight men and women in business suits take to the stage, led by First Assistant US Attorney Tracy Wilkison. She's a colleague of Tony Lewis, and, like him, she's spent years tracking the work of the Lazarus Group, accumulating evidence in the hope of one day being able to announce to the world that someone – a real, physical person as opposed to an online persona – is being charged. Today is that day. As she stands at the podium, to her left is a screen displaying an FBI Cyber 'Most Wanted' poster. The man in the picture is Park Jin Hyok, the hacker alleged by the US to have been behind the Sony attack, the heist on Bangladesh Bank and the WannaCry global ransomware outbreak.

Of course, Park's face is by now well familiar to Wilkison, Lewis and the rest of the team investigating the Lazarus Group. They've spent many months crawling over his details in their effort to piece together the inner workings of the hacking crew. But this is the first time the public have seen Park. He stares out from the TV screen, expressionless and unreadable. Meanwhile, Wilkison maps out the charges against him, outlining the campaign of cybercrime she and her colleagues allege that he helped to wage.[11]

The allegations are quickly denied by North Korea. 'The act of cybercrimes mentioned by the Justice Department has nothing to do with us,' read an article published shortly after the US press conference by KCNA, the official news organization in North Korea and therefore the closest thing to a government response. It said Park Jin Hyok was 'a non-existent entity'. 'Our State has long made it as its policy to oppose all kinds of cyber-attacks and fully ensure cyber-security,' read the article, which painted the Americans' accusations of hacking as an attempt to bully and besmirch North Korea: 'the US is forcibly linking the cybercrimes with the DPRK; their purpose is to tarnish the prestigious external image of the DPRK, using cyber-security issue as a pretext and thus justify their policy of "maximum pressure".'[12]

One thing is abundantly clear: none of America's allegations are ever likely to be tested in court. It's extremely unlikely Park will ever be arrested. He's almost certainly back in North Korea, beyond the reaches of the US justice system. So perhaps the idea of charging Park was to fire a shot across North Korea's bows – to exert 'maximum pressure', as the North Koreans said. If that's the case, it's questionable how successful this tactic was. Because, according to investigators, far from winding in their necks after the September 2018 revelations from the US, the cyber-attackers not only continued their hacking spree but expanded their network of criminal accomplices in a way that would make headlines around the world.

The story of the Lazarus Group has been a tale full of bizarre twists, but the craziest is yet to come. The shadowy, hidden realm of North Korea's hackers is about to intersect with the flashy, champagne-fuelled world of Instagram celebrity. It's a striking turn of events that perfectly illustrates the global scale of modern cyber-crime, and gives a worrying insight into just how pernicious this new underworld economy has become.

In January 2019 the Canadian fraudster Big Boss got a new message from Kim Il, the Lazarus Group's fixer-in-chief. The hacking gang was getting ready to hit another bank and needed some more help. But this time it wasn't going to use the trick of stealing customer information and creating cloned cards for an ATM attack. The Lazarus Group was switching back to the tactic it had deployed against Bangladesh Bank: straightforwardly transferring money out of the bank and into other accounts. But the hackers had clearly learnt from their frustrating experience in Manila, where many of the transfers had failed because they made a slip-up by using the flagged word 'Jupiter'. For their next attack they were looking for assistance from someone who could make sure the transfers went through without such hitches. Did Big Boss know anyone who could help? Indeed he did: a man listed in his iPhone contacts book only as 'Hush'. Big Boss had worked with Hush before, and knew he had access to bank accounts that could be used for laundering.[13]

Excitedly, Big Boss messages Hush from his iPhone, informing him that a new heist is in the offing, and telling him that the hackers plan to transfer the money in batches of around €5m. Can Hush find bank accounts run by accomplices that are able to accept that kind of money? Hush wastes no time. He replies the same day with details of an account at a bank in Romania that his contacts have made ready to receive the cash. Within a couple of days Big Boss is messaging Hush again. The hackers have told him that, when they hit the bank, they're going to keep transferring money for as long as they can until the bank stops them. 'If they don't notice, we keep pumping,' he tells Hush. Big Boss is now worried that a single Romanian account might not be enough and asks Hush if he can supply more, telling him (*sic*): 'Brother tonight is my dead line to submit anything more. Do u want add one more or just stick to that one u gave me?' Hush responds with the details of another account primed to facilitate the laundering, this time in Bulgaria. Meantime, Big Boss has been working with other contacts: he now has six accounts lined up, including Hush's, all set to receive up to €5m each. He goes back to his paymasters via Kim Il, provides them with the account details and tells them he's all set to go. They give him the date for the heist, which he sends on to Hush: 'big hit in 12th feb'.[14] Once again, thanks to Big Boss's help, the hackers have the infrastructure all arranged for the job.

On Tuesday, 12 February 2019, thousands of miles away from Big Boss's native Canada, a few shopkeepers in Malta start to notice something amiss with the machines they use to take card payments from customers. The machines are on the blink. They'd been provided to the shops by Bank of Valetta.[15] It's one of Malta's largest banks, and a key player in the tiny Mediterranean island's economy. Half of the country's transactions go through this one financial institution.[16] 'Malta is very dependent on the bank,' Abigail Mamo, CEO of the Maltese Chamber of Small and Medium Enterprises, later told BBC News. 'It has so many clients, everyone has accounts there.'[17] And so, as the day wears on, the issues are mounting up. In addition to the card machines, people start to experience problems using payment cards issued by Bank of Valetta. But when customers try to call the bank, they can't get through, according to Mamo.[18]

Bank of Valetta is under attack. It's become the latest target for the Lazarus Group. In October 2018, several months before Malta's shoppers and retailers started to experience problems with their cards, employees at Bank of Valetta had received some important-looking emails with a Word document attached. They appeared to come from the Autorité des Marchés Financiers (AMF), the French financial markets regulator, because they'd been sent from addresses using @amf-fr.org. However, the AMF's real email addresses use @amf-france.org. Spot the difference? It seems some within Bank of Valetta did not. The Word document came loaded with a computer virus; any bank employee who fell for the phishing email and opened the document would have exposed the bank to the attackers. Thanks to this well-worn tactic, the hackers have broken in and are now busy transferring out as much as they can before Bank of Valetta's IT team catch on and stop them.[19]

Meanwhile, Big Boss is watching money start to roll into the accounts he and Hush have lined up for the hackers. 'Wire is completed . . . We did it. 500k euro Should be on ur side by now,' he tells Hush, referring to the Romanian account.

Towards the end of the day, Big Boss tells Hush that the bank still hasn't figured out what the hackers are up to, meaning they're going to keep the heist going: 'Brother, we still have access and they didn't realize, we gonna shoot again tomoro am,' he writes.

But then the plot runs into trouble. The bank finally grasps the scale of the problem, possibly alerted by all the reports of malfunctioning card machines in Malta. It manages to shut out the hackers.

And the media have cottoned on too, as more people have reported problems with their cards. 'Look it hit the news,' Big Boss tells Hush. 'Damn,' is Hush's response.[20]

The hackers tried to transfer around €13m from Bank of Valetta. But the bank manages to claw some of the money back, according to the Maltese Prime Minister, by stopping some payments and asking the recipient banks to reverse others.[21] It comes as a disappointment to Big Boss, who tells Hush: 'To[o] bad they caught on or it would been a nice payout.'[22]

But, despite Bank of Valetta's efforts, some of the stolen money gets through, including £800,000 sent to accounts in the UK set up by Big Boss's other contacts. Here, accomplices have been lined up to take it to the next stage of the laundering process. And they waste no time in doing so, according to British police. Before the UK bank accounts can be blocked by the authorities tracing the Malta hack, the launderers pull out the stolen money and go on an impressive spending spree, hitting high-end stores such as Harrods and Selfridges and buying Rolex watches, according to the National Crime Agency. They also shell out on Jaguar and Audi cars.[23] The purchases have something in common: they're all high-value goods that are easily transported – just the kind of products money launderers love.

Compared to the millions of euros they'd planned to steal, however, the haul from the Bank of Valetta job is far from the giant payday that the hackers had hoped for. But this isn't the fault of Big Boss and Hush. They'd performed their end of the bargain, and were probably looking forward to further, more profitable adventures with the cybercriminals who'd brought them in on the Cosmos and Bank of Valetta raids.

But it is not to be. Unknown to Big Boss and Hush, the net is already closing in on them.

Years before the Malta bank job, police in the US had been investigating a completely unrelated crime when they got a lucky break. It put them on the trail of a criminal network that would ultimately lead them right to Big Boss. But the revelations wouldn't stop there:

the biggest surprise of all would be when they went after Hush. Even as the crooks counted their winnings from the Bank of Valetta raid, the police were homing in on the pair. It had all started with a seemingly random encounter by a bank employee in Florida.

Jennal Aziz was recently married and living in Orlando in the spring of 2017 when she heard from an old high-school friend called Kelvin Desangles. The pair reacquainted themselves and caught up on each other's lives. Desangles was now a successful businessman, he said, running an investment firm in Georgia – a 'tight ship', as he described it to Aziz. She, meanwhile, had been a branch manager at Sun City Bank for several years. On hearing this, Desangles asked her for a favour: could she provide him with information on the bank's customers? He would then use this data to pitch his investment firm to them. Aziz would receive a commission in return. Of course, such an arrangement was a massive breach of the bank's own rules and a huge invasion of privacy. But, for reasons best known to Aziz, she went along with it (though she never received any money in return). It's not as though she wasn't suspicious: at one point she texted Desangles to ask: 'Are u doing anything shady?' But it seems she was reassured by his affectionate reply. 'Come on juju seriously,' Desangles texted back. 'I would never.'[24]

In fact, unknown to Aziz, Desangles had an extensive criminal history and had been sentenced to more than two years in jail for carrying out fraud – which was exactly what he intended to do with the account holders' details he'd convinced Aziz to supply.

Working with a network of accomplices, Desangles would use the illegally obtained data to impersonate the bank's customers and withdraw money from their accounts. In December 2017 Desangles's gang hit the jackpot. They gained information about a rich doctor living in Florida. A plan was hatched: one of the gang would memorize the doctor's details, walk into a bank branch in Dallas where the victim had an account, pretend to be the doctor and withdraw $216,000. Unfortunately for the gang, the person they picked to do the job was a police informant. He agreed to wear a wire for the cops, who now began monitoring the gang's communications. They discovered an intriguing connection: one particular gang member seemed to be pulling the strings. He paid for the flights to Dallas, paid for the hotel room there, and repeatedly called the gang member who would be doing the impersonation to make sure he was ready to carry out the job.[25] But this mysterious Mr Big wasn't in the US like the rest of the gang. He was in Canada. It turned out the man helping to run Desangles's bank scams was Big Boss. The police team didn't know it yet, but they'd just stumbled upon the man who'd go on to help North Korea's hackers steal millions from Cosmos Bank and Bank of Valetta.

The FBI began to look into Big Boss's activities, and it didn't take them long to discover his cosy working relationship with Hush, the man who'd organized the bank accounts through which the money had been laundered.

Unsurprisingly, following their work on Cosmos Bank and Bank of Valetta, Big Boss and Hush were busy planning their next raid. This time they were exploiting a new tactic that had proved extremely lucrative, not just for them but for cybercriminals the world over. It's called Business Email Compromise, and the crime Big Boss and Hush were about to commit is a case-study example of it.

In October 2019 a law firm in New York State had been representing a client in a property deal. The deal was about to go through, and the law firm needed to make a payment to the client's bank of just under $1m. An employee of the firm emailed the bank to check the payment information. This was where it all started to go wrong.

Unknown to the law firm, Big Boss, Hush and their accomplices had infiltrated its communications. It's still unclear how exactly they did so, but it meant they could monitor the messages being sent in and out of the firm. The gang noticed that the employee was about to transfer a large sum of money, so it created an email address that looked very similar to that of the bank, and tricked the employee into corresponding with this spoofed address. It then sent the employee the bank-account details into which to pay the money – an account which was controlled by the gang. The law firm wanted to be sure it was using the right account, so it even went so far as to confirm the details using the fax and phone numbers it had been given. But of course those numbers had been provided by the gang too, so when the firm called up it was the hackers they were talking to, who gave the law firm the okay to make the transfer. Convinced that the bank details were correct, the law firm duly sent the money, which disappeared into the accounts of Big Boss, Hush and their gang. The sim was then divvied up between the conspirators.[26]

As all this was going down, Big Boss and Hush were in constant contact. 'Sup bro,' asked Hush on 17 October, 'money came in?' Big Boss confirmed that it had, and offered to send Hush a screenshot of the transfer. But he'd have to wait, he said, because Big Boss was in the airport, having flown from Los Angeles to Atlanta and didn't have a strong enough signal to send it. Hush anxiously waited for the screenshot confirming his payment. But the picture never came. Because, unknown to Hush, his partner in crime was now under arrest. The police had finally decided to move in on Big Boss. They'd been waiting in the airport and the fraudster was picked up before he could get back in touch with his accomplice.[27]

The man who'd helped Hush to engineer bank scams around the world was now unmasked by the cops as Ghaleb Alaumary, a stubbly, jowly Canadian in his mid-thirties who'd been living in Ontario. From there, he'd played a pivotal role in a string of bank frauds and multiple cases of the kind of Business Email Compromise scam explained above.[28]

But that left one big question: who was Hush?

With Big Boss in custody, the FBI began to analyse the iPhone through which he'd been in regular contact with his mysterious accomplice. It found a link to an account on the photo-sharing social media service Snapchat, under the username 'hushpuppi5'. Big Boss had saved the contact in his phone with the name 'The Billionaire Gucci Master!!!' The FBI investigators then found links to an Instagram account in the name 'hushpuppi'.[29] What they saw next must have knocked their socks off.

Hushpuppi was a so-called Instagram influencer whose account had 2.3 million followers. His photos showed a tall, heavy-set black man with a beard, whose life seemed like something from an outrageous reality TV series. There were hundreds of photos of him posing in designer clothes, being ferried around in chauffeur-driven luxury cars, and occasionally boarding a helicopter or a private plane for a trip to some exotic location. He'd hung out with famous footballers, attended the glitziest of events and, if his Instagram feed was to be believed, been showered with luxury goods by the world's most exclusive brands. In many of the photos he was careful to stand with one foot turned subtly sideways so that his millions of followers could admire every detail of the expensive shoes he was wearing. 'More than two dozen images showed [him] in front of, on top of, or inside other luxury vehicles, including multiple models of Bentley, Ferrari, Mercedes, and Rolls-Royce,' the FBI later reported.[30]

On the surface, Hushpuppi gave his audience unrivalled insights into the lifestyle of the mega-rich. What was less open to inspection was precisely how he had the money to fund it all. But, frankly, very few people cared. In the world of social media marketing, Hushpuppi appeared to be simply another one of the 'Instacelebs' – a class of meritless narcissists who've inexplicably been handed the keys to a modern perpetual-motion machine: their wealth brings them fame, and their fame brings them yet more riches. The key question is, of course, how do you kick-start the machine? As the old saying goes, making the first million is the hard part. And it was this chapter of his life story that Hushpuppi wasn't sharing with his fawning fans. Because it turned out that, away from his gaudy displays of gluttonous consumerism, Hushpuppi had been hiding a very dark, secret life for many years.

He was born Ramon Olorunwa Abbas in Nigeria on 11 October 1982, and by his thirties had become involved in Internet scam gangs. Such fraudsters were dubbed 'Yahoo boys', because Yahoo provided the free email accounts which were widely used by the scammers.[31] But Abbas was destined for bigger things than scratching around for online suckers from the Internet cafés of Lagos. Around 2014 he travelled to Malaysia and transformed himself into Hushpuppi, before moving on to a country in which overt displays of wealth are practically an art form: Dubai. He lived in the perfect setting for a man obsessed with bling, the Palazzo Versace. 'This is a house built by Versace,' remembers one interviewer given a glimpse into Abbas's world. 'The dustbins were Versace, the cups were Versace, the soap holders were Versace, spoons and forks could be done by Versace.'[32]

On Instagram he talked of how blessed he felt to enjoy such trappings of wealth, and how he hoped others could follow in his footsteps. At the same time, Abbas was running a global scam empire that fuelled the luxury lifestyle of his alter ego. Away from the public gaze, Abbas was a committed crook who showed his victims no mercy as he bled them for every penny to fund his extravagance, as illustrated by just one of his schemes. In late 2019 Abbas had developed contacts with a man who was raising funds to build an international school in Qatar. Abbas conned him into paying $330,000 into a Canadian bank account. The Nigerian then spent part of the loot on a Richard Mille watch worth $230,000. With the spare change he bought a St Kitts and Nevis passport, one of several passports he owned. He then went back to his victim, stinging him for a further $300,000.[33] His greed seemed almost insatiable. According to one estimate, over the years Abbas and his gang had defrauded almost 2 million people.[34] At one point he and Alaumary even discussed ripping off an unnamed UK Premier League football club to the tune of £100m.[35]

All of this came to light as the FBI uncovered more and more detail about Abbas and his connections to Alaumary. But, unlike his accomplice, Abbas wasn't going to the US. The Americans would need the help of their counterparts in Dubai to make the arrest.

On 6 June 2020 the Palazzo Versace received a visit from a group very different from the usual crowd. Instead of Valentino frocks and Muaddi heels, this bunch were clad in black balaclavas, helmets and bulletproof vests with SWAT written on the back. They raided the set of rooms that were home to Abbas. His Instagram followers had always seen this glamorous suite as the backdrop for his carefully curated videos. Now it was crawling with Dubai police officers cuffing suspects with cable ties and loading computer equipment into evidence bags. Abbas himself, wearing a wrinkled white T-shirt, was filmed being taken away in handcuffs. Quite a comedown for the 'Billionaire Gucci Master'.

The cops also seized 21 computers, 47 smartphones and 13 luxury cars. All of this was captured on video and later released on YouTube. The Dubai police clearly didn't scrimp when it came to the special-effects budget: the four-minute clip looks like a cross between *CSI: Dubai* and a *Fast & Furious* movie. The sweeping Steadicam shot of Abbas's luxury vehicle collection is worth the watch alone.[36]

Thanks to Abbas's celebrity status, his arrest garnered headlines around the world (along with a fair amount of *Schadenfreude* in his native Nigeria and elsewhere). His next stop was the US. On 3 July 2020 the Americans announced he had been brought to Los Angeles to face charges. 'Abbas finances [his] opulent lifestyle through crime . . . he is one of the leaders of a transnational network that facilitates computer intrusions, fraudulent schemes, and money laundering, targeting victims around the world,' trumpeted the Department of Justice announcement.[37]

But there was no mention of North Korea, or of Ghaleb Alaumary. And for months after Abbas's arrest the US authorities said nothing more.

Behind the scenes they were piecing together the links they claimed bound together this global criminal network. The case against Park Jin Hyok two years previously had revolved around just one man (albeit a man accused of carrying out three sprawling cybercrime campaigns). This time the Department of Justice was attempting to connect the dots of a criminal enterprise that, it alleged, stretched from North Korea to almost every continent on earth, over a span of more than a decade, generating more than $1.3bn in profits.[38]

On 17 February 2021 the Department of Justice went public with its case.

It outlined the charges against Alaumary and Abbas, and described the links connecting the pair to the Lazarus Group. And it also claimed to have fresh information on the hackers themselves: alongside the photo of Park Jin Hyok there were now two new additions – Jon Chang Hyok, aged thirty-one, and Kim Il, twenty-seven (this time it was less clear how the US agencies had obtained their photos).³⁹ Jon is shown outdoors bundled up in a heavy, black, fur-lined overcoat, possibly insulating himself from North Korea's harsh winter conditions. According to the Department of Justice, Kim Il is the real identity of Julien Kim and Tony Walker. He is shown in a grainy passport photo. Even compared with Park's youthful demeanour, the pair seem achingly young. As I looked at Kim, I found it hard to believe this was the man who had spent months duping financiers, technologists and shipping experts across Asia into setting up the fake Marine Chain scam, and who went on to orchestrate multimillion-dollar raids on banks across the world. I found myself asking whether, aged twenty-seven, I would have had the confidence to go through with it all, let alone the skill. Then I immediately realized the futility of the exercise: there's no way I could ever put my privileged life alongside that of someone raised in North Korea and make any comparisons.

By the time the Department of Justice released its charges, Alaumary had already pleaded guilty to money laundering. He was later sentenced to eleven years and eight months in prison. Abbas also pleaded guilty and at the time of writing still awaits his sentence, which could be as much as twenty years. Kelvin Desangles, the man who led police to Alaumary, got four years and nine months, and Jennal Aziz, the woman who fed him the bank customers' details, received a six-month sentence.⁴⁰

Absent from the list of those sent to prison were, of course, Jon Chang Hyok and Kim Il. Just like Park Jin Hyok and the rest of the Lazarus Group's alleged hackers, they're presumed to be safely back in North Korea, way beyond the reach of any outside criminal-justice system. It's unlikely that will ever change.

Much as I'd love to interview them and find out their side of the story, at the moment it seems like a pipe dream. And so today my only option is to look at them on the FBI Cyber's 'Most Wanted' website, where their photos sit alongside those of all the other suspects who, the US claims, are terrorizing cyberspace from legally unreachable hideaways: the Russians in their military uniforms, the Nigerians in their T-shirts, the Chinese with their spectacles, the Iranians with their stubble. Trapped in amber, these men (and, yes, they're all men) stare back at me. I want to know what their stories are, where they started out, and how their lives led them to end up in the sights of the FBI. But instead all I have is their alleged crimes, listed in the sterile jargon of the state along with the barest biographical details: name, age, location. There's something else that's missing too: the stories of their victims – the ruined careers, the destroyed businesses, the invaded privacy, the emptied bank accounts – are nowhere to be seen.

Conclusion

North Korea's alleged computer hackers get away scot-free, while their accomplices (or some of them, at least) get caught in the net. It's a pattern we've seen again and again throughout this book. As a result, the Lazarus Group remains free to continue the global hacking campaigns attributed to it by the FBI, the United Nations and many security researchers.

We may not know where or when they'll strike next, but, from what we've seen in this book, there's one thing you can count on: innovation. In a little over a decade the Lazarus Group's hackers have risen from low-level defacement hacks to destructive cyber-attacks and billion-dollar thefts exploiting the very latest financial technology. These guys are quick learners, and they don't stand still for long.

As North Korea closed off its borders due to the coronavirus pandemic, some suspected that their skills would come in very handy for the regime. With its physical supply routes cut off and its network of smugglers and sanctions-dodgers hamstrung by COVID restrictions, some saw North Korea's high-tech criminal activity as the ideal way for the regime to keep its coffers topped up. With the country even more isolated than usual, surely the kind of seamless, cross-border crypto-crime described in Chapter 15 would be a lifeline?

It's not clear, however, that this was the case. From what we know, the bulk of the alleged cryptocurrency activity was carried out in 2018 and early 2019, and it tailed off in 2020 as coronavirus took hold. There are some logical reasons for this. After all, stealing cryptocurrency isn't an end in itself for Pyongyang. The stolen digital money is only useful in so far as it can be used, for example, to buy goods not available in North Korea, and therefore those goods still have to be moved across the border. That requires the kind of hands-on activity and physical infrastructure that was hampered by virus lockdowns.

But, according to security researchers, the pandemic spurred North Korea's hackers in a different direction. They were trying to break into companies researching and manufacturing vaccines, according to South Korea's National Intelligence Agency, including Pfizer (which declined to comment on the reports).[1] It's worth noting that it was far from the only country accused of targeting coronavirus resources. As the virus circled the world, governments' hacking teams went into overdrive, according to tech researchers. Not only were they attempting to snoop on their adversaries' medical and political responses to the pandemic, but they were also using coronavirus as a powerful new lure to trick victims into opening dodgy attachments and clicking on virus-related links, allowing the hackers access to the kind of sensitive information they're perpetually seeking.

If North Korea was indeed hacking vaccine manufacturers as alleged, it's not clear how much it helped them. Given the endemic secrecy surrounding daily life in the country, it's impossible to know how badly it's been affected by coronavirus. But, remarkably, during the pandemic its leaders have not only maintained their missile-testing programme but also advanced it. At the time of writing North Korea has just launched a long-range cruise missile which some fear can carry a nuclear warhead. If the US is correct in its estimate of the Lazarus Group's profits – around $1.3bn – it's highly likely some of that money would have funded this missile and the other weapons which now threaten global peace. Even during a pandemic, North Korea is still very much at war, and its hackers are part of the military machinery.

In this context, there are those who see a worrying potential future for the Lazarus Group's gifted young operatives. 'During peaceful times they can use their hacking ability to create income,' says former North Korean Ambassador Thae Yong Ho. 'But if it turned into wartime, they can easily turn their potential to use as a cyber-attack on the South Korean system.' We saw a worrying fore-shadow of such tactics in Chapter 4, when researchers claimed to have found North Korean viruses inside the South's military net-work. The viruses weren't detonated. But, in any future conflict, the cyber-warriors' tools might be a key weapon.

Halting these hackers seems like an impossible task. After all, des-pite the US rhetoric, the Department of Justice press conferences, the criminal indictments and the release of suspects' photos, it's obvious that America stands no chance of proving its case in court and putting Park, Kim, Jon and their accomplices behind bars, even if they were to be found guilty. So why bother? What's the point in making such a very public hullabaloo?

There are a number of reasons: first, the allegations can become a weapon in the diplomatic game. In any negotiations the US can bring up these cybercrime charges and demand answers from North Korea. If it's not happy with the response, the US can then argue that North Korea is acting in bad faith. From a global PR point of view, the US can use these allegations to paint North Korea as a cyber-menace on the world stage. Think of all the countries affected by the events described in this book: Bangladesh, Pakistan, Sri Lanka, the Philippines, Slovenia and more. The US can start to build a coalition of North Korea's cyber-victims, creating a powerful alli-ance to put pressure on Pyongyang.

But there's another, more prosaic reason why the US put these charges out: to burn down the hackers' infrastructure. Alongside the press conference and the photo of Park, the Department of Just-ice released a 179-page criminal complaint against him. It was packed with detail: the email, Facebook and Twitter accounts he'd allegedly been using; the viruses he's accused of having written; the tactics the FBI claim he used to break into his victims' digital networks. There was yet more detail in the charges against Kim Il and Jon Chang Hyok. The US has gone so far as to list the hundreds of Bit-coin wallets it claims were used in the cryptocurrency-exchange attacks. If the FBI's claims are true, all of that infrastructure is now useless to the Lazarus Group. Its Gmail and social media accounts have been shut down, and even if it spins up new ones, organizations will now be on the lookout for the group's viruses and tactics, and be better able to defend against its attacks.

This is the modern face of law enforcement when it comes to cybercrime. In many cases, making an arrest is impossible: even if the suspect can be identified, they're often in a jurisdiction that's not going to play ball when it comes to legal proceedings (something that hackers may well take into account if they have a choice about where to live). Instead, police and prosecutors must fight a war of attrition, chipping away at the hackers' infrastructure by taking down servers, disabling viruses and closing off email accounts.

The tactics of law enforcement are an inevitable response to the fact that the adversary they're up against can't be defeated by traditional means. Hackers are a classic guerrilla threat. Armed only with a laptop and an Internet connection, a tiny player can use a bewildering arsenal of cyber-tools to take down a high-profile target – be it a Hollywood movie studio, a national bank or a hospital emergency room. Then they can disappear back into the digital undergrowth, confident that law enforcement will struggle to find them, much less prosecute them.

The more reliant we all become on digital data, computers, and the connections between them, the more vulnerable we get and the easier these hackers will find it to exploit novel ways to carry out a successful attack. Such incidents will inevitably become a growing threat to global security. After all, it can't have escaped the attention of the world's most bellicose and antagonistic regimes that the Lazarus Group's hackers were able to knock out key parts of the developed world's infrastructure by digital means without ever setting foot in enemy territory. Neither will it have escaped the notice of cybercrime gangs that rich national banks and fast-growing crypto-currency exchanges turned out to be ripe and vulnerable targets. Thanks to its parlous financial situation – the legacy of its years of self-induced isolation and aggression – North Korea represents perhaps the perfect illustration of this modern menace. But it's far from alone in its ability to unleash hacker tactics worldwide.

Law enforcement is changing as a result. Just as the hackers use innovative and non-conventional means to carry out their crimes, the police and intelligence agencies often have to think differently when it comes to fighting the online crooks.

Inevitably, that means relying on private industry. The servers, the email accounts and the social networks which the hackers exploit are all owned by private companies. And so it's private companies which have to work with police to tackle the hackers. Some of the greatest minds in the world are building the tools to keep us safe: filters to block the dodgy emails, software that can spot a hacker's movements and so on. There is also a growing community of what might be called 'armchair cyber-analysts', like the Reddit user Arsenalfan5000 who tipped people off to Marine Chain's murky set-up. And yet cybercrime continues. Why? Because one of the great things about being a hacker is that every new Internet connection, every new email address, every new social media account, represents another potential way into a target. Ultimately, there is no government, police force or company that can spot and stop every attempt by the attackers. And so it's the people on the other end of those email addresses and social media accounts – you and I, in other words – who are ultimately the last line of defence.

Think about the hacks covered in this book: Sony, Bangladesh Bank, NiceHash and many of the others. What got the hackers over the very first hurdle was a dodgy email, inadvertently opened by an employee who let the hackers inside without even knowing it.

This is the stark reality of digital life. The power that many of us enjoy in our super-connected world – the power to communicate globally, to share our lives with those we love, to access our bank accounts, photos and private data day or night – comes with responsibility. As we've seen in the preceding chapters, online we are all targets and we can all be attacked. Now we must all learn how to defend. The good news is that, by reading this book, you already understand way more about the cybercriminals' tactics than they ever wanted you to know. And the more knowledge you acquire, the safer you'll become.

Acknowledgements

This section is by far the least comprehensive in the book, for a number of reasons: first, because my memory for names is atrocious; and, second, because the inevitable security risks involved in covering North Korean hackers mean that it's not safe to credit by name many of those to whom credit is very much due. If you're missing an acknowledgement for either of these reasons, please accept my apology and your free drink when next we meet.

This book came about as a result of a BBC World Service podcast called *The Lazarus Heist*, and I cannot be thankful enough to all of those who helped bring it to life, polish it up and get it into listeners' ears – especially to our producer, Estelle Doyle, who has a mystifying yet much-appreciated ability to somehow do approximately six to seven hours' more work than should be feasible in any one day. And to all those from the editorial, commissioning, marketing, digital and business-affairs teams, as well as our script consultants: thank you. Most of all, thank you to all the many listeners.

The BBC team also introduced me to someone without whom the series (and therefore this book) would have been very greatly diminished. My co-host, Jean H. Lee, spent years in North Korea working for the Associated Press news agency, opening the only US text/photo news bureau in the country. Every conversation with Jean brings amazing new insights into this secretive land. Her expertise and knowledge are unrivalled in my opinion, and I am deeply grateful to her, not only for her insights but also for the incredible interviews she delivered via her contacts, some of which you have read in the preceding pages.

As it became clear the podcast was to become a book, Lydia Yadi and Celia Buzuk at Penguin Business did an incredible job of cool-headedly steering the process despite the tight deadlines. Thank you both.

I'd also like to thank all our interviewees from *The Lazarus Heist* podcast for sparing their time and offering their experiences and expertise, especially those quoted in this book: David Asher, Bob Hamer, Priscilla Moriuchi, Celina Chavanette, Dan Sterling, Bruce Bennett, Tatiana Siegel, Ben Waisbren, Amy Heller, Tony Lewis, Rakesh Asthana, Congresswoman Carolyn Maloney, Eric Chien, Kyung Jin Kim, Ferdinand Topacio, Rodolfo Quimbo, Moyara Ruehsen, Muhammad Cohen, Ajmalul Hossain, Alan Katz, Patrick Ward, Tony Bleetman, Marcus Hutchins, Mike Hulett and Marko Gašparič.

Thanks also to Jihyun Park for taking the time to tell me her incredible story, Son Taek Wang for recalling his experience of the days of Dark Seoul, Jared Cohen for recounting his trip to Pyongyang to Jean H. Lee, Thae Yong Ho for giving her his insights from within the regime's top tiers, and Hyun-Seung Lee for telling her of his escape and the experiences that preceded it.

And, finally, thanks to the techies and experts: Nirmal John, Martyn Williams; Don Smith and Rafe Pilling at Secureworks; Adrian Nish and Saher Naumann at BAE Systems; and Ryan Sherstobitoff.

Notes

Introduction

1. National Crime Agency and the Strategic Cyber Industry Group, 'Cyber Crime Assessment 2016', 7 July 2016, pp. 6, 7.

1 Jackpot

1. Asseem Shaikh, 'Cosmos Bank Case: Two More Held, Got Rs 35,000 for ATM Withdrawals', *Times of India*, 15 September 2018; 'One More Arrest in Cosmos Bank Heist', *Times of India*, 5 January 2019.
2. ibid.
3. 'Pune Police Eye More Arrests for Cosmos Online Heist', *Times of India*, 13 September 2018.
4. Government of India, Ministry of Statistics and Programme Implementation, 'Real GDP and Per Capita Income Over the Years', www.mospi.nic.in, accessed 29 July 2021.
5. Cosmos Co-Operative Bank Ltd, '113th Annual Report: 2018–19', p. 27.
6. Asseem Shaikh, 'Cosmos Bank Cloned Card Heist Planned in Thane', *Times of India*, 12 December 2018.
7. ANI News Official, 'Cosmos Bank Chairman Calls Cyber-hack "International Attack on Banking System"', YouTube, 14 August 2018.
8. J. Crespo Cuaresma, O. Danylo, S. Fritz, et al., 'What Do We Know about Poverty in North Korea?', *Palgrave Communications*, 6, 40 (17 March 2020).

9. United Nations Security Council, 'Report of the Panel of Experts Established Pursuant to Resolution 1874 (2009)', 30 August 2019.

10. Cosmos Bank, 'About Us', www.cosmosbank.com, accessed 4 October 2021.

11. Cosmos Co-Operative Bank Ltd, '114th Annual Report: 2019–20'.

12. Oleg Kolesnikov, 'Cosmos Bank SWIFT/ATM US$13.5 Million Cyber-attack Detection Using Security Analytics', Securonix Threat Research Team [n.d.]; ANI News Official, 'Cosmos Bank Chairman Calls Cyber-hack "International Attack on Banking System" ', op. cit.

13. Brian Krebs, 'FBI Warns of "Unlimited" ATM Cash-out Blitz', Krebs on Security, 12 August 2018.

14. 'Woman Held in Cosmos Bank Online Heist Case', *Times of India*, 2 April 2019.

15. Cosmos Co-Operative Bank Ltd, '113th Annual Report', op. cit., p. 27.

16. Sushant Kulkarni, 'Cosmos Malware Attack: SIT Arrests Two "Who Withdrew Money with Cloned Cards", Search on for Others', *Indian Express*, 12 September 2018.

17. Although this situation had started to change, in large part due to the Indian government's banknote demonetization in November 2016.

18. Cosmos Bank, 'Cosmos Bank: Message from the Directors – English', YouTube, 1 October 2018.

19. Cosmos Co-Operative Bank Ltd, '113th Annual Report', op. cit., p. 27.

20. ibid., p. 3.

21. Cosmos Co-Operative Bank did not respond to my requests for information or an interview.

22. 'Accused in Cosmos Case Involved in Union Bank Cyber Scam: Pune Police', NDTV, 19 September 2018.

23. Geetha Nandikotkur, 'Cosmos Bank Heist: No Evidence Major Hacking Group Involved', Bank Info Security, www.bankinfo security.com, 29 August 2018.

24. United States Cybersecurity and Infrastructure Security Agency, 'Cybersecurity and Infrastructure Security Agency Alert (TA18-275A) HIDDEN COBRA – FASTCash Campaign', 2 October 2018.

2   Going Broke

1. Jihyun Park's remarkable story of escape and survival is almost certainly worth a book in itself, and I am deeply indebted to her for patiently telling it to me.
2. Robert L. Worden (ed.), 'North Korea, A Country Study' (Federal Research Division, Library of Congress, 2008), p. 38; Shannon McCune, 'The Thirty-eighth Parallel in Korea', *World Politics*, 1, 2 (January 1949), pp. 223–32.
3. Bradley Martin, *Under the Loving Care of the Fatherly Leader: North Korea and the Kim Dynasty* (Saint Martin's Griffin, 2006), p. 51.
4. Worden, op. cit., p. 72.
5. Martin, op. cit., p. 56.
6. Worden, op. cit., p. 46.
7. ibid., p. 45.
8. Steven Casey, 'Selling NSC-68: The Truman Administration, Public Opinion, and the Politics of Mobilization, 1950–51', *Diplomatic History*, 29, 4 (September 2005), pp. 655–90.
9. Kim Il Sung, 'On Eliminating Dogmatism and Formalism and Establishing *Juche* in Ideological Work', *Kim Il Sung Works. Volume 9: July 1954–December 1955* (Foreign Languages Publishing House, 1982).
10. Martin, op. cit., p. 157.
11. Worden, op. cit., p. 63.
12. Eric Croddy, 'Vinalon, the DPRK, and Chemical Weapons Precursors', www.nti.org, 1 February 2003.
13. Martin, op. cit., p. 126.
14. Korean Institute for National Unification, 'White Paper on Human Rights in North Korea', August 2012.

15. Martin, op. cit., p. 326.
16. There are signs that this is changing. In her book *North Korea: Like Nowhere Else* (September Publishing, 2021), Lindsey Miller describes her two years spent in the country as the partner of a diplomat. She recalls showing photos of Hong Kong on her smartphone to a North Korean she became friendly with, who spent many minutes scrutinizing the pictures (p. 19). However, as a foreigner, Miller would have been exposed only to a small cross-section of North Korean society, as she herself acknowledges.
17. Worden, op. cit., p. 79.
18. ibid., p. 77.
19. ibid., p. 32.
20. Anna Fifield, *The Great Successor: The Secret Rise and Rule of Kim Jong Un* (John Murray, 2020), p. 192.
21. Worden, op. cit., p. 48.
22. ibid., p. 141.
23. Clyde Haberman, 'North Korea Delivers Flood Aid Supplies to the South', *New York Times*, 30 September 1984.
24. Filip Kovacevic, 'Sport and Politics on the Korean Peninsula: North Korea and the 1988 Seoul Olympics', The Wilson Centre, 9 June 2021. North Korea had suggested staging half of the Olympic events north of the border. When that failed, it boycotted the whole thing and called for other communist countries to follow suit: only a handful played ball, and they didn't include the big beasts of China and the USSR.
25. Pavel P. Em and Peter Ward, 'City Profile: Is Pyongyang a Post-socialist City?', *Cities*, 108, 1, (January 2021).
26. Martin, op. cit., p. 432.
27. Worden, op. cit., p. 56.
28. Almost literally – some report that the women were given the rank of Lieutenant of the Bodyguard Division (Paul Fischer, *A Kim Jong Il Production: The Extraordinary True Story of a Kidnapped Filmmaker, His Star Actress, and a Young Dictator's Rise to Power* (Flatiron Books, 2015), p. 97).

29. Martin, op. cit., p. 315.
30. Chris Hughes, 'Perverted North Korea Leader Kim Jong Un Plucks Teenage Girls from Schools "With Straight Legs" to be His Sex Slaves', *Daily Mirror*, 20 September 2017.
31. Martin, op. cit., pp. 200–201.
32. ibid., p. 321.
33. Don Oberdorfer, *The Two Koreas: A Contemporary History* (Addison Wesley, 1998), p. 347.
34. Worden, op. cit., p. 141.
35. Martin, op. cit., p. 244.
36. Worden, op. cit., p. 66.
37. Fifield, op. cit., p. 124.
38. 'World Food Programme and North Korea: WFP has Fed Millions', www.reliefweb.int, 25 October 2000.
39. Worden, op. cit., p. xxxii.

3 Superdollars

1. Te-Ping Chen, 'Smoking Dragon, Royal Charm', The Center for Public Integrity, https://publicintegrity.org/health/smoking-dragon-royal-charm/, 20 October 2008.
2. 'Statement of Michael Merritt, Deputy Assistant Director, Office of Investigations, United States Secret Service, before the Subcommittee on Federal Financial Management, Government Information and International Security, Committee on Homeland Security and Government Affairs, United States Senate', 25 April 2006.
3. Sheena E. Chestnut, 'The "*Sopranos* State"? North Korean Involvement in Criminal Activity and Implications for International Security', Honors Program for International Security Studies, Center for International Security and Co-Operation, Stanford University, 20 May 2005, p. 83.
4. Philip H. Melanson and Peter F. Stevens, *The Secret Service: The Hidden History of an Enigmatic Agency* (Basic Books, 2005).

5. Stephen Mihm, 'No Ordinary Counterfeit', *New York Times*, 23 July 2006.

6. 'Fake Dollars Found in Japan', UPI Archive, 8 April 1996.

7. United States General Accounting Office, 'Iran, Syria and the Trail of Counterfeit Dollars', House Republican Research Committee, cited in 'Counterfeit US Currency Abroad: Observations on Counterfeiting and US Deterrence Efforts. Statement of JayEtta Z. Hecker, Associate Director, International Relations and Trade Issues', 27 February 1996.

8. John K. Cooley, 'Ask North Korean Defector about Those Counterfeit Dollars', *New York Times*, 10 May 1997.

9. Glenn Schloss, 'North Korea's Macau-based Trading Venture Opens Its Doors to Deny Reports of Espionage and Shady Deals', *South China Morning Post*, 3 September 2000.

10. Nicholas D. Kristof, 'Is North Korea Turning to Counterfeiting?', *New York Times*, 17 April 1996.

11. Carl Rochelle, 'Redesigned $100 Bill Aimed at Foiling Counterfeiters', CNN, 25 March 1996.

12. Mihm, op. cit.

13. Richard Lloyd Parry, 'Car Chase Leads to Pyongyang's Superforgers', *Independent*, 8 June 1996.

14. 'Hijacker Admits Guilt after Thirty Years', BBC News, 15 December 2000.

15. Bradley Martin, *Under the Loving Care of the Fatherly Leader: North Korea and the Kim Dynasty* (Saint Martin's Griffin, 2006), p. 499.

16. Parry, op. cit.

17. 'Former Japanese Red Army Member Acquitted', AP, 24 June 1999.

18. 'Obituary: Yoshimi Tanaka', *Japan Times*, 3 January 2007.

19. Martin, op. cit., p. 583.

20. Media Burn Archive, 'Inside the US Bureau of Engraving and Printing, 1991', YouTube, 4 January 2013.

21. 'The Superdollar Plot', *BBC Panorama*, 20 June 2004.

22. 'KBA-NotaSys Becomes Koenig & Bauer Banknote Solutions', www.koenig-bauer.com, 11 March 2020.

23. 'About Roberto Giori', www.robertogioricompany.com, accessed 28 June 2021.

24. United States Bureau of Engraving and Printing, 'US Currency: How Money is Made – Paper and Ink', www.bep.gov, accessed 2 July 2021.

25. Mihm, op. cit.; David E. Kaplan, 'The Wiseguy Regime', *US News & World Report*, 15 February 1999, via www.scaryreality.com, accessed 2 July 2021.

26. Mihm, op. cit. SICPA confirmed to me that it does supply the US government, but would not comment beyond that, citing confidentiality.

27. *BBC Panorama*, op. cit.

28. ibid.

29. ibid.

30. *United States of America* v *Seán Garland*, filed 19 September 2005.

31. *BBC Panorama*, op. cit.

32. Bobbie Hanvey, 'The Ramblin' Man: Interview with Seán Garland', Downtown Radio, 5 August 2007, via www.workerspartyireland.net, accessed 5 July 2021.

33. *The Attorney General* v *Seán Garland*: Judgment of Mr Justice Edwards, 27 January 2012.

34. ibid.

35. *BBC Panorama*, op. cit.

36. ibid.

37. Workers' Party, 'Letter to International Comrades on the Death of Comrade Seán Garland', 14 December 2018.

38. Counterfeit cigarettes are an extremely lucrative line of business for smugglers. Bob Hamer says that at the time of Operation Smoking Dragon a carton of knock-off cigarettes could be bought for $7 or $8, and its contents sold as the real thing for $70 or $80. Given that estimates of the global illicit trade run to 600 billion individual cigarettes in 2006 (Framework Convention Alliance, 'How Big Was the Global Illicit Tobacco Trade Problem in 2006?', July 2006), that's a lot of profit, which potentially finances the illicit import of drugs, guns and more.

39. Another of Hamer's FBI colleagues had also arranged to buy superdollars from a man reportedly serving as a go-between for the North Korean government, further convincing US law enforcement that the money was coming from Pyongyang (Chen, op. cit.).

40. 'Operation Smoking Dragon, Dismantling an International Smuggling Ring', www.fbi.gov, 7 May 2011, accessed via www.archive.org, 5 July 2021.

41. Chen, op. cit.

42. 'Operation Smoking Dragon, Dismantling an International Smuggling Ring', op. cit.

43. 'Statement of Michael Merritt', op. cit.

44. Jay Solomon and Hae Won Chit, 'In North Korea, Secret Hoard of Cash Props Up a Regime', *Wall Street Journal*, 14 July 2003.

45. Dick K. Nanto, 'North Korean Counterfeiting of US Currency', Congressional Research Service, 12 June 2009.

46. David Asher, 'The Impact of US Policy on North Korean Illicit Activities', Heritage Foundation, 18 April 2007.

47. Donald Greenlees and David Lague, 'Trail Led to Macao as Focus of North Korean Corruption', *New York Times*, 13 April 2007.

48. US Department of the Treasury, 'Treasury Designates Banco Delta Asia as Primary Money-laundering Concern under USA Patriot Act', 15 September 2005.

49. Nanto, op. cit.

4   Dark Seoul

1. 'South Korea Network Attack "A Computer Virus"', BBC News, 20 March 2013.

2. 'Richardson: North Korea Trip is Private, Humanitarian', AP, 4 January 2013.

3. Bradley Martin, *Under the Loving Care of the Fatherly Leader: North Korea and the Kim Dynasty* (Saint Martin's Griffin, 2006), p. 627.

4. Choe Sang-Hun, 'North Korea Says Diplomat Who Defected is "Human Scum"', *New York Times*, 20 August 2016.

5. Martin, op. cit., p. 295.

6. Joachim Fest, *Hitler: A Career* (*Hitler: Eine Karriere*) (Interart/ Werner Rieb Produktion, 1977). At time code 1.08.30: 'He did not give the people their rights, what he gave them was the fascination of geometry.'

7. DPRK Video Archive, 'Attain the Cutting Edge', YouTube, 4 July 2011.

8. For an overview of CNC's history, with some great footage and a startlingly incongruous rave soundtrack, see Chris Smelko, 'The History of CNC', YouTube, 2 October 2006.

9. *Kim Jong Il Biography: Volume 4* (Foreign Languages Publishing House, 2017), p. 310.

10. Martin, op. cit., p. 86.

11. Congressional Research Service, 'Redeploying US Nuclear Weapons to South Korea: Background and Implications in Brief', 14 September 2017.

12. International Atomic Energy Agency, 'Fact Sheet on DPRK Nuclear Safeguards', www.iaea.org, accessed 5 July 2021.

13. 'Chronology of North Korea's Missile, Rocket Launches', Yonhap News Agency, 5 April 2017.

14. James Pearson and Hyonhee Shin, 'How a Homemade Tool Helped North Korea's Missile Program', Reuters, 12 October 2017.

15. 'Frozen North Korean Funds to be Released', *Guardian*, 10 April 2007.

16. German Federal Institute for Geosciences and Natural Resources, 'Nordkorea: BGR registriert vermutlichen Kernwaffentest', 1 June 2016. 'A magnitude of 5.1 was determined. This corresponds roughly to a charge of 14,000 tons of the chemical explosive TNT. The current test is thus well above the values of 2006 (700 tons).'

17. The UN failed to define 'luxury goods', but usefully the European Union later drew up a list, which includes Asti Spumante

and shoes worth more than 20 euros ('Council Regulation (EU) 2017/2062 of 13 November 2017, Amending Regulation (EU) 2017/1509 Concerning Restrictive Measures against the Democratic People's Republic of Korea'). Admittedly, the wording is somewhat ambiguous: 'shoes (regardless of their material) of a value exceeding EUR 20 each' – which could of course be interpreted as 20 euros per shoe, or per pair.

18. 'Obituary: Kim Jong Il', BBC News, 19 December 2011.

19. Gus Lubin, 'North Korea Has Biggest Party Ever to Celebrate Unveiling of Kim Jong Un', *Business Insider*, 11 October 2010.

20. A similar debate affects the number given for Kim Jong Il's age at his death, with some reporting it as seventy rather than sixty-nine. The US Treasury pegged Kim Jong Un's birth at 8 January 1984 when it sanctioned him for human-rights violations. Interestingly, while North Korea's Ministry of Foreign Affairs website gives official dates of birth for Kim Il Sung (15 April 1912) and Kim Jong Il (16 February 1942), it does not list one for Kim Jong Un ('Panorama of the Democratic People's Republic of Korea', www.mfa.gov.kp, accessed 5 July 2021). But media outlets have reported the official date as being 8 January 1982 (Riley Beggin, 'Everything You Need to Know about North Korean Leader Kim Jong Un', ABC News, 9 June 2018).

21. Jeongyol Ri, speaking to Jean H. Lee, my co-host for *The Lazarus Heist* podcast, BBC World Service, 2021.

22. 'North Korea's Ruling Elite are Not Isolated', Recorded Future, 25 July 2017.

23. Geoff White, *Crime Dot Com: From Viruses to Vote-Rigging, How Hacking Went Global* (new edn, Reaktion Books, 2020), p. 67.

24. An affiliate of 38 North, a North Korea-focused website that is, in turn, backed by a US think-tank. See www.northkoreatech.org.

25. 'North Korea Boosted "Cyber-forces" to 6,000 Troops, South Says', Reuters, 6 January 2015. It's worth pointing out that most countries – including the US and the UK – have cyber-experts in their military and intelligence agencies who are allowed to use offensive capability.

26. 'China IP Address: Link to South Korea Cyber-attack', BBC News, 21 March 2013.

27. ibid.

28. 'North Korea's Artillery Attack on the South', CNBC, 29 November 2010.

29. John Reed, 'The Five Deadly D's of the Air Force's Cyber-arsenal', *Foreign Policy*, 12 April 2013.

30. Ryan Sherstobitoff, Itai Liba and James Walter, 'Dissecting Operation Troy: Cyber-espionage in South Korea', McAfee White Paper, www.mcafee.com/enterprise/en-us/assets/white-papers/wp-dissecting-operation-troy.pdf.

31. Whois is a piece of online terminology, a query that a user can run to find out details of a website, sometimes including its registered owner.

32. Sherstobitoff, op. cit.

33. ibid.

34. Youkyung Lee and Elizabeth Shim, 'Websites in Two Koreas Shut Down on War Anniversary', AP, 25 June 2013.

5 Hacking Hollywood

1. *United States of America* v *Park Jin Hyok*, Criminal Complaint, 8 June 2018, p. 24.

2. ibid., p. 49.

3. ibid., p. 25.

4. Seth Rogen and I had a somewhat bizarre Twitter conversation about other fiction films in which a real-world leader is bumped off. The only instances we came up with were the *Hot Shots* movies, in which Saddam Hussein is murdered both in the original and in the sequel. Although in the latter film, for reasons too complex to explain here, the victim is a hybrid: Saddam Hussein mixed with his pet dog. Rogen and I were therefore unsure whether this counts towards the tally of murdered 'real-world' leaders.

5. United Nations General Assembly Security Council, 'Letter Dated 27 June 2014, from the Permanent Representative of the Democratic People's Republic of Korea to the United Nations, Addressed to the Secretary-General', 27 June 2014.

6. 'North Korea Pardons US Reporters', BBC News, 4 August 2009.

7. *United States of America* v *Park Jin Hyok*, op. cit., p. 34.

8. ibid., p. 48.

9. ibid., p. 25.

10. Sony Pictures Entertainment did not respond to my requests for a comment or an interview.

11. *United States of America* v *Park Jin Hyok*, op. cit., p. 26.

12. Mark Seal, 'An Exclusive Look at Sony's Hacking Saga', *Vanity Fair*, 4 February 2015.

13. ibid.

14. Kevin Roose, 'Hacked Documents Reveal a Hollywood Studio's Stunning Gender and Race Gap', Splinter, 1 December 2014. Splinter was part of the Fusion.net stable.

15. Seal, op. cit.

16. ibid.

17. Sam Biddle, 'More Embarrassing Emails: The Sony Hack B-Sides', Gawker, 17 April 2015.

18. Dominic Rushe, 'Amy Pascal Steps Down from Sony Pictures in Wake of Damaging Email Hack', *Guardian*, 5 February 2015.

19. Jen Yamato, 'Sony Hack: "Christmas Gift" Reveals Michael Lynton Emails Stolen Days before Attack', Deadline, 16 December 2014.

20. Ken Lombardi, 'Fall Movies 2014', CBS News, 29 August 2014.

21. *United States of America* v *Park Jin Hyok*, op. cit., p. 32.

22. Brent Lang, 'Major US Theaters Drop *The Interview* after Sony Hacker Threats', *Variety*, 17 December 2014.

23. Sony News and Information, 'Consolidated Financial Results Forecast for the Third Quarter Ended December 31, 2014, and Revision of Consolidated Forecast for the Fiscal Year Ending March 31, 2015', 4 February 2015, p. 6.

24. Arik Hesseldahl, 'Sony Pictures Investigates North Korea Link in Hack Attack', Recode, 28 November 2014.

6   Fallout

1. 'Sony Archives', WikiLeaks, 16 April 2015.
2. 'Sony Pays $8m over Employees' Hacked Data', BBC News, 21 October 2015.
3. Jacob Kastrenakes and Russell Brandom, 'Sony Pictures Hackers Say They Want "Equality", Worked with Staff to Break In', The Verge, 25 November 2014. The communication with the alleged hacker was somewhat odd – The Verge wrote that the messages came from an email address associated with the hackers, but that the email provider allowed messages to be sent from the email address without the use of a password, meaning the messages could have been sent by someone who had nothing to do with the hack at all.
4. 'Was FBI Wrong on North Korea?', CBS News, 23 December 2014.
5. Tatiana Siegel, 'Five Years Later, Who Really Hacked Sony?', *Hollywood Reporter*, 25 November 2019.
6. Ian Spiegelman, 'Some in Hollywood Still Don't Believe North Korea was behind the Massive Sony Hack of 2014', *Los Angeles Magazine*, 25 November 2019.
7. *United States of America* v *Park Jin Hyok*, Criminal Complaint, 8 June 2018, p. 2.
8. 'President Obama 2014 Year-End News Conference', via www.c-span.org, 19 December 2014.
9. Bradley Martin, *Under the Loving Care of the Fatherly Leader: North Korea and the Kim Dynasty* (Saint Martin's Griffin, 2006), p. 272.
10. *Kim Jong Il Biography: Volume 1* (Foreign Languages Publishing House, 2005), p. 269.
11. Robert Cannan and Ross Adam, *The Lovers and the Despot*, 2016.

12. There are some points of distinction between the two films. In *The Interview* an actor playing Kim Jong Un is shown dying in graphic detail. In *Team America* it is a puppet version of Kim Jong Il that is impaled, and thereafter a cockroach speaking in Kim's voice is seen crawling from the corpse's mouth and exiting stage right in a tiny rocket ship. Whether this mitigates the offensiveness of his death is a debate best left to film scholars.

13. In the wake of the Sony hack, there was an Internet outage in North Korea, which some believed was a US-led retaliation. However, the US government has never confirmed this, and, given the limited nature of Internet connectivity in North Korea, it's quite difficult to discount the possibility this was an outage due to less malicious causes.

14. 'North Korea Slams New US Post-Sony Hack Sanctions', Reuters via CNBC News, 4 January 2015.

7   Casing the Joint

1. 'Interview with Zubair Bin Huda, First Information Report', Motijheel Police Station, 15 March 2016.

2. 'The Bangladesh Cyber Heist: Five Years Later, Insights from Ground Zero', World Informatix Cyber Security, 2021.

3. Asthana would later call in his strategic partner, FireEye, which would do more work on the hacking investigation.

4. It should also be noted that such security breaches don't necessarily indicate a flaw in the SWIFT software itself. If a hacker or a corrupt employee is able to penetrate the bank's security and log in to SWIFT, as far as the software is concerned they'll appear like a legitimate user. Nonetheless, in the wake of the Bangladesh Bank hack, SWIFT has taken steps to help institutions beef up security around the software, controlling who has access to it and what can be done when (making transfers outside business hours, which was what happened at Bangladesh Bank, can be prohibited, for example).

5. INQUIRER.net, 'Bangladeshi Ambassador: It's the Poor People's Money', YouTube, 15 March 2016.
6. 'Bangladesh: Reducing Poverty and Sharing Prosperity', World Bank, 5 November 2018.
7. *United States of America* v *Park Jin Hyok*, Criminal Complaint, 8 June 2018, p. 58.
8. The CV and attendant virus were actually inside a zip file. This is a way of compressing file sizes so large documents can be sent more easily. But it can also be a useful way of evading organizations' cyber-defences. In order to see whether there's anything malicious inside the zip file, the defender's software must first unpack the contents, and not all anti-virus software programs can do this.
9. The naming of malware is an endlessly fascinating business. Other examples of alleged North Korean viruses identified by FireEye include BLINDTOAD, CHEESETRAY and SORRYBRUTE ('APT-38: Un-Usual Suspects', FireEye, 2018). CageyChameleon and Leery Turtle are two of my other favourites ('Attributing Attacks against Crypto Exchanges to LAZARUS – North Korea', ClearSky, 24 May 2021).
10. The fascinating story of Stuxnet and the theories behind who unleashed it are covered in Kim Zetter's excellent book *Countdown to Zero: Stuxnet and the Launch of the World's First Digital Weapon* (Broadway Books, 2015).
11. Sergei Shevchenko, 'Two Bytes to $951m', baesystemsai.blogspot.com, 25 April 2016.
12. *United States of America* v *Park Jin Hyok*, op. cit., p. 43.

8 Cyber-slaves

1. Tesco has recently reined back its international operation in locations such as China ('Tesco Completes China Exit with $357m Stake Sale', Reuters, 25 February 2020).
2. *United States of America* v *Park Jin Hyok*, Criminal Complaint, 8 June 2018.

3. ibid., p. 140.

4. 'Australian Sentenced for Trying to Sell North Korean Missile Parts', Reuters, 27 July 2021.

5. *United States of America* v *Park Jin Hyok*, op. cit., p. 156.

6. www.chosunexpo.com, 10 November 2004, accessed via www. archive.org, 13 August 2021.

7. *United States of America* v *Park Jin Hyok*, op. cit., 8 June 2018, p. 136.

8. I attempted to contact the company for comment. Its website subscription had lapsed and ownership of the site has now been taken over by a security researcher. There was no answer from the phone numbers previously listed on the site.

9. Cyber's 'Most Wanted', www.fbi.gov.

10. 'South Korean Accused of Doing Business with North Korean Hackers', *Chosun Ilbo*, 6 May 2011.

11. 'South Korea Arrests Five over Gaming Scam "Linked to Hackers in North"', AP via *Guardian*, 4 August 2011.

12. 'Russian Firm Provides New Internet Connection to North Korea', Reuters, 2 October 2017.

13. 'Korea (Democratic People's Republic of) IP Address Ranges', IP2Location, lite.ip2location.com, accessed 4 October 2021.

14. 'International Mathematical Olympiad: 32nd IMO 1991 Country Results' and '51st IMO 2010 Country Results', www.imo-official. org, accessed 11 August 2021. There is some debate over the 2010 cheating accusation, which some attendees felt was an unfair decision by the competition jury; see 'North Korea's Disqualification at IMO 2010', www.artofproblemsolving.com, 14 July 2010.

15. ibid.

16. United Nations Security Council, 'Note Verbale Dated 18 June 2019 from the Permanent Mission of Myanmar to the United Nations Addressed to the Chair of the Committee', 19 June 2019; Anastasia Napalkova, 'The Secret World of Russia's North Korean Workers', BBC Russian Service, 25 April 2019.

17. United States Mission to the United Nations, 'Fact Sheet: UN Security Council Resolution 2397 on North Korea', 22 December 2017.
18. ibid.
19. *United States of America* v *Park Jin Hyok*, op. cit., p. 146.
20. ibid.

9   *The Getaway*

1. 'Transcript of the Republic of the Philippines Senate, Committee on Accountability of Public Officers and Investigations (Blue Ribbon)', 17 March 2016, pp. 17–22.
2. ibid., p. 16.
3. 'Details of the Thirty Payment Instructions (PI) Not Executed by FRB NY', letter sent from Bangladesh Bank to Bangladesh's Ambassador to the Philippines, 29 March 2016.
4. 'Transcript of the Republic of the Philippines Senate', op. cit., 17 March 2016, p. 49.
5. ibid., 5 April 2016, p. 189.
6. ibid., 29 March 2016, p. 46.
7. ibid., 17 March 2016, p. 33.
8. 'Hacked: The Bangladesh Bank Heist', Al Jazeera, accessed via Dark Screen, YouTube, 29 May 2018.
9. 'Transcript of the Republic of the Philippines Senate', op. cit., 5 April 2016, pp. 79, 80.
10. Manolo Serapio Jr and Enrico Dela Cruz, 'Philippines Central Bank Fines Rizal Bank over Bangladesh Cyber-heist Failings', Reuters, 5 August 2016.
11. 'Transcript of the Republic of the Philippines Senate', op. cit., 15 March 2016, p. 94.
12. *Bangladesh Bank* v *Rizal Commercial Banking Corporation et al.*, Complaint, 31 January 2019, p. 50.
13. 'Transcript of the Republic of the Philippines Senate', op. cit. 17 March 2016, p. 182.

10   *Baccarat Binge*

1. I've changed Tony Lau's name. He still works in the casino industry and does not want to jeopardize his chances of future work.
2. This has now changed, as per Congress of the Philippines, Republic Act No. 10927, 25 July 2016.
3. You can also bet on a tie, and on whether the player's or the banker's cards are a pair. These bets are higher odds (i.e., riskier for the gambler but with a potentially higher return) and are less common.
4. 'Transcript of the Republic of the Philippines Senate, Committee on Accountability of Public Officers and Investigations (Blue Ribbon)', 29 March 2016, p. 126.
5. As the investigation unfolded, the Solaire Casino's owner, Bloomberry Resorts Corporation, said it had no idea it was dealing with stolen funds, and is co-operating with the authorities. The Midas Casino did not respond to my requests for comment or an interview.
6. 'Transcript of the Republic of the Philippines Senate', op. cit., 29 March 2016, p. 50.
7. ibid., 12 April 2016, p. 198.

11   *The Plot Unravels*

1. 'About Us', www.shalikafoundation.org, accessed 16 March 2019.
2. 'Agreement Letter Signed with the Name Shalika Perera', dated 8 April 2015, kindly provided by Shihar Aneez.
3. Dairy Farm Project, Laggala, Matale, www.shalikafoundation. org, accessed 30 March 2019.
4. 'Information Given to Magistrates' Court by Sri Lanka Police', 31 March 2016, kindly provided by Shihar Aneez.
5. ibid.

6. 'Donation of Funds', dated 2 February 2016, provided by Shalika Perera.

7. 'First Sri Lankan CID Report Submitted to the Court', 17 March 2016, kindly provided by Shihar Aneez.

8. 'Information Given to Magistrates' Court by Sri Lanka Police', op. cit.

9. 'First Sri Lankan CID Report Submitted to the Court', op. cit.

10. ibid.

11. ibid.

12. *Bangladesh Bank* v *Rizal Commercial Banking Corporation et al.*, Complaint, 31 January 2019, pp. 32–5.

13. Workshop by JICA and BB, www.bb.org.bd, accessed 28 August 2021.

14. Sayaka Chatani, Assistant Professor, Department of History, National University of Singapore, speaking to Jean H. Lee for our BBC World Service podcast *The Lazarus Heist*.

15. 'Ludic loop' is a phrase attributed to Natasha Dow Schüll, cultural anthropologist and Associate Professor in the Department of Media, Culture, and Communication at New York University, author of *Addiction by Design: Machine Gambling in Las Vegas* (Princeton University Press, 2012). Broadly speaking, it describes the experience of a repeated activity in which the prospect of a reward is both exciting and uncertain, as when using a one-armed bandit gambling machine, or swiping down a mobile-phone screen to check for updates.

16. 'A person who gambles shall be punished by a fine of not more than 500,000 yen or a petty fine; provided, however, that the same shall not apply to a person who bets a thing which is provided for momentary entertainment' in 'Chapter XXIII: Crimes Related to Gambling and Lotteries, Article 185 (Gambling)', *Penal Code* (Act No. 45 of 1907).

17. 'Pachinko Parlor Sales are about 20.7trn yen', Pachinko Industry Web Reference, www.pachinko-shiryoshitsu.jp, accessed 26 August 2021.

18. Tara Francis Chan, 'Japan's Pinball Gambling Industry Rakes in Thirty Times More Cash than Las Vegas Casinos', Business Insider, 26 July 2018.
19. Sega Sammy Holdings Inc., 'FY Ending March 2017, 3rd Quarter Results Presentation', 7 February 2017.
20. Simon Scott, 'Ball and Chain: Gambling's Darker Side', *Japan Times*, 24 May 2014.
21. Subroemon, 'Japanese *Yakuza*' (subbed), YouTube, video dated on screen as 19 October 2006.
22. Ed Caesar, 'The Incredible Rise of North Korea's Hacking Army', *New Yorker*, 19 April 2021.
23. Another complicating factor for any potential prosecution is that the alleged offence was committed in Sri Lanka, but Sasaki is in Japan, raising a whole series of issues around extradition, competing legal systems and standards of proof.

12   The Las Vegas of the East

1. 'Transcript of the Republic of the Philippines Senate, Committee on Accountability of Public Officers and Investigations (Blue Ribbon)', 29 March 2016, p. 177.
2. ibid., p. 48.
3. Alan Katz and Wenxin Fan, 'A Baccarat Binge Helped Launder the World's Biggest Cyber-heist', Bloomberg News, 3 August 2017.
4. 'Republic of the Philippines Senate Committee Report on the US$100 Million that was Laundered in the Philippines', 6 June 2016, p. 70.
5. 'Transcript of the Republic of the Philippines Senate', op. cit., 5 April 2016, p. 103.
6. Gaming Inspection and Co-ordination Bureau Macao SAR, 'Monthly Gross Revenue from Games of Fortune in 2019 and 2018', www.dicj.gov.mo, accessed 1 September 2021; Nevada Gaming Control Board, 'Nevada Gaming Abstract 2019' (total

revenue is shown as $24.5bn, but this includes income from rooms, food and beverage sales).

7. After Shoxx, '1991 Interview with Korean Air Flight 858 bomber Kim Hyon-Hui', YouTube, 15 November 2019.

8. Rupert Wingfield-Hayes, 'The North Korean Spy Who Blew Up a Plane', BBC News, 22 April 2013.

9. Kim Hyun Hee, *The Tears of My Soul* (William Morrow & Co., 1993).

10. ibid.

11. Sanctions against the bank were finally lifted in 2020 (Min Chao Choy, 'US Lifts Sanctions against Macao Bank Accused of North Korea Money Laundering', NK News, 13 August 2020).

12. Mike Chinoy, speaking with my co-host Jean H. Lee for *The Lazarus Heist* podcast.

13. Paul Fischer, *A Kim Jong Il Production: The Extraordinary True Story of a Kidnapped Filmmaker, His Star Actress, and a Young Dictator's Rise to Power* (Flatiron Books, 2015), p. 52.

14. Bradley Martin, *Under the Loving Care of the Fatherly Leader: North Korea and the Kim Dynasty* (Saint Martin's Griffin, 2006), pp. 688, 694.

15. ibid., p. 685.

16. This seems a little unfair on Kim Jong Nam, because his half-brother, Kim Jong Un, had visited Euro Disney during the time when he was being educated in Europe (Anna Fifield, *The Great Successor: The Secret Rise and Rule of Kim Jong Un* (John Murray, 2019), p. 14). But of course his trip didn't turn into an international incident.

17. ibid., p. 216.

18. 'Kim Jong Nam Murder: Vietnamese Woman Pleads Guilty to Lesser Charge', BBC News, 1 April 2019.

19. 'CCTV Footage Shows Deadly Assault on North Korean Leader's Half-brother', Reuters, 20 February 2017.

20. 'North Korean Leader's Slain Half-brother was a CIA Informant: *Wall Street Journal*', Reuters, 11 June 2019.

13   *WannaCry*

1. 'NHS Cyber-attack: "My Heart Surgery was Cancelled"', BBC News, 12 May 2017.
2. 'WannaCry Cyber-attack Compromised Some Russian Banks: Central Bank', Reuters, 19 May 2017. Sberbank said it had been attacked by a virus but that its systems were not infected; Danny Palmer, 'WannaCry Ransomware Crisis, One Year On: Are We Ready for the Next Global Cyber-attack?', ZDnet, 11 May 2018.
3. Julian King, EU Commissioner for the Security Union, speaking at the Europol–Interpol Cybercrime Conference in The Hague, www.ec.europa.eu, 27 September 2017.
4. 'Cyber Threat Alliance Cracks the Code on Cryptowall Crimeware Associated with $325 Million in Payments', www.cyberthreatalliance.org, 28 October 2015.
5. Secureworks Counter Threat Unit Research Team, 'WCry Ransomware Analysis', 18 May 2017. WannaCry also used AES algorithms to encrypt files, separately to the Windows Crypto API. In the code, 'Wanna' is actually spelt 'Wana'.
6. Ruth Alexander, 'Which is the World's Biggest Employer?', BBC News, 20 March 2012.
7. William Smart, 'Lessons Learned Review of the Wannacry Ransomware Cyber-attack', Department of Health & Social Care, NHS Improvement, NHS England, February 2018, p. 5.
8. Secureworks, 'WCry Ransomware Analysis', op. cit.
9. Many companies are now trying to address this using 'bug bounties'. If a hacker finds a flaw in the company's systems and is prepared to behave ethically by reporting their findings, the firm will pay the hacker a fee for information to help fix it.
10. 'Tor Browser Bounty', www.zerodium.com, 13 September 2017.
11. As Moriuchi points out, the US government has recently started to change its practices with regard to exploits: 'When they discover a vulnerability and are able to develop an exploit for it, they have to go through a process right across the intelligence

community and the military where different agencies get to weigh in and say [whether] it's worth it or not to keep this from the public.'

12. Michelle Nichols, 'US Prepared to Use Force on North Korea "If We Must": UN Envoy', Reuters, 4 July 2017.

13. Kate Samuelson, 'Here are All the Times Kim Jong Un and Donald Trump Insulted Each Other', *Time*, 22 September 2017.

14. David E. Sanger, Choe Sang-Hun and William J. Broad, 'North Korea Tests a Ballistic Missile that Experts Say Could Hit California', *New York Times*, 28 July 2017.

15. Michael Kan, 'Security Researcher Who Stopped WannaCry Avoids Jail Time', *PC Mag*, 27 July 2019.

14 Old Tricks, New Money

1. I heartily recommend watching the *Washington Post*'s full livestream recording of the event on YouTube, if only for the viewers' comments; a mix of sarcastic humour, paranoia and heartfelt hope (*Washington Post*, 'Moon Jae-in and Kim Jong Un Meet for Historic Summit of the Koreas', YouTube, 26 April 2018).

2. Upasana Bhat, 'North Korea's Athletes at the Winter Olympics', BBC Monitoring, 8 February 2018.

3. 'North Korea Nuclear Test Tunnels at Punggye-ri "Destroyed"', BBC News, 24 May 2018. Opinion within North Korea was less optimistic. As reported in Channel 4's *Dispatches: Life Inside North Korea*, many in the North believed the tunnels were destroyed because they were no longer needed following successful nuclear tests. The voices reported in the documentary were sceptical of the entire rapprochement narrative in 2018.

4. NiceHash says it encouraged users not to keep their money in the company's wallets, but to regularly withdraw it and keep it somewhere else.

5. *United States of America v Jon Chang Hyok, aka 'Quan Jiang', aka 'Alex Jiang', Kim Il, aka 'Julien Kim', aka 'Tony Walker', and Park Jin Hyok, aka 'Jin Hyok Park', aka 'Pak Jin Hek', aka 'Pak Kwang Jin'*, 8 December 2020, p. 22.

6. 'How to Steal $500m in Cryptocurrency', Bloomberg News, 31 January 2018.

7. F-Secure Labs, 'Lazarus Group Campaign Targeting the Cryptocurrency Vertical, Tactical Intelligence Report', 18 August 2020.

8. *United States of America v 113 Virtual Currency Accounts*, 2 March 2020.

9. ibid., p. 9.

10. ibid., pp. 11, 12.

11. *United States of America v Tian Yinyin and Li Jiadong*, 27 February 2020.

12. UN Security Council, 'Report of the Panel of Experts Established Pursuant to Resolution 1874 (2009)', 30 August 2019, p. 29.

13. ibid., p. 117.

14. ibid., p. 132.

15. ibid., p. 125.

16. 'Supply Chain and Logistics Innovation Forum', meetup.com, 22 March 2018.

17. INSKIT Intelligence, 'Shifting Patterns in Internet Use Reveal Adaptable and Innovative North Korean Ruling Elite', 25 October 2018.

18. UN Security Council, 'Report of the Panel of Experts', op. cit.

19. ibid., 2 March 2020, p. 214.

20. 'Operation AppleJeus: Lazarus Hits Cryptocurrency Exchange with Fake Installer and MacOS Malware', Kaspersky, 23 August 2018.

21. *United States of America v Jon Chang Hyok*, op. cit., pp. 19–22.

22. KuCoin CEO Johnny Lyu via Twitter, 3 October 2020; 'Lazarus Group Pulled Off 2020's Biggest Exchange Hack and Appears to be Exploring New Money-laundering Options', Chainalysis, 9 February 2021.

23. 'The 2021 Crypto-crime Report', Chainalysis, February 2021.

24. KuCoin CEO Johnny Lyu via Twitter, op. cit.

25. 'South Korean Intelligence says North Korean Hackers Possibly Behind Coincheck Heist – Sources', Reuters, 5 February 2018.

15   *Going Back for More*

1. CNBC International TV, 'Trump and Kim Meet for the First Time / Trump–Kim Summit', YouTube, 12 June 2018.

2. 'Trump Warns North Korea Will be "Met with Fire and Fury"', CBS News, 8 August 2017.

3. Kate Samuelson, 'Here are All the Times Kim Jong Un and Donald Trump Insulted Each Other', *Time*, 22 September 2017.

4. ' "He Wrote Me Beautiful Letters and We Fell in Love": Donald Trump on Kim Jong-un – Video', Reuters via the *Guardian*, 30 September 2018.

5. Josh Lederman and Hans Nichols, 'Trump Meets Kim Jong Un, Becomes First Sitting US President to Step into North Korea', NBC News, 30 June 2019.

6. *United States of America v. Jon Chang Hyok, aka 'Quan Jiang', aka 'Alex Jiang', Kim Il, aka 'Julien Kim', aka 'Tony Walker', and Park Jin Hyok, aka 'Jin Hyok Park', aka 'Pak Jin Hek', aka 'Pak Kwang Jin'*, 8 December 2020.

7. ibid., p.18.

8. *United States of America v Ghaleb Alaumary*, Plea Agreement, 17 November 2020, p. 13.

9. There is some discrepancy in the amount reported by different sources. Cosmos Co-Operative Bank itself claims that around $11m was withdrawn, but in the Department of Justice case against Ghaleb Alaumary it was stated as $16.3m from the 'Victim Indian Bank' (ibid., p. 9).

10. ibid., p. 9.

11. Department of Justice, 'North Korean Regime-backed Programmer Charged with Conspiracy to Conduct Multiple Cyber-attacks and Intrusions', 6 September 2018.

12. 'A Smear Campaign for What?', KCNA, 14 September 2018, accessed via KCNA Watch, kcnawatch.org.

13. *United States of America v Ramon Olorunwa Abbas, aka 'Ray Hush-puppi', aka 'Hush'*, Criminal Complaint, 12 March 2020.

14. ibid., pp. 19–20.

15. Bertrand Borg, Vanessa MacDonald and Claire Caruana, 'BOV Goes Dark after Hackers Go after €13m', *Times of Malta*, 13 February 2019. Bank of Valetta did not respond to my questions and request for an interview, stating that criminal proceedings are ongoing.

16. 'Watch: BOV Hackers' €13m in Transactions "Being Reversed" – Muscat', *Times of Malta*, 13 February 2019.

17. 'Hush Money: The Rise and Fall of an International Fraudster', *File on Four*, BBC Radio 4, 14 September 2021.

18. Borg, MacDonald and Caruana, 'BOV Goes Dark', op. cit.

19. Alexandre Neyret, 'Stock Market Cybercrime, Definitions, Cases and Perspectives', Autorité des Marchés Financiers, 28 January 2020.

20. *United States of America v Ramon Olorunwa Abbas*, op. cit., p. 21.

21. 'Watch: BOV Hackers' €13m in Transactions "Being Reversed" ', op. cit.

22. *United States of America v Ramon Olorunwa Abbas*, op. cit., p. 21.

23. National Crime Agency, 'Further Arrests Made by NCA in Bank Cyber-heist Money Laundering Probe', 31 January 2020, accessed via www.archiveorg.

24. *United States of America v Jennal Aziz*, Sentencing Memorandum, 18 February 2019, pp. 3–6.

25. United States District Court, Southern District of Georgia, Savannah Division, 'Affidavit in Support of Criminal Complaint (in the Matter of the Criminal Complaint Filed against Kelvin Desangles, aka "Kevin Desanges")', 7 December 2017.

26. *United States of America v Ramon Olorunwa Abbas*, op. cit., pp. 14–16.

27. ibid., p. 18.

28. *United States of America v Ghaleb Alaumary*, op. cit., p. 15.

29. *United States of America* v *Ramon Olorunwa Abbas*, op. cit., p. 4.

30. ibid., p. 5.

31. 'Hush Money', *File on Four*, BBC Radio 4.

32. ibid.

33. *United States of America* v *Ghaleb Alaumary*, op. cit., pp. 14–17.

34. Dubai Police, 'Dubai Police Take Down "Hushpuppi", "Woodberry", Ten International Cyber Criminals', YouTube, 25 June 2020.

35. *United States of America* v *Ghaleb Alaumary*, Information, 17 November 2020, p. 12.

36. Dubai Police, 'Dubai Police Take Down "Hushpuppi"', op. cit.

37. Department of Justice, 'Nigerian National Brought to US to Face Charges of Conspiring to Launder Hundreds of Millions of Dollars from Cybercrime Schemes', 3 July 2020.

38. Department of Justice, 'Three North Korean Military Hackers Indicted in Wide-ranging Scheme to Commit Cyber-attacks and Financial Crimes across the Globe', 17 February 2021.

39. ibid.

40. Department of Justice, 'International Money Launderer Sentenced to More than Eleven Years in Prison for Laundering Millions of Dollars in Cybercrime Schemes', 8 September 2021.

Conclusion

1. 'North Korea Accused of Hacking Pfizer for Covid-19 Vaccine Data', BBC News, 16 February 2021.

Index

PENGUIN PARTNERSHIPS

Penguin Partnerships is the Creative Sales and Promotions team at Penguin Random House. We have a long history of working with clients on a wide variety of briefs, specializing in brand promotions, bespoke publishing and retail exclusives, plus corporate, entertainment and media partnerships.

We can respond quickly to briefs and specialize in repurposing books and content for sales promotions, for use as incentives and retail exclusives as well as creating content for new books in collaboration with our partners as part of branded book relationships.

Equally if you'd simply like to buy a bulk quantity of one of our existing books at a special discount, we can help with that too. Our books can make excellent corporate or employee gifts.

Special editions, including personalized covers, excerpts of existing books or books with corporate logos can be created in large quantities for special needs.

We can work within your budget to deliver whatever you want, however you want it.

For more information, please contact
salesenquiries@penguinrandomhouse.co.uk